SLAVE OF DESIRE

SLAVE OF DESIRE

Sex, Love, and Death in *The 1001 Nights*

Daniel Beaumont

Madison • Teaneck
Fairleigh Dickinson University Press
London: Associated University Presses

Associated University Presses
440 Forsgate Drive
Cranbury, NJ 08512

Associated University Presses
16 Barter Street
London WC1A 2AH, England

Associated University Presses
P.O. Box 338, Port Credit
Mississauga, Ontario
Canada L5G 4L8

The paper used in this publication meets the requirements of the American National Standard for Permanence of Paper for Printed Library Materials Z39.48-1984.

Library of Congress Cataloging-in-Publication Data

Beaumont, Daniel E.
Slave of desire : love, sex, and death in The 1001 nights / Daniel Beaumont.
p. cm.
Includes bibliographical references and index.
ISBN 0-8386-3874-0
1. Arabian nights. 2. Love in literature. 3. Sex in literature. 4. Death in literature. 5. Discourse analysis, Narrative. I. Title.

PJ7737.B43 2002
398.22—dc21 2001051248

PRINTED IN THE UNITED STATES OF AMERICA

to my mother and father

Contents

Preface

THIS BOOK COMBINES MANY OF MY INTERESTS: NARRATIVE, PSYCHOanalytic thought, and philosophy, as well as my love of the book best known as *The Thousand and One Nights*. By exploring its stories within the theoretical frames of Jacques Lacan and Slavoj Žižek, I hope to reveal their sophistication and complexity—and to dispel as far as possible its general reputation as "folk literature" or "children's literature." It is neither.

I have used the Arabic edition known as the Second Calcutta, but have consulted other Arabic editions and many translations. My reasons for my choices are spelled out in greater detail in the first chapter. The translated passages are my own, and are based on the so-called Second Calcutta edition unless otherwise noted.

I have tried to minimize the transliteration of Arabic words, and yet some of it necessarily remains—an unhappy compromise between the needs of the specialist with knowledge of Arabic and those of the general reader with literary interests. In deference to the former, I must adhere to a consistent system of transcription in which the pronunciation is not always obvious at first glance. In general, I give the full transliteration only the first time a name or word occurs and thereafter use as simple a form as possible. The system of transliteration is that used by *The International Journal of Middle East Studies* with a few small changes. The feminine *nisbah* is given as îyah, not iyya, and the *ta marbutah* is represented as "-ah," not "-a." The definite article *al-* for so-called "sun letters" remains al-, thus *Hârûn al-Rashîd*, not *Hârûn ar-Rashîd*. Titles for individual stories are given in quotation marks: "The Merchant and the Jinni." These are usually my translations of titles inserted into the Calcutta II edition but not found in the manuscripts; sometimes the title is my own invention if a story lacks one in that edition.

I should like to thank people who have helped me in various ways with this book. Foremost in this regard is Walter Andrews who read drafts of all the chapters but one; his comments and encouragement were a great help to me. Andras Hamori also read a portion of this work and commented on it in very helpful ways. Theresa

LaPietra read the entire manuscript and made numerous corrections. Tom DiPiero, Emil Homerin, and Anne Merideth all helped me in different ways.

Lastly I must thank my wife Cathy and my daughter Lily for their help—and their patience.

Acknowledgments

THE AUTHOR GRATEFULLY ACKNOWLEDGES THE FOLLOWING:

Sigmund Freud © Copyrights, The Institute of Psychoanalysis and the Hogarth Press for permission to quote from *The Standard Edition of the Complete Psychological Works of Sigmund Freud*, translated and edited by James Strachey.

Jokes and Their Relation to the Unconscious by Sigmund Freud, translated by James Strachey. Copyright 1960 by James Strachey, renewed 1988 by Alix Strachey. Used by permission of W. W. Norton & Company, Inc.

Beyond the Pleasure Principle by Sigmund Freud, translated by James Strachey. Copyright 1961 by James Strachey. Used by permission of Liveright Publishing Corporation.

Écrits: A Selection by Jacques Lacan, translated by Alan Sheridan. Copyright © 1966 by Les Éditions du Seuil. English translation copyright © 1977 by Tavistock Publications. Used by permission of W. W. Norton & Company, Inc.

The Seminar of Jacques Lacan: Book I: Freud's Papers on Techniques 1953–1954 by Jacques Lacan, translated by John Forrester. Copyright © 1975 by Les Éditions du Seuil. English translation © 1988 by Cambridge University Press. Used by permission of W. W. Norton & Company, Inc.

The Seminar of Jacques Lacan, Book II: The Ego in Freud's Theory and in the Technique of Psychoanalysis 1954–1955 by Jacques Lacan, translated by Sylvia Tomaselli. Copyright © 1978 Les Éditions du Seuil. English translation copyright © 1988 by Cambridge University Press. Used by permission of W. W. Norton & Co., Inc.

The Seminar of Jacques Lacan, Book III: The Psychoses by Jacques Lacan, translated by Russell Grigg. Copyright © 1981 Les Éditions du Seuil. English translation copyright © 1993 by W. W. Norton & Company, Inc. Used by permission of W. W. Norton & Co., Inc.

The Seminar of Jacques Lacan, Book VII: The Ethics of Psychoanalysis by Jacques Lacan, translated by Dennis Porter. Copyright © 1986 by Les Éditions du Seuil. English translation copyright © 1992 by W. W. Norton & Co. Used by permission of W. W. Norton & Co., Inc.

The Four Fundamental Concepts of Psycho-Analysis by Jacques Lacan, translated by Alan Sheridan. Copyright © 1973 by Les Éditions du Seuil. English translation copyright © 1977 by Alan Sheridan. Used by permission of W. W. Norton & Co., Inc.

The Sublime Object of Ideology by Slavoj Žižek. Copyright © Verso 1989. Used by permission of Verso.

The Metastases of Enjoyment by Slavoj Žižek, Copyright © Verso 1994. Used by permission of Verso.

"Dancing Girls at Cairo" by David Roberts, used by permission of the British Library.

Chapters 3 and 8 appeared in journals in somewhat different forms. Chapter 3, "King, Queen, Master, Slave," appeared in *Neophilologus,* Vol. 82, No. 3, July 1998, pp. 335–56; it is used here with the kind permission of Kluwer Academic publishing. Chapter 8, *"Peut-on tuer avec des noyaux de dattes?"* first appeared in *Comparative Literature,* Vol. 50, No. 2, Spring 1998, pp. 120–35.

SLAVE OF DESIRE

1

Alf Laylah wa Laylah or *The Thousand and One Nights*

By the night when she hides with her veil,
By the day when he reveals,
By that which created male and female—
Truly your paths are varied
—Qur'ān, Surah "Night" (92: 1–3)

LIKE ONE OF THE JINN WHO SUDDENLY MATERIALIZE AND VANISH IN ITS pages, *Alf laylah wa laylah* or *The Thousand and One Nights* is a book that is in many ways difficult to pin down. Indeed, exactly what texts and what stories constitute the *Nights* has always been the subject of some disagreement, and so whoever would write about *The Thousand and One Nights* must say exactly what entity he means by that title. I have relied for the most part on the Arabic edition printed in Calcutta in the 1830s and known as Macnaghten's Second Calcutta edition, but I would certainly not claim that the Second Calcutta is the definitive *Nights*. I have used two other important nineteenth-century Arabic editions, the Bulaq and the Breslau editions, and I have also consulted some of the major European translations such as Burton and Lane. But the only way to respond to the question of what I mean by *The Thousand and One Nights* is to give some account of the history of the book. That account will also refer to the European editions, not only because I have made use of some of them but, more importantly, because it can be argued that these translations influenced modern Arabic versions of the *Nights*, such as the Second Calcutta edition.

THE MEDIEVAL ARABIC *NIGHTS*

The first thing to be said is that *The Thousand and One Nights* is a rather exceptional work in the context of medieval Arabic literature. It happens sometimes that a person takes up the study of a language because of his love for a single work, but if someone were tempted to begin the task of learning Arabic because of his love of *The Thousand and One Nights*, he should be forewarned that the book is sui generis. He will really find nothing else like it in the literature, one reason being that the *Nights* seems to have absorbed a number of once independent medieval Arabic fictions; the story of "Sindbad" is probably the most famous example. The borders of this text were not, it seems, ever very well defined. Hence the size of the *Nights*. Unfortunately, in the case of the *Nights* its marginality in this respect has also worked to veil its history in a good deal of obscurity. Indeed, in recounting its history in the medieval period, there is no need to summarize; a fairly complete account will read like a summary, since most of its medieval history is unknown and is likely to remain unknown. To retell the story, let us think of it for the moment as a piece of architecture—a palace, as Borges calls it. "To erect the palace of *The Thousand and One Nights*, it took generations of men, and those men are our benefactors, as we have inherited this inexhaustible book, this book capable of so much metamorphosis," Borges said of one of his favorite books.[1]

The "palace" of the *Nights*, in the form in which we now know and enjoy it—which is to say the nineteenth-century Arabic editions printed in Egypt, India, and Germany that have served as the basis for all but one of the translations since Galland—that structure with its spacious pavilions, its charming recesses, its secret chambers and mysterious passages must have been the work of many literary hands, and it must have been the result of a development in Arabic alone that lasted seven or eight centuries. Evidence about the development of the book may be divided into two categories: testimony by medieval writers and what in a legal hearing would be called "material evidence"—here, textual evidence—those stories in *The Thousand and One Nights* that show some relation to other works in medieval Arabic literature and to works in other literatures.

Earliest mention of a text with a clearly antecedent relation to the contemporary work is found in a papyrus dating from the ninth century A.D. The papyrus mentions two characters, Dînâzâd and Shîrâzâd—later to become Dunyâzâd and Shahrazâd—and has a few lines of narrative in which the former asks the latter to tell a story.[2] There is also mention of a title that anticipates the title we now know: "The Book of Stories from the Thousand Nights."

About a century later two writers in Baghdad, al-Masʿûdî and Ibn al-Nadîm, mention the same work. In his book *Meadows of Gold* (*Murûj al-dhahab*), the historian Masʿudi (d. 956) states that among the translations made in Baghdad of stories from Persian, Indian, and Greek sources was a book called "A Thousand Tales" *(Alf khurâfah)*, also known as "A Thousand Nights" (*Alf laylah*).[3] Mas'udi says that it is the story of a king, his vizier, the vizier's daughter and her slave, and that the last two are called Shirazad and Dinazad. They are not yet sisters, as they will be later. In his bibliographic work *The Catalogue* (*Al-Fihrist*), Ibn al-Nadim (d. circa 995) mentions a work translated from Persian called "The Thousand Stories." He also gives a summary of the frame story, but he criticizes it as "a coarse book, without warmth in the telling."[4]

For the next seven centuries, there are only two even briefer references to its existence. In the twelfth century, a loan record for a Jewish bookseller in Cairo mentions the title "The Thousand and One Nights"—the earliest mention of its present title: "Majd ibn al-'Azîzî has *The One Thousand and One Nights*."[5] And in the early fifteenth century the Egyptian historian al-Maqrîzî (d. 1442) cites authors who indicate the work was in circulation in Cairo in the late eleventh century.[6] These brief references separated by long periods when the book all but vanishes from view suggest an analogy with an unconscious thought that only infrequently and briefly makes its presence known in conscious thought and then quickly vanishes again beneath the force of repression—and repression is not mere metaphor here, as we shall see.

On the basis of these facts, we know that there are three main layers to the book: a translation of a group of Persian stories (which themselves incorporated Indian stories), a Baghdad layer, and a Cairo layer. D. B. Macdonald, in an important article published in 1924, "The Earlier History of the Arabian Nights,"[7] further divided its development into five stages: a Persian core "The Thousand Stories" (*Hazâr Afsânah*); an Arabic version of this; the frame story of "The Thousand Stories" with new Arabic stories added to it; a late Fatimid version (twelfth century); and the Syrian recension whose sixteenth-century manuscript was the basis of the first European translation, that of Galland. Stages two and three correspond to the Baghdad layer, while four and five are part of the later Egyptian layer. To this we may add a sixth and final stage, suggested by Nabia Abbott, a stage that extends into the sixteenth century and introduces the materials from popular epics.

The infrequency of the medieval references to the work cited above, their brevity, and their tone all point to the insignificance of the work in the eyes of recognized practitioners of medieval Arabic literature. Yet it seems to have been a popular work—the work has not completely shed this paradoxical reputation in Arab countries even today.

In addition to these testimonies, there is also the textual evidence: stories in the *Nights* that bear unmistakable links to other works in medieval Arabic literature and to works in other literatures. Here it will be useful to distinguish between three categories.

The first category would contain stories that reveal its links with a few specific works in medieval Arabic literature. For example, "The Story of the Steward," told within the longer story of "The Hunchback," is roughly the same story recounted as fact by the tenth-century author al-Tanûkhî (d. 994) in his book *Happiness after Hardship* (*Al-Faraj ba'd al-shiddah*). It is the story of a husband who offends the delicate sensibility of his wife on their wedding night by forgetting to wash his hands after having eaten a certain spicy stew called *zîrbâjah*.[8] Years later, the same dish is served at a banquet and the other diners demand that he eat some of it; the unfortunate man washes his hands one hundred and twenty times, then tells the story of his disastrous wedding night.

Another story narrated within "The Hunchback," "The Story of the Lame Young Man," also shares its plot with stories and anecdotes found elsewhere in the literature. In the other versions this plot makes use of a certain stew called *maḍîrah*, which similarly provokes the recounting of a painful story. However, in "The Story of the Lame Young Man," as regards its plot function, the dish of stew is transformed and split into two human characters: a judge and his daughter.[9] A purportedly factual *madirah* anecdote which focuses on a clash between guest and host over the provocative dish is fairly widespread in medieval anecdotal literature. An example can be found in the anecdotal work *The Misers* (*Al-Bukhalâ'*) by the eleventh century writer al-Khaṭîb al-Baghdâdî (d. 1071).[10] Interestingly, the anecdote there is attributed to the same author, Tanukhi, who has the analogue of the previous story, "The Story of the Steward," in one of his books. The story "The Madirah Maqamah," found in a late tenth or early eleventh-century work *Al-Maqâmât* by al-Hamadhânî (d. 1008), makes use of the same *madirah* plot.[11] The eleventh-century physician Ibn Buṭlân (d. 1066) also makes use of this plot in his comic work *The Physicians' Banquet* (*Da'wat al-aṭibbâ'*). And, finally, it is also found in an anonymous thirteenth-century work *Wonderful Stories* (*al-Ḥikâyât al-'ajîbah*).

Finally, more such textual links are found in the story "The Sleeper Awakened," a story that Galland translates, but which is not found in two of the major nineteenth-century Arabic editions, the Bulaq or the Second Calcutta editions. The story is comprised of two parts. In the first part, the main character, Abû 'l-Ḥasan, is drugged by the caliph Hârûn al-Rashîd and tricked into believing that he is the caliph. In the second part, Abu 'l-Hasan tricks Harun into thinking that he and his wife have died. The first part of the story is also found in a work by a seventeenth-century Egyptian author al-Isḥâqî (d. 1651). Ishaqi writes when Egypt is a province in the Ottoman Empire, and in his work *Accounts of Previous Rulers of Egypt*, he gives the first half of the story as fact in the section devoted to Harun al-Rashid. The second half of the story seems to be an elaboration of an anecdote told of the Abbasid poet/buffoon Abû Dulâmah that is found in the famous work of Abû 'l-Faraj al-Iṣfahânî (d. 967), *The Songs* (*Al-Aghânî*).[12] The relative lateness of Ishaqi makes the occurrence there more interesting from the perspective of literary history, for with him we are within a few decades of Galland's discovery of the manuscript of the *Nights* in Istanbul. Another brief passage in Ishaqi is also of interest in this context. In an account of a visit to a graveyard by an anonymous narrator said only to be one of the "people of refinement," the narrator states that the purpose of his visit is "to visit the dead and reflect on the lessons of what has passed . . . and to remember the destroyer of delights, the separator of societies, he who makes orphans of son and daughters."[13] The phrase "the destroyer of delights" (*hâdim al-ladhdhât*) is found at the end of numerous stories in *The Thousand and One Nights*, and indeed the version here with mention of the "maker of orphans" (*muyattim al-banîn wa 'l-banât*) is, word for word, the same as the version of this sentence that comes at the end of the last story Shahrazad tells, the story of "Maʿrûf the Cobbler."[14] The nature of Ishaqi's work is also telling; much of it is patent fiction passed off as historical and edifying anecdote. These things suggest that Ishaqi knew the *Nights* in a version very much like the one we know, and we are only a few decades removed from the date when Antoine Galland, the first European translator of the *Nights*, purchases his Syrian manuscript in Istanbul.

The second category of textual evidence contains stories in *The Thousand and One Nights* that make use of and revise the plots of extremely well-known stories in Islamic culture; stories about figures like Abraham, Joseph, and Solomon are examples.

Finally, in the third category are the stories that make use of plots which are even more widely spread, the "Cinderella" plot, the "Phaedra" plot, and so on.

What do these textual links suggest about the development of the text of *The Thousand and One Nights* at any particular stage in the

Middle Ages? Unfortunately, not very much more than I have already said. The latter two categories of material tell us nothing at all since the material is pervasive throughout the period. With regard to the first, more specific, category, the safest assumption would seem to be that the storytellers involved in the creation of the *Nights* sometimes made use of "factual" anecdotal collections for plots, revising them freely to suit their purposes. But even this modest conclusion must carry a caveat.

The earliest manuscripts of *The Thousand and One Nights* date from the fourteenth century, and most of the works cited above for containing analogues are earlier. Yet as we have seen, on the basis of the testimony of earlier authors we know that some sort of collection with a title *The Thousand Nights* existed centuries prior to the fourteenth century. So lacking any knowledge of what the book contained in, say, the tenth and eleventh centuries, it is not absolutely certain that material moved only in one direction, out of established writers and works and into the *Nights*. For, a priori, it is not impossible that an author like Tanukhi and a *One Thousand and One Nights* storyteller drew upon a common store of material. Or a third possibility: it is not out of the question that some material might have moved in the other direction, out of the *Nights* and into the "factual" works of a writer like Tanukhi. After all, writers do lie sometimes. In fact, in some instances in Tanukhi's *Happiness after Hardship* I think this third possibility is the most likely one—that it is Tanukhi who is borrowing from some version of *The Thousand and One Nights*. For example, in the first chapter Tanukhi tells as fact a brief story about a traveler who is shipwrecked. The story has two parts. In the first, a voice from the sky shouts at the man and his fellow travelers that they should throw their money overboard in order to gain a piece of knowledge that will be of spiritual benefit to them. But only the one man does so. Then, when a storm destroys the ship, he is saved while all the others drown. In the second part, the saved man washes ashore on a desert island and finds a subterranean chamber that contains a treasure and a beautiful girl (also shipwrecked).[15] While these elements are found in various combinations in many stories in *The Thousand and One Nights*, this story is basically that of "The Story of the Second *Qalandâr*" told in "The Porter and the Three Ladies of Baghdad." In this case, since the story is an obvious fiction for which he gives no sources, it seems likely that Tanukhi has borrowed the second part from one of two places, either from some version of the *Nights* or from a store of narratives (perhaps as yet unwritten) that the *Nights* also uses; this he joined to a Sufi conversion tale. In view of its similarity to "The

Story of the Second Qalandar," it is tempting to say that the first case is what happened, and that, therefore, "The Story of the Second Qalandar" must have existed in the tenth century. But given the ubiquity of these plots and motifs, given the instability of the texts, especially in a manuscript culture, and given the question of oral and written versions and their possible interaction—given all these factors, who can say for certain what happened in any particular case?

Thus, while the textual evidence—its demonstrated links with other works—may tell us something about the sorts of literature that furnished the raw materials for the storytellers of *The Thousand and One Nights* and how they reworked it, that evidence does not, in my opinion, tell us much about the specific content and shape of the text at any particular stage prior to the fourteenth century, roughly the date of the earliest Arabic manuscript.

The European Nights

The first appearance of *The Thousand and One Nights* in Europe in 1704 was not unlike the uncanny appearance of the jinni in the first story Shahrazad tells. The jinni is a paradoxical being, now tiny and now enormous; he towers over the merchant and yet his son is so small that the merchant's date pit has killed him. A similar sort of paradox attached to Antoine Galland's French translation of an Arabic manuscript. The book immediately enjoyed huge popular success, yet, as Georges May points out, it drew scarcely any critical or scholarly attention.[16] The disparity between popular success and critical attention, which recalls its status in medieval Arabic literature, has waxed and waned over the course of almost three centuries but has never entirely disappeared—a fact all the more problematic when one considers that the publication of Galland's translation is an early landmark in what Raymond Schwab was to call "The Oriental Renaissance." And there are other complications and paradoxes, for ever since Galland's translation the book has led an unusual double life in Europe and the Arab world. Indeed, to speak of "doubles" here merely hints at the complicated relations between various European translations and Arabic editions.

In 1704 Antoine Galland began to publish his translation of a manuscript he had purchased in Istanbul while serving there as an assistant to the French ambassador to the Ottoman Empire. The first six volumes of Galland's translation contained 234 Nights, after which he abandoned the divisions of Nights in the last six volumes. Given the title however, some of his readers may well have wondered when the rest of the *Nights* would appear. And at this point things get a little complicated.

There are basically two opposed explanations of what happened next. The first and simplest is that Europeans seeking the rest of the book more or less found it, either in manuscript form or in the form of persons—Arabs—who knew more stories that had made their way into the work by this time. The result was the "complete editions" published in the nineteenth century, the Arabic editions of Bulaq and Second Calcutta and Breslau—the latter two we should note were the work of Europeans. According to this version of its history, the late medieval *Nights* looked much like the texts of Bulaq and the First and Second Calcutta and Breslau. This version has its contemporary defenders who have made some important arguments (and revisions) to support it.

Those adherents must deal in one way or another with a "revisionist" version put forth recently by Muhsin Mahdi that opposes the first explanation on almost all the important points. Mahdi devoted years to the study of Galland's manuscript sources, some of which are now lost, and to the reconstruction of a prototype manuscript for *The Thousand and One Nights*. The results of those labors were a reconstructed Arabic text faithful, in Mahdi's view, to the presumed antecedent of Galland's manuscript, a fourteenth-century Syrian manuscript, and a book detailing his views on the history of the *Nights*.[17] His conclusions as to which stories belong in *The Thousand and One Nights* are based on this research. Mahdi argues that European demand for a "complete version" of the work distorted the Mamluk-era original.[18] Europeans wanted a book with literally one thousand and one nights of stories, which the work, in Mahdi's view, did not have through most of its existence. The result was the creation of Arabic manuscripts in the eighteenth and nineteenth centuries that delivered more nights and more stories, and, as Mahdi puts it, the book came to be a "catch all" for popular narratives to meet European demand. In his view, the medieval *Nights* was a much smaller and more coherent work, perhaps one-quarter the length of the nineteenth-century editions. In this view, the number "one thousand and one" for much of its history simply meant "a lot," in accordance with the rather free use of numbers in medieval Arabic literature. But after Galland the number proved fateful, and, if Mahdi is right, the subsequent history of *The Thousand and One Nights* followed "the path of the signifier," so to speak. From that point on, the work's dual versions in European translations and in Arabic manuscripts became intertwined in a very complicated relation, with its popularity in Europe creating a demand for a "complete version." Mahdi's comparison of his presumed "original" with the Bulaq edition and Macnaghten's Second Calcutta, which are based on later Egyptian manuscripts, leads him to conclude that a huge number of the stories in modern versions of *The Thousand and One Nights* do not "belong" in it. Thus, Mahdi's version of the *Nights* and a nineteenth-century Arabic edition like the Second Calcutta confront each other as uncanny doubles with a claim to the same name. It is rather like the Amphitryon-like moment in "The False Caliph" when Harun al-Rashid is confronted with his double in the form of the false caliph.

Mahdi's investigations have done much to clarify the modern history of the text. It seems clear that European demand influenced, to some degree, the shape and content of subsequent Arabic editions. He has also produced an Arabic text that is probably closer in style to the medieval work than any of the nineteenth-century editions.[19] But recent criticism of his "revisionist" version raises some important objections to it. Robert Irwin argues that Mahdi's conclusions proceed from mistaken assumptions about what sort of book *The Thousand and One Nights* was in the medieval period. Mahdi's work on the transmission of the manuscripts is based on theories about manuscript transmission developed from the study of texts by known and esteemed classical authors; but, as Irwin says, the *Nights* never was accorded the sort of respect that such texts enjoyed, hence we cannot assume that its manuscripts were copied and transmitted with anything like the same sort of care.[20] Moreover, there is manuscript evidence for medieval versions of the *Nights* with many more nights than Mahdi would allow. In her recent book, Eva Sallis points out that there are manuscripts predating Galland with many more nights. Moreover, these manuscripts contain stories—"ʿUmar ibn Nuʿmân," for example—that must be regarded as relatively late additions. Hence, she argues that the "expansion" beyond Mahdi's "core" of stories "was a feature of *Nights* compilation earlier than the eighteenth century."[21] In other words, well before the "European demand" created by Galland's work, Middle Eastern writers had already created a text much longer than Mahdi's "original" Mamluk-era text.

Although Mahdi's argument does not bear directly on the analyses that follow, my position on it is largely that of Irwin and Sallis. Even were Mahdi right about what constituted the real medieval *Nights*, only the logic of the specialist could impel someone to reach the conclusion that such stories as "The Seven Voyages of Sindbad" or "Aladdin and His Lamp" do not "belong" in *The Thousand and*

One Nights. At this point in its history, this seems rather like mounting a campaign to change the name of the West Indies to rectify Columbus's error. The most recent English translation of the work, which is based on Mahdi's Arabic text, illustrates my point.

In 1990 Husain Haddawy published a translation called *The Arabian Nights* based on Mahdi's reconstructed Arabic text. In his introduction, Haddawy naturally enough subscribes to Mahdi's position; he writes of the Egyptian manuscript tradition that it "produced an abundance of poisonous fruits that almost proved fatal to the original."[22] "Aladdin and His Lamp," he tells us, must be regarded as a "forgery" (xiii). Five years later, however, Haddawy brought out a second volume, *The Arabian Nights II* containing—yes, the "forgeries" and "poisonous fruits."[23]

For my part, the diversity of stories in the later manuscripts does not bother me, and I think, in any case, there is rather more unity to be found in the nineteenth-century Arabic editions than Mahdi is ready to allow—a point I will argue in chapter 8. Even later stories like "Jûdar and His Brothers" show features that relate them stylistically and thematically to earlier stories. But more importantly, given the general aversion of the medieval Arabic literary elite for outright fictions, we should be happy if the book did act as a kind of "catch-all" for stories. For, setting aside the popular *sîrah*s like "'Antar" and his literary kin (which admittedly are not to my taste), if a story did not find its way into *The Thousand and One Nights*, it likely did not survive.[24] Beginning probably from a core of translated and reworked stories, the book must have grown by process of accretion—the Ottoman royal palace Topkapi may furnish an architectural image for the process; what were originally independent structures are gradually joined together. And what we know of the later history does not seem to depart from this pattern. Insofar as the later additions preserve more stories, I think they are welcome additions to the palace. After all, in such a vast structure, if one does not care for a certain passage, one can move along.

For the reader who is interested in a more detailed history of the text, there is a fairly extensive literature. Unfortunately, much of it is printed in old and obscure journals. Besides Mahdi's work, a few of the more important works in English and French may be mentioned here. The article in the new edition of *The Encyclopedia of Islam* under its Arabic title *Alf laylah wa laylah* is a good place to start. Irwin and Sallis offer the best and most recent "anti-revisionist" accounts. Irwin devotes a chapter in *The Arabian Nights: A Companion* to both the development of the Arabic work and its European editions. I would recommend Irwin's whole book without hesitation; it is an excellent work. The second chapter of Sallis's book offers a very readable and current account of the history of the Arabic text with a good discussion of various manuscripts. The first chapter by André Miquel in the work *Les mille et un contes de la nuit* speculates in a very interesting way on the reasons for the "eclipse" of the work in Arabic in the Middle Ages. Mia Gerhardt's book, *The Art of Story-telling*, published in 1963, also discusses the history of the work, though her account is superseded in some degree by recent work. Lastly I will mention a book by David Pinault, *Story-telling Techniques in The Arabian Nights*, which tries to show us how the storyteller worked; Pinault's analysis is based on a detailed examination of differences between manuscripts.

In my view, despite the antiquity of many of the plots in *The Thousand and One Nights*, the stories as we have them now seem to wear the garb of the late medieval period in the Arab-Islamic world; that is, the eras of the Mamluks and the Ottomans. Thus, stories about the Abbasid caliph Harun al-Rashid, who ruled about five centuries before the Mamluks established their power, may reflect popular notions about how a Mamluk sultan lived in the fourteenth century rather more than they reflect such images of the way Harun lived five hundred years earlier. Not that ornate palaces, gardens, wine drinking, cup bearers, and slave consorts were not features of the Abbasid court, but as found here these features often seem like those of the Mamluks or the Ottomans. An obvious example comes in the frame story, in the scene in which King Shahriyâr's wife commits adultery in the garden with a black slave; the lover and the enclosed garden are stock elements in any Ottoman Turkish *gazel* or love poem. On the general question of the work's historical context, I might finally remark that the Ottoman period is viewed in the Arab world now as one of cultural decadence, a view propounded by Arab nationalism. However, the very existence of this book is testimony, I think, to cultural vitality in that period.

On the basis of the preceding discussion of the various versions of the *Nights*, my reader may well wonder at this point which Arabic text or texts (and which translations) are in my view the "real" *Nights*. My answer is simple: all of them. *The Thousand and One Nights* is a multiple text, and I see no reason to exclude any standard Arabic edition or any of the translations based on it, no matter how controversial they may be. I have for the most part relied on Macnaghten's Second Calcutta edition, an edition based, it seems, on the Bulaq edition and a now-lost manuscript probably copied sometime shortly after 1830. The manuscript belonged to the late Egyptian recension on which the Bulaq edition was also based.

Those manuscripts are now known as Zotenburg's Egyptian Recension (ZER) after the scholar who studied them. But I have made free use of other editions (and of various translations) as it suited my purposes and in accordance with my "maximalist" position.

So much for literary history. Much more important for this study are the reasons *why* the book had such a shadowy existence in the pre-modern Arabic literature. That is to say, the historical problems posed by the book's orphan-like existence in Arabic literary culture are of less importance for what follows than the characteristics of the book that made it an orphan. These call for some discussion here because, as I have said, my readers should know that *The Thousand and One Nights* is an exceptional, even aberrant work with respect to some of the most important conventions of medieval Arabic literature.[25] Hence, that the stories say the things I contend they do stems in many ways from the fact that this work is the "repressed" of the literature. The factors that contribute to this status may be discussed under three headings: its genre, its linguistic style, and its content. Foremost is genre, and this raises the question of the place of narrative in medieval Arabic literature.

Narrative in Medieval Arabic Literature

The early development of medieval Arabic literature was part and parcel with the development of Islam. While there existed a rich poetic tradition in pre-Islamic Arabia and a body of narratives that accompanied it and purported to provide the factual background of the poetry, this material seems to have been preserved in oral form until it began to be written down in the late eighth and early ninth centuries—that is, at the same time that, with one exception, the other early texts of Arabic literature are being written. The one exception, of course, is the Qur'an.

The death of Muhammad in 632 A.D. furnishes a reference point. The Qur'an is the only major text that we know to have existed in some *written* form in the century after his death. It is, we should note, a work that contains little narrative as compared to the Bible.

After the Qur'an, the next major work we possess is *The Life of the Prophet* (*Sîrat al-nabî*), composed in the first half of the eighth century by Ibn Isḥâq (d.767), but available to us in the recension of Ibn Hishâm (d. 828 or 833), who made his own cuts and additions. Close on its heels comes a book by al-Wâqidî (d. 823) called *The Raids* (*Al-Maghâzî*) describing the raids Muhammad and his followers made on the pagan tribes of western Arabia.

Because of their priority and the importance of their subject matter, these works established precedents for the use of narrative that would have lasting effects throughout the Islamic Middle Ages. They are made up of the earliest narratives in Arabic, traditions about what Muhammad and his followers said and did in the course of conquering western Arabia. These narratives are known as *akhbâr*; *al-akhbar* in modern vernacular simply means "the news." The singular *khabar* means a piece of information recounted for someone—the same term is used in Arabic grammar to mean the predicate of a sentence. In the early literature a *khabar* is a short narrative, usually a half page or less in length, and hence confined to the pithy recounting of a single incident. Because of its religious significance and to buttress its factual claims, each *khabar*-narrative came to be preceded by a feature known as the *isnâd* or "chain," a series of names representing a kind of bucket brigade of tradents who, it is claimed, have passed the narrative along to the writer from an eyewitness to the original event. Both with respect to narrative form and the *uses* to which narrative may be put, these traditions exerted enormous influence on subsequent narrative literature. Thus, in its beginning, narrative literature in Arabic purports to confine itself to fact, to the recounting of real events by eyewitnesses, real people. If one accepts everything at face value in works such as Ibn Ishaq's *Life of the Prophet* and Waqidi's *Raids*, then Ibn Ishaq and Waqidi, the "authors," have composed very little of their books' texts, having simply copied verbatim the "accounts" from other people and other written sources.

For various historical and ideological reasons, it proved very difficult for narrative literature to free itself of these conventions.[26] The theoretical and practical problems these conventions pose for the development of fictional narrative should not be underestimated. First of all, narratives are always about "real events."[27] Within the literature proper, a generic space for fiction never really opened up. That which never happened is simply a lie. Curiously, *The Thousand and One Nights* is in agreement with this attitude—it has "internalized" the prejudice, so to speak. Shahrazad does not make up stories. As Abdelfattah Kilito writes: "It sometimes happens that characters in the *Nights* make up a story, that is to say, they affirm that they know it to be false. Invention is then synonymous with lying."[28]

Secondly, the device of the *isnad* poses a formal obstacle for beginning a fiction. It bars the way to the space where a fiction unfolds. This can be seen in some of the few fictional narratives composed by recognized authors. Thus Ibn Butlan, deferring to the need for an *isnad*, begins his *The Physicians' Banquet*, "One of them said. . . ." One of whom? We can imagine a novel beginning with those words, but we would expect shortly to be given at least a hint as to the identity of "one of them" within the fiction. That never happens in Ibn Butlan's work. We never learn anything about "one of them," for this "one of them" exists in some extratextual place. The French Symbolist Paul Valéry remarks somewhere that he could not write fiction because he could never bring himself to write a sentence like, "The marquise went out at five." Being so used to the conventions of fiction, we may underestimate the amount of literary development that prepares the way for someone to begin with a sentence like that.

The *isnad* can also pose a problem with respect to the length of a narrative if one must represent a fiction as fact. Here I might remark that speculation about length per se as a factor that distinguishes *The Thousand and One Nights* narrative from the anecdotal works of *adab* like those of Tanukhi misses the larger point. It is not a question of length in and of itself, but of length as an index of fictionality.[29] A second glance at a work like Tanukhi's *Happiness after Hardship*—which, as we have seen, contains some analogues with stories found in *The Thousand and One Nights*—shows this. The stories in Tanukhi are almost entirely anecdotal, by which I mean most are a page or less in length. They rarely have the scope or the detail found in the full-blown fictions of *The Thousand and One Nights*. The very length of a narrative would pose a problem vis à vis the assertion of fact staked out by the *isnad*. To focus on only one aspect, any *khabar* is likely to contain direct speech, but if such an account extends for many pages, one must grant the original eyewitness/reporter extraordinary powers of recollection to think that the reported speeches are the verbatim words of the various persons involved. The question must inevitably arise, "How could he (and all of the other persons in the *isnad*) have remembered all of this exactly as it was said?"

Other conventions pose other sorts of difficulties for the development of fictional narrative. Being supposedly a literature of hard fact, in a *khabar*–narrative no one would presume to make a statement about what someone else was thinking or feeling, for how would he know such a thing? Thus, only the grossest sorts of emotions are registered—"He was very angry"—and thought, unless it is spoken, remains absent. The continuing influence of these features will be seen in *The Thousand and One Nights*.

There may also have been ideological constraints. M. Arkoun has written: "The theological and philosophical tradition imposed an ontological weakness on the imagination. The Koran contributed to this weakening with its attacks against 'the poets whom the erring follow, who wander in every valley and who say what they do not do' (26:224–226)."[30] And a well-known episode in the *sirah* and *maghazi* literature shows Muhammad's anger with a storyteller who claimed his stories were "better" than Muhammad's. Naḍr ibn al-Ḥârith so vexed Muhammad that the latter ordered him killed.[31]

In time, to be sure, some obvious fictions came to exist within the literary canon; *Kalîlah wa Dimnah*, the fables translated by Ibn al-Muqaffaʿ (d. 756), and the *Maqamat* or "Seances" of al-Hamadhani (mentioned above) and al-Ḥarîrî (d. 1122) are the most notable examples. But such works are also exceptional. *Kalilah wa Dimnah* is a translation of a Persian work based on the *Panchatantra*, and Hariri was attacked for having made up his stories by Ibn al-Khashshâb (d. 1172).

As a result of all of these developments, in the general view of the literate minority inventing stories was not distinguishable from simply telling lies. And on all these accounts, *The Thousand and One Nights* just goes too far. Its excessively fictional character in this respect can be seen in the way the *Nights'* version of "The Sleeper Awakened" adds a second part to the story that Ishaqi has. Thus its genre, its clearly fictional nature, is the first major reason why *The Thousand and One Nights* is an exceptional work; there is no generic space in the medieval literary canon for it.

Another important factor has to do with its style; the sort of Arabic found in *The Thousand and One Nights* also counted against it. As far back as linguists can determine, Arabic seems to have been characterized by a considerable divergence between the written and spoken forms, a divergence in both vocabulary and grammar. The difference is perhaps most visible in the case endings that are preserved in the written language, but almost completely ignored in spoken dialects. With such a divergence, literacy is a rather more difficult and elusive goal to attain—something that remains the case today in the Arab world. In the Middle Ages, the spoken dialects were not even considered real languages by the literate minority. The power of that minority rested in their grasp of *al-ʿarabîyah*, the classical written language in which the official discourse of the culture was carried on, while the illiterate were excluded from speech, in their view, since they had no language proper. They were, in a sense, "unspeakable"—one could say "repressed" in the strict sense that they were denied the words to express themselves.

In such a vast work as *The Thousand and One Nights* there are many registers of language, but apart from perhaps conscious stylistic variations, the different manuscripts of *The Thousand and One Nights* all are salted with significant amounts of colloquial usages. These usages have led various scholars to speak of it as being written in "Middle Arabic," but that term, coined by a modern Western scholar, had no status at all among the authors who wrote "Middle Arabic"; those men were attempting to adhere to the classical grammar—they simply no longer mastered it. In the case of the *Nights* the writers may simply not have thought enough of it to go to the bother of adhering to *al-ʿarabiyah* with the result being "Middle Arabic." It may also have been in part the result, as Sallis suggests, of "the accretions of a random textual history."[32] In any case, the language of *The Thousand and One Nights* works against it. The influence of popular tongues, Syrian and Egyptian, is heard in it, and those sounds were, no doubt, repellent to the ears of the litterateurs who wrote in the "pure language" of *al-ʿarabiyah*.

Finally, there is the subject matter. Illicit sex and wine stain the pages. Hashish is used frequently. Despite the way the book is used as a stock reference for certain sorts of events ("It was like something out of *The Arabian Nights*"), many people are surprised by the real contents of the book. There is a widespread assumption that it is something like children's literature, but it is not.

On the other hand, whether the book is "a faithful mirror of medieval Islam," as one edition touts it, is difficult to say. In such a view, one of the reasons the *Nights* is so valuable is that it depicts many things that are not often treated in the literature proper. That literature, as I have said, was the product of an elite who seldom wrote about such homely subjects. But since the *Nights* is in many ways a unique source, the argument threatens to become circular if one claims it is a faithful picture of medieval Muslim society. Moreover, the book is a "catch-all" or *omnium gatherum*—to use Irwin's phrase—and as Irwin says, "one can use its texts, through selective quotation from stories, to support the argument that homosexuality was widely approved of, or to argue that it was indifferently accepted, or to argue that it was absolutely abominated."[33] In other words, one would have to take a Hegelian stance—("the truth is the whole")—to make it a "faithful mirror." It is some sort of reflection no doubt, but some literary refraction and distortion must be involved. The fantastic elements that abound also seem to pose some problems for this view of the book: jinn fly back and forth between China and the Near East in the course of a single night; humans are transformed into animals and back into humans; islands turn out to be whales; mountains pull the nails from ships' hulls by means of mysterious, magnetic powers. So, even while one "feels" the truth of its stories, as a source for social history *The Thousand and One Nights* must be used carefully. Yet this much is clear: its subject matter could be an affront to the pious writers who always made up a considerable portion of the literary elite, men who wrote books with titles like *The Condemnation of Fun* (*Dhamm al-lahû*).

For all of these reasons *The Thousand and One Nights* was a marginalized work in medieval Arabic literature, and that is one reason why it is so valuable. It escaped the self-censorship of more typical narrative works, and from the outset its pages are filled with desires and ideas that are rarely articulated elsewhere in the literature. Which could serve to justify the approach taken here, based as it is on the ideas of Jacques Lacan, but I shall not use that as a rationale. I will justify that on a more general basis in the next chapter. The third chapter analyzes the frame tale in terms of the master-slave dialectic. Chapters four, five, and six examine stories under the rubrics of love, the double, and wounds. Chapter seven deals with "The Hunchback" and its complex cycle of stories. Chapter eight is perhaps the true conclusion to the book; it considers various sorts of repetitions and recurrences in the book in relation to the question of the book's unity. The last chapter examines the relation between the epilogue wherein the frame tale is concluded and a coda-like sentence that is repeatedly used to conclude stories in the *Nights*. The chapter itself is something of a coda.

2

The Imaginary, the Symbolic, and the Real: An Overview of Lacan

THIS STUDY OF *THE THOUSAND AND ONE NIGHTS* COMBINES MY INTERests in medieval Arabic literature and psychoanalytic thought. More especially, it combines my interests in narrative and the work of Jacques Lacan. As such, it begins from the premise that certain basic psychoanalytic concepts are applicable across cultural boundaries and across time—indeed, I would say that they must be or psychoanalysis is nothing. There are, of course, numerous critiques of psychoanalysis that contend it is ahistorical, that it ignores cultural differences and falsely universalizes contingent, historical entities; more such critiques finding examples of these sins in Freud's work are being penned all the time. Attempts to bury Freud began even before he died, and they continue to this day. It is a little like the "Tale of the Hunchback." Everyone tries to get rid of the hunchback's body, but it is precisely the body in its traumatic form as corpse that continually disrupts the various social and historical contingencies of the story. So too Freud—and Lacan. The value of certain of their notions is precisely that they are ahistorical. One of these, to give only one example that is important for the analyses that follow, is that of the "traumatic kernel"—to use Slavoj Žižek's expression, the experience that defines the subject in his relation to the Law—that returns again and again in diverse "historicizations/symbolizations." To quote Žižek himself:

> In the Lacanian perspective, we should . . . designate as the most "cunning" ideological procedure the very opposite of eternalization: an *over-rapid historicization*. Let us take one of the commonplaces of Marxist-feminist criticism of psychoanalysis, the idea that its insistence on the crucial role of the Oedipus complex and the nuclear-family triangle transforms a historically conditioned form of patriarchal family into a feature of conjunction as an eternal, universal feature of the human condition: is not this effort to historicize the family triangle precisely an

attempt to elude the "hard kernel" which announces itself through the "patriarchal family"—the Real of the Law, the rock of castration? In other words, if over-rapid universalization produces a quasi-universal Image whose function is to make us blind to its historical, socio-symbolic determination, over-rapid historicization makes us blind to the real kernel which returns as the same through diverse historicizations/symbolizations.[1]

Thus, while I might justify this work on a more limited basis by arguing that *The Thousand and One Nights* as a "repressed" work in medieval Arabic literature is especially suitable for such a study, I would rather assert a broader applicability for psychoanalytic thought, and especially for the work of Lacan.

For this reason, some introduction to Lacan himself and Lacanian theory will be useful (though I will still attempt to gloss the meaning of various terms as they occur in the text). Such an introduction is perhaps especially useful given the rather sibylline quality of many of Lacan's formulations: that is, "The *real* is the impossible."

Three terms dominate Lacan's interpretation and development of Freudian thought: the *imaginary*, the *symbolic*, and the *real*. These provide a framework for a general introduction to his thought. The terms designate "orders" or "registers" that comprehend all of human experience, but their usual meanings do not begin to suggest their meanings within Lacanian theory. Although the three orders coexist, in Lacan's own career he placed varying degrees of emphasis on them. In his early career much of his writing and teaching was devoted to the imaginary; in his middle years much of his work focused on the symbolic, and finally in his later years, the real. This is the order in which I will treat them here.

The Imaginary

Jacques Lacan's career as a theorist of psychoanalysis began in 1936 with the introduction of the concept called "The Mirror Stage."[2] With this term Lacan designates the developmental stage in which the human infant, who is born "prematurely" (that is, helpless and without motor control) first conceives of himself as a whole being by seeing his image in a mirror—or, more likely, by gazing at the face of another human and thinking, roughly, "I am that." Of this moment two things must be said here. First, far from being a moment of triumphant integration, the moment "in which the *I* is precipitated in a primordial form" is an illusion, since the subject is still helpless and without control. As such it marks the first of a series of "misrecognitions" that will characterize the ego, and as such "prefigures its alienating destination" (*E*, 2). Indeed, Lacan compares the human child's reaction to its image with the reaction of a chimpanzee to its image and notes that the child is "for a time, however short, outdone by the chimpanzee in instrumental intelligence" (*E*, 1), for the chimpanzee realizes that the image is empty, while the human is captivated by it. Second, by means of the mirror stage, Lacan introduces the much larger concept of the *imaginary*, by which he does not mean anything related to the imagination, but rather that register of human experience that is solely composed of images.

As "mirror image" implies, imaginary relations are dyadic, and the ego is for Lacan an imaginary object: "The ego really is an object," he states emphatically.[3] He explains the functioning of the ego in this way:

> I would like to give you a representation of it [this "dialectic"] in an image . . . that of the blind man and the paralytic. Subjectivity on the level of the ego is comparable to this couple, which was introduced by the imagery of the fifteenth century—no doubt not without a reason—in a particularly emphatic manner. The subjective half of the pre-mirror experience is the paralytic, who cannot move himself about except in an uncoordinated and clumsy way. What masters him is the image of the ego, which is blind, and which carries him. Contrary to all appearances, and this is where the entire problem of the dialectic lies, it isn't, as Plato thinks, the master who rides the horse, that is the slave, it's the other way around. And the paralytic, whose perspective this is, can only identify with his unity in a fascinated fashion, in the fundamental immobility whereby he finishes up corresponding to the gaze he is under, the blind gaze. (*S*, 2:50)

Such references to Hegel's master-slave dialectic are scattered throughout Lacan's writings and teachings, especially in his early seminars, and they show the influence on Lacan of the most important interpreter of Hegel in France in the past century, Alexandre Kojève.

Kojève taught the seminar on Hegel's *Phenomenology of the Spirit* at the École des Hautes Études in the years preceding World War II. Besides Lacan, people such as Raymond Queneau, Georges Bataille, André Breton, and Maurice Merleau-Ponty attended the seminar, and Kojève's influence was considerable. Lacan found in Hegel's *Phenomenology*—or more precisely in Kojève's reading of the *Phenomenology*—a vocabulary for elaborating the relations of the subject and the other. Indeed, one of Lacan's most well known catchphrases, "Desire is the desire of the other," is a gloss on Kojève's reading of Hegel. "Desire is human," Kojève states, "only provided that it is directed toward another *Desire* and an *other* Desire."[4]

In 1947 Raymond Queneau published transcriptions of Kojève's seminars under the title *Introduction à la lecture de Hegel,* and this work, whose impress will be evident in this study, enables one to understand the influence Kojève had on Lacan and many others. Kojève's reading—a left-wing, atheistic, and anthropological reading—has been called idiosyncratic and even willfully wrong by some Hegelian scholars; but no matter, so long as it is understood that "Hegel" here means—unless otherwise indicated—"Kojève-Hegel."

The mirror stage comes to an end for Lacan with the beginning of oedipal conflict, at about eighteen months. Thus, in Lacan's revision of Freud, the effects of the Oedipus complex can only be understood as occurring on the already established subject of the mirror stage. The key for Lacan, as Richard Boothby says, is not that the child's desire for the mother is interdicted by the father, but rather that the child discovers that he/she lacks what the mother desires.[5] Prior to the oedipal stage, "If the desire of the mother *is* the phallus, the child wishes to be the phallus in order to satisfy that desire," Lacan writes (*E*, 289). But in the oedipal stage, the child realizes that the mother's desire is for a third party, the father. Thus, the fear of castration has a re-interpretation in Lacan in relation to his view of the "prematuration" of the human infant, its experience of itself in the months after birth as a number of uncoordinated parts. As Boothby writes, for Lacan "castration anxiety is not a fear over the loss of an original wholeness but reemergence of the sense of chaos and virtual dismemberment into which every human infant is born."[6] The Oedipus crisis is the moment when the mirror stage ends, and of this transformation Lacan writes:

> It is this moment that decisively tips the whole of human knowledge into mediatization through the desire of the other, constitutes its objects in an abstract equivalence by the co-operation of others, and turns the *I* into that apparatus for which every instinctual thrust constitutes a danger, even though it should correspond to a natural maturation—the very normalization being henceforth dependent, in man, on a cultural mediation as exemplified, in the case of the sexual object, by the Oedipus complex. (*E*, 5–6)

The upsurge of libidinal forces in the oedipal stage thus constitutes a threat to the imaginary organization of the ego. And whenever the subject finds himself in conflict with the Law, it is this sense of chaos and dismemberment that returns as the traumatic kernel. But the relation of the ego, as an imaginary function, to the *real* (to anticipate) of infantile experience from which it emerged has another important aspect.

The ego is experienced as a loss, but the nostalgia does not take the form of a fantasy of some Edenic wholeness. Rather, because of the chaotic and uncoordinated physical forces, the fantasy is one of dismemberment. Lacan's memorable phrase for this fantasy is *le corps morcelé*, "the fragmented body," and under its rubric he mentions everything from the homely example of toddlers' tendency to pull the limbs off their dolls to the paintings of Hieronymus Bosch. What is essential to understanding Lacan is that for him (and against ego psychology), the ego is not the subject. The ego is a symptom. It is a kind of callus that has hardened on the surface of the living subject.

The Symbolic

The intrusion of a third party occurs at a time when the child is also beginning to speak its first words, and not merely by coincidence, for the child can only understand its situation—that is, he can only conceptualize that he is *not* what the mother wants, that he *lacks* what the mother wants—by means of language. Thus, in the Oedipus complex, the child is integrated into the *symbolic order*.

The symbolic order is preeminently the order of language. In contrast to the imaginary order that is characterized by relations of sameness and resemblance, the symbolic is characterized by heterogeneity and absence. And thus, where the imaginary order is the order in which the ego endlessly refashions itself through identificatory processes, the symbolic order is where the subject is endlessly composed and recomposed or "articulated" in signifying chains. The symbolic order is the order of the unconscious, and this helps one to understand Lacan's assertion that "the unconscious is structured like a language." The structure of language then reproduces itself in the human subject; the dual axes of language described by his friend Roman Jakobson mean for Lacan that, "the symptom *is* a metaphor whether one likes it or not, as desire *is* a metonymy, however funny people find the idea" (*E*, 175).

Lacan's seminar in 1956 on the Poe story "The Purloined Letter" may be his best single excursus on the symbolic order and the subject. It has certainly been his single most influential piece of writing in this country. In Lacan's reading, the displacements of the Queen's stolen love letter may be taken as a "fable" to demonstrate "the decisive orientation which the subject receives from the itinerary of the signifier."[7] Besides *The Interpretation of Dreams*, the key Freudian texts for Lacan in this regard are *Jokes and Their Relation to the Unconscious*, *The Psychopathology of Everyday Life*, and *Beyond the Pleasure Principle*. In dreams, jokes, and "Freudian slips" Lacan sees evidence of how the linguistic processes of metaphor and metonymy structure the unconscious and hence determine the subject. In *Beyond the Pleasure Principle*, Lacan reinterprets the "death drive" as an effect of the symbolic order, the insistent return of the linguistic sign. As Žižek puts it:

> "death drive" is not a biological fact but a notion indicating that the human psychic apparatus is subordinated to a blind automatism of repetition beyond pleasure-seeking, self-preservation, accordance between man and his milieu. Man is . . . an animal extorted by an insatiable parasite (reason, *logos*, language).[8]

Necessary for the proper functioning of the symbolic order—of language—in the human subject are what Lacan calls *points de capiton*, after the buttons in a cushion that keep the stuffing from shifting around. Most prominent of these is the one Lacan calls the *nom-du-père*, the Name-of-the-Father. Lacan uses the term to designate the symbolic father, and the pun in French with "The No-of-the Father" is intended to underline the symbolic father as representative of the Law (since the murder/death of the father inaugurates the Law in *Totem and Taboo*). The Name-of-the-Father for Lacan evokes the fundamental relation of the subject to language and Law; that the Law underwrites and defines the subject's desire. The way in which this term relies upon Freud and at the same time greatly expands on him is instructive regarding Lacan's so-called "return to Freud." A comparison of Lacan and Freud on the voices heard by the paranoiac Schreber may help to clarify this. Freud says that "it was incorrect to say that the perception which was suppressed internally was projected outwards; the truth is rather, as we now see, that what was *abolished* internally returns from without."[9] Lacan's understanding is somewhat different; it is not a matter of repression, but what he calls *foreclosure*, taking over a term Freud used elsewhere, *Verwurfung*.[10] He says that what was "foreclosed" was not any signifier but the Name-of-the-Father, the fundamental signifier that defined and articulated the relations of the subject's desire to the symbolic order and the Law. "It's a matter of understanding . . . what happens for a subject when the question comes to him from where there is no signifier, when it's a hole, a lack, that makes itself felt as such" (*S*, 3:203). Without it, there is a hole in the symbolic order, and those effects that ought to have been articulated in language return as hallucinations in the *real*, the third Lacanian order.

The Real

The *real* is probably the most difficult of the triad of orders to explain, for elusiveness is precisely one of its foremost qualities for Lacan. If the imaginary in Lacanian theory has little to do with our usual sense of "imaginary," the Lacanian real has even less to do with our usual notion of reality as designating that which is outside the mind. The easiest way to get at Lacan's concept of the real is by defining it negatively—though we will not be satisfied with this. The real for Lacan is all that which resists and eludes man's symbolic representations of the world.

It will be useful, however, to go back to the mirror stage in order to situate the real in Lacanian theory; in the mirror stage the real is the mass of chaotic sensations, the very flow of life, which at that point is replaced by the ego, which results from the subject's identification with an external, alienated image. In terms of the symbolic order, the real is both purely positive presence, the living body that is "dissected" and "divided" by the process of symbolization, by discourse, yet at the same time, since the symbolic process (discourse) can never totalize its object, the real is that remnant which eludes the symbolic process. Hence, the real is, despite its positivity, also a lack, a hole in the symbolic order. And since the real designates things without regard to their symbolic representation, and therefore without regard to their place in any conceptual system, Lacan can say that in the real "everything is always in its place." For a thing can only be misplaced with regard to some symbolic ordering of reality that yields an expectation of where it is to be found. All of which leaves out one important aspect of the Lacanian real: the subject's most frequent experience of the real is traumatic. In psychoanalysis, Lacan says the real first presented itself "in the form of that which is unassimilable in it—in the form of the trauma. . . ."[11] This comment is taken from chapter 5 of *The Four Fundamental Concepts of Psycho-Analysis*, which is perhaps Lacan's most provocative exposition of the real.

The chapter's title is "Tuché and Automaton," two terms taken from Aristotle's *Physics*. In the second book of the *Physics*, Aristotle discusses *tuché*—"chance" or "luck"—in terms of the unintended consequences of human actions; a man goes to the market to buy or sell something and happens to meet a man who owes him money. *Automaton*, Aristotle says, is a much broader term that refers to events involving beasts and inanimate objects. He gives the example of a stool that falls and happens to land on its feet; *automaton* refers then to random events in the broadest sense. As Malcolm Bowie says, at first it may seem as though Lacan has switched terms "the wrong way around," for by *tuché* he means an encounter with the real that is beyond the network of signifiers for which he reserves the term "automaton."[12] But all's well that ends well, and Lacan's use of the terms shows what he means. *Tuché* is a chance encounter with the real, for good or ill, which is unassimilable to the network of signifiers in which the subject is articulated. Automaton designates the return of the sign, the insistence of the signifying network. The most telling example of how the real is always experienced as *tuché*, as accident, is Lacan's rereading of the well-known "burning child" dream Freud discusses in *The Interpretation of Dreams*.

Freud describes the situation as this: A man whose child has just died of some illness leaves someone to keep a vigil over the child's body while he goes to sleep in the next room, keeping the door open between them. The man dreams that the child is standing close to his bed, and taking him by the arm whispers, "Father, don't you see I'm burning?" (*SE*, 5:509). A moment later the man awakes to find that the man he set to keep watch over his child has also fallen asleep and a candle has fallen over and begun to burn his dead child's arm. For Freud this sorrowful dream nevertheless constitutes evidence for his theory that dreams are the fulfillment of a wish, since the man, in his attempt to incorporate the real event into yet another dream, thereby paradoxically restores his dead child to life: when he awakes the child will be dead again. But Lacan's reading takes this even further. Freud conjectures that the phrase "don't you see I'm burning?" probably contains some allusion to the fatal illness of the child, and taking this up Lacan asks, "Is not the missed reality that caused the death of the child expressed in these words?" (*FFC*, 58). Lacan asks, "Is not the dream essentially an act of homage to the missed reality—the reality that can no longer produce itself except by repeating itself endlessly, in some never attained awakening?" (*FFC*, 58). Desire is still manifest in the dream for Lacan, but it "manifests itself in the dream by the loss expressed in an image at the most cruel point of the object" (*FFC*, 59).

In sum, the real is apprehended only retroactively by means of a traumatic residue of a missed encounter.

Readers of Freud will realize that with the real we are very close to that same enigmatic place that Freud would return to many years later in *Beyond the Pleasure Principle*. After formulating a subject who functions/oscillates between the venerable poles of pleasure and unpleasure, Freud takes up the puzzling question of why people repeat in their dreams some trauma.

Lacan's term for the subject's relation to this traumatic real is *jouissance*, weakly translated as "enjoyment." *Jouissance* is not pleasure (*Lust*), for it is not subject to the homeostasis of the Freudian "pleasure principle." Rather, it is, as Slavoj Žižek says, "precisely '*Lust im Unlust*'; it designates the paradoxical satisfaction procured by a painful encounter with a Thing that perturbs the equilibrium of the 'pleasure principle.' In other words, enjoyment is located 'beyond the pleasure principle.' "[13] Hence, *jouissance* has no end other than itself, and while it is outside the subject, it somehow uncannily is also inside him. Furthermore, it somehow defines that experience that is necessary to his very identity and without which he threatens to dissolve. As we shall see, the story of "The Third Qalandar" told within "The Porter and the Three Ladies of Baghdad" provides an example; *jouissance*, we may say, is why the Third Qalandar repeatedly breaks the enigmatic prohibitions placed upon him.

Again, Lacan coins a term to designate how the real object is apprehended by the subject, and to evoke the manifold aspects of this relation. His term is *objet petit a* (for *autre*—"other"), later reduced to *objet a*, and finally to simply the *a*. Initially Lacan calls it the *petit a* to distinguish it from the upper-case *A* meaning *Autre* (or the "Big O," as it is translated in English), which stands for the symbolic order. The *objet a* is what is left over of the real object of our desire after it has been submitted to symbolization. Since symbolization eviscerates it of the real, *objet a* becomes the positive expression of a lack. One commentator describes *objet a* as the void around which our desire endlessly orbits, always falling towards it, yet never attaining it.

Lacan and Literature

In a paper delivered to a group of literary scholars, "The Agency of the Letter in the Unconscious, or Reason since Freud," Lacan says that "Freud constantly maintained to the end of his days that such training [literary training] was the prime requisite in the formation of analysts, and that he designated the eternal *universitas litterarum* as the ideal place for its institution" (*E*, 147). Not surprisingly, references to literary works are copious in Lacan's seminars and in the *Écrits*. There are also more extended discussions of literary works: the "Seminar on the 'Purloined Letter' " is the best known in this country, but Lacan also wrote extensive analyses of *Antigone* and *Hamlet* and devoted a seminar to Joyce. His discussions of literary works are subtle and incisive, that is to say on a par with Freud's—and in contrast with much psychoanalytic criticism.

For those readers with a further interest in Lacan, a more than glancing acquaintance with Freud is of course helpful; as far as Lacan's own works, I would recommend reading the seminars first and then the *Écrits*. This was the advice given me by my colleague and friend Tom DiPiero, and it proved very helpful. The literary flourishes of the *Écrits* are more comprehensible after one is acquainted with his style of expression in his seminars.

For me, Freud and Lacan are the most provocative readers of the last century. Obviously, I hope that application of certain of their concepts to *The Thousand and One Nights* will yield a new understanding of this singular work. Due in part to Lacan's philosophical bent, and due in part to my own interests and readings, concepts and passages drawn from a variety of important Western thinkers—Descartes, Kant, Hegel inter alia—also play a prominent role in this study, though usually within the frame of some psychoanalytic concept. Hence, readers who are skeptical about psychoanalysis may find themselves surprised by the way in which certain narrative situations in *The Thousand and One Nights* seem to mirror concepts found in the works of such modern Western thinkers. Regarding these correspondences, only two explanations come to my mind. Either the human subject has certain universal features, as psychoanalysis holds, features that ineluctably express themselves in products of the mind such as *The Thousand and One Nights*, or they must conclude that a marginalized medieval Arab writer (or writers) of popular fictions anticipated such concepts and theories in his stories. The only further justification I will offer for my approach here is its results. These results will, I hope, bring to light the provocative and even disturbing qualities of this work, and will show how this marginalized medieval work still speaks to us.

3

King, Queen, Master, Slave

THE FRAME STORY OF *THE THOUSAND AND ONE NIGHTS*, THE STORY OF King Shahriyar and the woman named Shahrazad, has probably drawn more comment and analysis in Western literary criticism than any other single piece of Arabic writing, including the Qur'an. This might seem an anomaly given the great disparity in the status of the two works in Muslim Arab culture, but it is perhaps understandable in view of certain factors. There is, of course, the provocative nature of the story itself. The difference in the role of narrative art in the two cultures has probably also helped to determine this situation; fictional narrative is central in Western culture, while the Qur'an tells few stories, and tells them rather differently from *The Thousand and One Nights*. Finally, the *Nights* has had considerable influence on Western literature and art, something that cannot be said of the Qur'an.

The story begins, like numberless folktales, by describing two brothers who are kings. The language, aside from a bit of rhymed prose (Arabic *saj*ʿ) at the outset, is plain, even a little sloppy, and descriptions of people and things are perfunctory. But soon enough the narrative takes a turn, and we realize we are reading something rather different from what we usually understand by the term "folktale." The narrative veers off into betrayal, orgy, and murder, the stuff of tragedy, and yet the narrative tone is often comic—even apart from the epilogue that ends, in the usual way of comedy, with a wedding. Doings that might at least raise an eyebrow are related in a matter-of-fact narrative style not wholly dissimilar to the style in contemporary fiction known as "hard-boiled": "He cut off their heads, and killed them in the bed. Then he ordered that his departure be made . . ." (1:2). "She called out, 'Masʿûd', and a black slave came to her. They embraced and he mounted her" (1:3). "She asked, 'Do you realize what these are?' They said, 'No,' and she said, 'Each ring belonged to a man who fucked me, putting cuckold's 'horns' on this jinni' " (1:5). The story cannot be transformed into children's literature without a little editing, and one wonders if the innocuous beginning was not contrived to lull the reader.

No doubt the perennial interest of the story derives from the complex ways in which sexuality and violence figure in it, and, in recent years, psychoanalytic and feminist readings have focused on these issues.[1] The former sorts of readings put the concept of "desire" at the center of their readings of the story; through Shahrazad's storytelling, Shahriyar learns about the nature of his desire and this, in some fashion, straightens him out. Feminist readings, on the other hand, tend to emphasize how the mastery of Shahrazad counters patriarchy in the story. This is not to efface the differences of these individual readings, but simply to situate the comments that follow. In my view, Shahrazad's method—rather like psychoanalysis—is not so much the revelation of something, be it desire or mastery, but the revelation of a *lack* of something.

More specifically, what I wish to counter in those previous readings and analyses is the relative short shrift given to the role of the slave in the narrative. Those analyses that lay more emphasis either on the relation of desire and narrative on one hand, or on gender relations on the other hand, tend to overlook another dyad that is of at least equal importance, the relation of master and slave. The slave is taken merely as a necessary prop so the queen may commit adultery. But the plot cannot be understood simply in terms of the desire and dynamics of gender, or the "male-female power dynamic."[2] It must take into account the roles of master and slave. Analyses that overlook the role of the slave also misconstrue the manner in which death figures in the narrative and miss the importance of the wager in the narrative scheme.

My method here will be to read the story of Shahriyar and Shahrazad against Hegel's myth of the master-slave relation as interpreted by Kojève and Lacan.

Shahriyar's crisis, occasioned by his wife's infidelity, is the heart of the tale, and the story divides itself into two parts in relation to his crisis. The first part describes how it develops and its results; the second part begins with Shahrazad's entrance and narrates her response to this crisis. The key events in the first part of the story are a series of sexual triangles. In the first three instances, the triangles are composed of a king, queen, and slave; the fourth triangle alters this arrangement. In the second part of the story, Shahrazad's actions offer an implicit critique of those triangles and she offers a different sort of triangle to Shahriyar. This is, I will argue, a version of the *Fort/Da* game, the simple game of making a spool disappear and reappear invented by Freud's grandson in reaction to the absences of his mother.

After formal gestures common to all medieval Arabic texts—namely, invocation ("Praise be to God and may peace be upon His messenger") and justification ("accounts of people in the past provide lessons for those in the present")—the story begins: "There was once in times long past a king who had two sons. . . ." The two brothers, apart from their different ages, are described in very similar terms except for one characteristic; the older brother Shahriyar is said to be *afras* (1:2). This might mean simply "more of a horseman" or perhaps "more knightly" in a broader sense, or, again, it may refer to the concept of *firâsah*, a term that meant the ability to divine hidden qualities based on physiognomy. This meaning probably evolved out of some meaning like "horse sense" for the ancient Arabs. In the later medieval period, the word encompassed a Sufi meaning of spiritual insight, of seeing the immaterial beyond the material, but also the broader ability to see below the surface; a chief use of this skill in the later Middle Ages, as Irwin notes, was the assessment of slaves for sale.[3] In view of the role of the slave in this story, something of the latter sense may be implied here. Yet, as will be seen, one would not want to make Shahriyar too perspicacious, for his bloody modus operandi is preceded by a critical instance of misperception.

In any case, after the death of the father, the older brother Shahriyar inherits a vast kingdom, because he is older, no doubt—but perhaps also because, being *afras*, he is worthier?—while the younger brother Shahzaman gets Samarkand, which seems to be something less. We also learn that the brothers are both married, though we do not learn the names of their wives; this is perhaps less surprising in Shahzaman's case, since his wife loses her head almost as soon as she is introduced. No children are mentioned either—more significantly, no sons.[4] The two brothers are said to rule for twenty years, and then the older brother Shahriyar misses his younger brother Shahzaman. Shahriyar sends his minister to ask his younger brother to visit him. Shahzaman agrees and soon departs. But, in the middle of the night before he has gone far, he realizes he has forgotten something in his palace that he wished to bring—some versions tell us it is a gift for his brother, a pearl—so he returns to his palace.

When Shahzaman returns, he finds the queen "asleep in bed, embracing a black slave," and, as the text has it, "the world blackened in his face" (*iswaddat al-dunyâ fî wajhihi* 1:2). He draws his sword and cuts off their heads. Then he sets out again, though, to be sure, now in a rather different mood than before. When he arrives at his brother's palace his gloom is a disappointment to his brother Shahriyar. The latter is puzzled by his brother's mood, but does not at first ask him its cause, nor does Shahzaman disclose it. And although the crisis of Shahzaman would seem to be preeminent, with mention of the disappointment of Shahriyar the focus begins to shift, and the nature of Shahriyar's disappointment merits closer consideration.

With no explanation forthcoming, Shahriyar is left with only what he can *see* in his brother, an image of gloom that disappoints him. At this moment their relation is constituted predominately on the plane of the image, and, thus, we can say that his disappointment lies in that register of experience that Lacan calls the imaginary order. As stated in the previous chapter, the imaginary is the dominant mode of experience for the infant before he can speak, and imaginary relations are dyadic, characterized by presence and sameness. If we recall the insistence of the text on the similarity of the two brothers, then the imaginary quality of their relation becomes even clearer. Indeed, given the emphasis on their similarities at the very outset, we can see that the episode shares a number of obvious qualities with Lacan's mirror stage. In the image of his brother, Shahriyar hopes to see what is missing in himself. But he is disappointed in this; Shahzaman is manifestly indifferent to the sight of Shahriyar. This causes Shahriyar to say to himself, "That's because of his separation from his land and his kingship" (*dhâlika bi-sabab mufâraqatihi bilâdahu wa mulkahu* 1:2–3). One of Lacan's commentators, Richard Boothby, remarks that the imaginary is "the register of power *par excellence*," and this is seen in Shahriyar's speculations about the cause of his brother's condition.[5] Shahriyar speculates that it is due to his brother's missing his *mulk*, his power, as he says. His brother's gloom then is not a matter, in Shahriyar's view, of missing another, but of missing a part of himself.

A few days pass and Shahzaman's condition worsens. He refuses to eat or drink, his body begins to weaken and he loses color. The symptoms of his malady are similar to those of "lovesickness" as they are described elsewhere in *The Thousand and One Nights*, in other works of medieval Arabic literature, and indeed, even in European literature, yet we cannot say he is suffering from lovesickness. Nevertheless, he slowly wastes away as would a lover suffering from unrequited love. So, instead of seeing his brother's pleasure at seeing him, Shahriyar sees weakness and decline. Finally he asks his brother what is the matter. Shahzaman tells him only, "I have a wound inside me" (1:3). Shahriyar's response to his brother's illness is to propose that they go hunting. This, he thinks, should cheer him. But Shahzaman, in no mood for such things, declines, and Shahriyar goes by himself.

While his brother is hunting, Shahzaman sits down beside a window that overlooks a garden and ponders his sad lot. And, in this mood, he sees his brother's wife enter the garden leading twenty slave girls and twenty slave men. By a fountain they remove their clothes. Then the queen calls out, "Oh Masʿûd!" and a black slave climbs down from a tree in the middle of the garden and mounts her.[6] Such a tree will figure again in the story, and at this point one can scarcely not think of the tree in the center of the garden in Genesis—in which case, it can be seen that the woman calling to the slave in the tree revises the situation of Genesis where the woman answers the call of the snake. The similarity of this episode with Genesis might even suggest a broader similarity with those creation myths in which some primordial misdeed sets history in motion—"history" now being the stories of *The Thousand and One Nights*. However, in the period when the *Nights* was in its later stages of development, the image of lovers in a garden was pervasive in Ottoman and Persian poetry and painting, and this image was also understood as a reflection of paradise. The image, then, seems from one angle very archaic and at the same time not so archaic at all, and in this it is very typical of the *Nights*. In any event, whether the allusion is archaic or contemporary or both, the act has the aura of desecration about it.

What is the effect on Shahzaman of what he sees? He watches in fascination, and he says to himself, "By God, my misfortune is lighter than this misfortune! This is greater than what happened to me." And the result is "the jealousy and gloom in him were undone" (1:3). The spectacle of his brother's wife fornicating with a black slave in the midst of an orgy has cheered him up. We should consider again the similarity between Shahzaman's sickness and lovesickness in the *Nights* and other works of medieval Arabic literature just noted, for the proximity of love and hate, so often noted in literature and by Freud and Lacan, is seen again here.

In *The Thousand and One Nights* love, which is everywhere and always love at first sight, begins with the image; love is set in motion by the image of the beloved. But love turns to lovesickness if the lover cannot possess his beloved. Thus, the only cure is being united, being joined to the beloved. Shahzaman, it would seem, suffers from the polar opposite, hate, and his hate is to a degree "palliated," if not cured, in a parallel way by finding sadistic expression. The "psychology" manifest in this episode is worth remarking. No justification or explanation is offered for Shahzaman's reaction; it is presented as absolutely obvious. Seeing someone else suffer something as bad or worse makes him feel better. His reaction, which is not without an element of triumph, is something like, "See! I'm not the only idiot!" The therapeutic if not curative effect of this is clear; Shahzaman begins to eat and drink again and his color returns. When his brother Shahriyar returns and notices his younger brother's improved color, he asks him again about his condition. Shahzaman hesitates, but, when Shahriyar persists, he reveals both the cause of his illness and the cause of his recovery.

The Gaze

Shahriyar says, "I wish to look with my [own] eye" (1:4). Shahzaman tells him to pretend to go hunting, but to come back instead and hide with him. Then he says "you will see it and realize it with your own eyes." Shahriyar goes into a tent outside the city: "He sat down in the tent and said to his slave boys, 'Don't bring anyone in.' Then he disguised himself (*tanakkara*) and he went off unseen (*mukhtafin*) to the palace" (1:4). There he joins his brother by the window. The point of the ruse is that Shahriyar cannot see what he wants to see so long as he is *seen*, and in this what Lacan calls the *gaze* comes into play, a factor whose influence was already suggested by the role of the window and the tree in the previous scene.

The gaze is a manifestation of the scopic drive. It is not simply gazing at another human, nor is it to be reduced to seeing another who sees oneself. Rather, Lacan says: "There is never any simple duplicity of terms. It is not only that I see the other, I see him seeing me, which implicates the third term, namely that he knows that I see him. The circle is closed. There are always three terms in the structure, even if these three terms are not explicitly present" (S, 7:218). Moreover, the gaze does not require that the eyes of the other be seen: "The gaze is not located just at the level of the eyes. The eyes may very well not appear, they may be masked. The gaze is not necessarily the face of our fellow being, it could just as easily be the window behind which we assume he is lying in wait for us. It is an *x*, the object when faced with which the subject becomes object" (*S*, 2:220).

Shahriyar's disguise is an attempt to escape the power of the gaze; the verb used is *tanakkara,* which means "to make oneself unrecognizable," and hence, "to disguise." Similarly the participle *mukhtafin* is also used to denote Shahriyar's being unseen. And since he is *seen* as king, he must in a way "abdicate." He cannot exercise his power as king here, because as king he cannot see what he wants to see. What is more, he pretends to go hunting, an activity in which the function of the gaze is critical. Of course, he really is hunting, and he does bag his quarry, so to speak—there is some irony here, I should think.

The gaze continues to figure in the episode after he steals back into the palace and joins his brother to watch the scene in the garden. The comportment of his wife, the queen, in the context of the gaze presents a contrast to her husband's behavior, for she fornicates with the black slave beneath the window of the palace—that is, she submits to the gaze. There is further irony here, I think; the king who does nothing wrong must hide behind the window in disguise, while the queen who fornicates does so openly. This is not a stable situation, however, for the queen's behavior has its effect; her actions make Shahriyar feel himself the object of the gaze once more.

The dialectic of the gaze is seen in this turn of events. What one sees can, in turn, transform the situation and make the one who sees become the helpless object of the gaze.[7] And how do we know that Shahriyar is the object of the gaze? Because he now feels shame.

Admittedly, the text does not tell us this immediately. It tells us first that he "loses his mind" (literally, "his reason flew from his head" 1:4). But evidence of shame, of the fact that he now feels himself to be the object of the gaze again, is found in what he proposes to his brother. He says to Shahzaman, "Come, let us travel as we are, for we have no need of kingship (*mulk*) unless we can gaze upon someone to whom the like [of what happened to us] happened. And if not, then death is better for us than life." He wants to maintain his disguise, for they will travel "as they are." Deranged and ashamed, he steals out of the palace with his brother by means of a secret door.

At this point, it would be well to take stock of the three scenes of scandal. One event is common to all three scenes: the wife fornicates with a black slave under the gaze of the husband. In other words, the "same thing" has now happened *three* times. And here Peter Brooks's suggestion may be apposite: coincidence seems to be surpassed in three, and hence three is the lowest number by which one may designate a *series*.[8] The repetition here has an uncanny aspect as well. As Freud noted, the very fact of the recurrence of certain events causes "the idea of something fateful and inescapable when otherwise we should have spoken only of 'chance' " (*SE*, 18:237).

At the same time, certain differences between the scenes should not be overlooked. Where Shahzaman's wife lies with her black lover in the privacy of her own chamber, Shahriyar's wife couples in the open air in the company of a troupe of slaves who form, as it were, a chorus of infamy—an effect of amplification that anticipates Sade insofar as it seems to aim at some limit of absolute transgression.

In any event, where Shahzaman can speak of a "wound inside," Shahriyar suffers an external wound also, shame before others. Does this account for the difference in their reactions?[9]

The Triangles

The key to understanding the triangles is to understand how the terms *husband* and *wife* and *master* and *slave* are distributed among those three characters. In each of the first three instances, the white male who is both husband and master discovers that the desire of the wife who is a white female is for the slave who is a black male. Thus we can say that the discovery that the desire of the wife is for another has a correlate in terms of the master-slave relation, the discovery that the wife is also a master to whom the slave must submit. In other words, even though the position of the wife in marriage correlates to a degree with that of the slave insofar as she is "possessed" and is part of the king's *mulk*, at the same time, as wife and queen, she also has a status apart from that. And it is this other status that determines her relation to the slave; insofar as she is the king's wife she is a master to him and can compel his obedience. Thus, while the king as husband discovers that he cannot command the desire of the wife, he also discovers that the wife, as another master, may compel the slave to submit to her desire. Therein lies the difference between a husband and a master, and also between a wife and a slave.

After all, it is not the case that the slave renounces pleasure per se, rather the disquieting thing about servility is that the slave's *jouissance* is secondhand, deriving as it does from the *jouissance* of the master.

In any case, to simply equate the relation of husband and wife with that of master and slave is a mistake.[10] In doing so, one overlooks the fact that it is not merely a matter of pairs but also of triads upon which various pairs are imposed. The dyad of master-slave cannot simply be aligned with any of those of gender; it is not reducible to any of the gender-based dyads, and none of the latter is reducible to it. It is always a question of three, not two. Indeed, on a certain level of abstraction, it is a matter of mere arithmetic; when you divide four (signifiers) by three (persons) something is left over. The wife's status is ambivalent; if she were a slave, she would be a concubine (*jâriyah*). The only real slave is the black man, who must submit to her desire because she is another master, since she is the wife of the king.

The racism involved is unmistakable. The scandal is clearly worsened by the fact of the slave's blackness.[11] The view that slavery was a divine punishment imposed on blacks was known in medieval Islam. The author Masʿudi, who was also acquainted with the medieval *Nights*, said people knowledgeable about tradition (*ahl al-athr*) said that, "Noah called on God to make his son Ham ugly and black and to make his [Ham's] son a slave to Shem's son." The reason for this curse was that the wind lifted Noah's skirt and Ham laughed at what he saw. But Masʿudi says that blacks deny this.[12] In any case, racist ideas circulated, and this scene shows their influence. Due to that influence, there is the sense of a taboo being broken here, but there would not be the same scandalous effect if it were merely two slaves fornicating. The taboo effect depends on the woman being the wife/queen who can compel the slave's obedience. On the other hand, given the instances of irony that have preceded, we should be wary of simply ascribing the racism to the nameless writer who gave us this version of the story. It is not out of the question that he—or she?—is consciously manipulating the racist elements here.

In any case, the uncanny repetition of an event turns the narrative in a new direction. When the orgy is over the two brothers ask themselves whether anyone else has ever suffered a worse fate, and Shahriyar proposes they travel the world to find out. This introduces another commonplace of the book, seeking similar examples to confirm one's own experience. However, in this instance, an element of sadism also seems present: "If I cannot witness similar pain, then my life is not worth living."

The two brothers travel until they reach a seashore, where they sit down beneath a tree in a meadow with a spring nearby it—recalling the tree and the fountain in the garden. Soon a towering black column appears on the sea and comes whirling toward the shore. They climb to the top of the tree and watch as the column transforms itself into a huge jinni bearing a trunk on his head. He opens the trunk, and takes out a chest, unlocks this second chest, and takes from it a beautiful young woman. After gloating that he kidnapped her on her wedding night, he rests his head on the girl's lap and falls asleep. The girl notices the two brothers up in the tree and signals to them that they must come down, or else she will wake the jinni who will kill them. When they come down, she tells them to "pierce her with their rapiers" or else, again, she will wake the jinni who will kill them. Again they comply.

Although at first glance this episode may seem similar to the previous instances, the similarity is purely biological; there are males and a female, and one of the males is black. The differences are more significant. If we compare it only with the instances of Shahriyar's wife—and from now on, we will confine ourselves to the case of Shahriyar, since Shahzaman is about to disappear from the narrative—it can be seen that many more elements have changed. In narratological terms, a formula has simply been negated: the queen and the slave die because they have sex; Shahriyar will die if he does not have sex with the girl. But to put it this way masks something important; Shahriyar now occupies the position of slave. How did he come to occupy it?

A brief detour through Kojève's commentary on Hegel will advance the argument here. In Hegel, what is truly human only appears in the struggle that yields a master and a slave. For, quoting Kojève:

> To be *human*, man must act not for the sake of subjugating a *thing*, but for the sake of subjugating another *Desire* (for the thing). The man who desires a thing humanly acts not so much to possess the *thing* as to make another *recognize* his *right* . . . to make another recognize him as the *owner* of the thing.[13]

The result of the conflict of these desires is a life and death struggle, which nevertheless does not end in death, since one party submits to the other: "One must suppose that the Fight ends in the victory of the one who is ready to go *all the way* over the one who—faced with death—does not manage to rise above his biological instinct of preservation. . . ."[14] The Master's superiority over the Slave is based on the Master's willingness to risk his life for a "nonvital" end—as Kojève puts it; that is, the recognition of his right: "The Master's superiority over Nature, founded on the risk of his life in the Fight for prestige, is realized by the fact of the Slave's *Work*."[15]

Now, as is known to readers of the *Phenomenology*, that Work will become the Slave's advantage over his Master, the Slave's means of becoming human and achieving a partial independence. The stages of this in Hegel—stoicism, skepticism/nihilism, Christianity—follow the Slave's attempt to come to terms with Slavery. We will set all this to one side, simply noting that Islam, in broad terms, offers a solution similar to that of Christianity. It makes slaves of all, as the very word *islâm* or "submission" implies, and offers their slavery to an Absolute Master, with freedom—of sorts—deferred to the hereafter.

In this new triangle we still find masters and slaves, and a black male (the jinni, represented as a "black column") and a white male and female, but it would be difficult to say a husband and wife are present any longer. The jinni is not the young woman's husband unless kidnapping is a form of marriage. Hence, it makes no sense here to speak of her as "an adulteress."[16] Adultery is the violation of a pact, but there is no pact here. She is his captive, and their relation is that of master and slave, not husband and wife. In this triangle, every social relation in the former triangles has been reduced to that of master and slave. At the same time, the hierarchy that formerly held is overturned; the black male is on top now, the master, and the white male is at the bottom, the slave. Wittingly or not, the story spins a pithy critique of medieval Islamic society.

The impress of late medieval Ottoman and Mamluk cultures on the *Nights* may be visible in this reduction of all relations to that of master and slave. The origins of the Ottoman and Mamluk states lie in the introduction of Turkish military slaves into the Abbasid court, a momentous development, for soon enough the slaves were choosing their master. But, curiously enough, when the slave became the master, he did not abolish the system of slavery, far from it. The slave instead made it pervasive. Vast numbers of the officials in the Ottoman state were technically slaves, and in Mamluk Egypt all members of the dynasty were slaves—though these slaves could rise to positions of considerable power.[17] Of the Ottoman state, Walter Andrews writes, "As the system of slavery grew to pervade the military and palace services, this peculiar master-slave relation appears to have become the dominant pattern of relationship throughout the central government. Even [free]-born Muslims . . . came to define their relation to the *padishah* (monarch) as that of slave to master."[18] Andrews also argues that "the practice of free Muslims referring to themselves as slaves, and most likely *thinking* of themselves as slaves . . . was far more widespread and permeated the cultural atmosphere of the empire to a far greater extent than is reflected in most historical secondary sources."[19] In later pages we will see how pervasive the master-slave relation is in the stories of *The Thousand and One Nights*. Here let us simply note again how this relation accords with perhaps the most fundamental conception of the relation of man and God in Islam. The word *islam*, as we said, means "submission," and *ʿabd*, the most common word for "slave," is the same word found in so many common Muslim names where it is in hyphenated form with one of the names of God: Abdallah or "Slave of God" and Abdur-rahman or "Slave of the Merciful." Likewise, the most common term for "worship" in the Qurʾan is *ʿibâdah*—literally, "service."

Those versions in which the slave in the garden descends from a tree to satisfy the wife's desire now can be seen to have prepared the way for this; Shahriyar climbs down out of the tree exactly as those black slaves have before him, something noted by Malti-Douglas.[20] But the precise significance is missed in her subsequent discussion, I think. For she goes on to say, "They have been reduced to the level of animality, perhaps their ultimate degradation, and a potent symbol of the meaning of becoming a sexual object."[21] But it is not "acting like an ape" in descending the tree or "becoming sex objects" that "assimilates their roles to that of the slave." Rather, they "enslave" themselves when they submit to her on account of their fear of death—the similarity of their descent from a tree to the slave's descent from a tree earlier is there to emphasize this. "Animal instinct" does not enter into the bargain solely on account of sexual desire; prior to that, before the two brothers know what the young woman wants, it comes into play more importantly in the form of the fear of death. Shahriyar does not become an animal on account of sexual desire, for desire is human ("Desire is desire of the other," and so forth), and becoming a "sexual object" for someone else does not reduce one to "animality"—that has nothing to do with it. We must wait until "The Story of the Merchant and the Jinni" for a human to be transformed into an animal. Shahriyar becomes a slave because he submits to his own fear of death.

If Shahriyar's subjective position in the "triangle of scandal" has changed, the positions of the black male and the white female have also changed, and we may ask what Shahriyar learns from his experience as a slave.

It is a bit of a disappointment. He doesn't manifest that other sort of *firasah* of which we spoke at the outset, and he certainly does not learn what we moderns (or "posts") wish he would learn. He manifests a certain resistance, so to speak. We could list the things he does not learn. He does not seem to reflect on the fact that as Lacan puts it, "A law is imposed upon the slave, that he should satisfy the desire and the pleasure [*jouissance*] of the other" (*S*, 1:223). Nor does he realize that the relation of wife to husband is not wholly dissimilar to that of slave to master (*pace* Farag), which fact might have struck him, since this "wife" happens to have been forcibly subjugated by her "husband."[22] Nor does he seem to reflect on what Lacan calls "the dissymmetrical position of the woman in the bond of love, especially in its most pre-eminently socialized form, namely the conjugal bond" (*S*, 1:261) whose result is that "adultery is punished in so dissymmetrical a manner" (*S*, 1:263). And again, as an aside, we might note that in medieval Islam this dissymmetry approaches a certain limit; though the term "adultery" or simply "fornication" (*zinâ* or *zinâ'*) is used of both males and females, husbands and wives, in fact there is a fundamental difference that is effaced in this, and this difference manifests itself in our story. The married man may sleep with his female slaves, but the wife may not sleep with her male slaves. Hence, for the Muslim husband to commit adultery/fornication takes a bit of contriving. And finally, Shahriyar does not reflect on the fact that human desire is necessarily mediated by the desire of the other—in Lacan's words, "Desire is the desire of the other." So, is Shahriyar just a bit dense or what?

The king is not a character in a realist fiction, and we cannot expect him to respond as such; this is a different sort of fiction. Like all characters in medieval Arabic narrative, he only "thinks" insofar as he speaks, and the only question we can pose is the question of what his speech and his actions tell us. And what happens next shows that he understands nothing.

When the young woman finishes with Shahriyar and his brother, she takes out a necklace on which are strung a great number of signet rings—five hundred and seventy, in the Second Calcutta edition—and she tells the two brothers, "Each owner of a ring fucked me, [thus] putting the 'horns' on this demon" (1:5). She then demands their rings, and the surrender of this emblem of one's identity may be taken as the final confirmation of their bondage.[23] Certainly, her collection of rings has a particular significance in a culture that ritually circumcises. She is the appropriator of the phallus—the phallic quality of the "huge black column" is obvious. Indeed, insofar as the phallus is the signifier par excellence ("the penis is a phallic symbol," as the joke goes), her appropriation of it here further underlines Shahriyar's abasement.

The size of her collection also points to one of the "truths" of *The Thousand and One Nights* and medieval Muslim-Arab culture, the voracity of the female sexual appetite—though again, in this case, there may be irony involved. But elsewhere in the *Nights* we will hear that "the physical appetite of women is stronger than the appetite of men" (*shahwat al-nisâ' aqwâ min shahwat al-rijâl* 1:837).

Something confirmed by a saying attributed to ʿAlî, the Prophet's son-in-law and the fourth caliph: "God created sexual desire in ten parts; he gave nine parts to woman and one part to man." And, indeed, in the late medieval literature of misogyny there are descriptions of the devouring and insatiable vagina, which show clearly the conception of the woman as a "pure lack." That is what makes woman so dangerous, and obviously lies behind the notorious linkage found in the word *fitnah,* which means both "seductive charm" and "social discord" and "political upheaval." The woman is isolated in the harem as much to protect her against her own potentially explosive desires as to protect her against other men.[24]

After they surrender their rings, she tells them how the jinni kidnapped her on her wedding night and placed her in the box and put the box inside a chest and put seven locks on the chest and then he hurled the chest to the bottom of the roaring sea:

> But he did not know that when a woman wants something, nothing will prevent her from getting it—as the poet said:
>
> > Have no faith in woman and trust not her pledges
> > Content or malcontent—it depends on her vagina
> > She hides deceitful desire and treachery in her clothes
> > Heed the story of Joseph with her tricks therein
> > Have you forgotten Adam's expulsion was on her account?
>
> (1:6)

The story of Joseph as told in the Qurʾan and elaborated in commentaries was one of the most important narratives in medieval Islamic culture, and mention of it here confirms my point that the wife as *wife* is also a master, and therefore not a slave. For if the slave rejects the wife's desire, the wife may then accuse him of an attempted seduction, even as Potiphar's wife does Joseph.

But Shahriyar takes nothing of this from the situation. He and his brother say to each other, "He is a [mighty] demon and yet something happened to him that was greater than what happened to us, something, in fact, that has not happened to anyone else!" (1:6). In other words, despite the fact that the jinni has kidnapped the girl, despite the anomalies noted above in the situation, the episode confirms for Shahriyar his own experience. He only sees another woman deceiving another powerful male. In the Mahdi edition, the two brothers marveling at the bottomless treachery of women then utter the same words: "Verily your wiles are great!" This "truth"—for it is nothing less than verse 28 from *Sûrat Yûsuf* in the Qur'an—is what the brothers take from the episode.[25] The Qur'anic verse is not found in the Second Calcutta edition, but the phrase haunts this episode in that edition through the mention of the story of Joseph and indeed the very rhyme of the poetry.

Shahriyar and his brother return to his palace—and now Shahzaman disappears. Without explanation, Shahriyar chops off the head of the queen and the heads of all her slaves, male and female. That evening, he marries a virgin, deflowers her—"takes her face" is the literal translation for *ya'khudhu wajhahâ*—and then kills her in the morning (1:6). And this becomes his "lifestyle," so to speak, for a period of three years—more than a thousand and one nights.

With this the first half of the story, describing Shahriyar's crisis, concludes. We might now consider the nature of that crisis.

Most readings, both psychoanalytic and feminist (or some combination of the two), take Shahriyar to be mad—and, indeed, the text has told us that he lost his reason, and how can one quarrel with that?[26] But this is not to say that Shahriyar is suffering from delusions or hallucinations. Shahriyar is not Schreber.[27] I would rather say that Shahriyar opts for what might be called a "paranoid solution" whose dimensions will become clearer if we consider the imaginary aspects of his crisis.[28]

It is a question of Shahriyar's desire and of his alienation in the mirror stage. As we said above, for Lacan the import of the mirror stage (and its correlate moment in Hegel's master-slave dialectic) is that the human subject only conceives himself as a unity through the other. Thus, at the moment when, as Lacan puts it, "the ego precipitates," a twofold alienation is installed in the subject. First, the subject is alienated due to the fact that he cannot conceive his unity without the other; secondly—and even more importantly perhaps—the subject is alienated insofar as the imaginary unity, his ego, is only formed by excluding from it—by *alienating*, that is—a considerable portion of the subject himself. Thus, alienation in Lacan's thought is more radical than it is in Hegel. In Hegel it is intersubjective, but in Lacan it is both intersubjective and intrasubjective; the subject is alienated not only from the other but also from himself. For our purposes here, the most important result of this "primordial alienation" for Lacan is an "aggressivity" in the subject that figures in all the ego's relations:

> At first, before language, desire exists solely in the single plane of the imaginary relation of the specular stage, projected, alienated in the other. The tension it provokes is then deprived of an outcome. That is to say that it has no other outcome—Hegel teaches us this—than the destruction of the other. (*S*, 1:170)

This, I would argue, is what constitutes the crisis of King Shahriyar. The oedipal dimensions of Shahriyar's crisis can now be explored in light of Lacan's reformulation of that stage in the child's development. As stated in the previous chapter, for Lacan the mirror stage is brought to an end in the oedipal crisis. The key for Lacan is not that the child's desire for the mother is interdicted by the father, but rather that the child discovers that he/she lacks what the mother desires. Prior to the oedipal stage, "if the desire of the mother *is* the phallus, the child wishes to be the phallus in order to satisfy that desire," Lacan writes (*E,* 289). But in the oedipal stage, the child realizes that the mother's desire is for the father. Shahriyar's crisis is oedipal in that it is brought on when Shahriyar discovers he lacks what the other desires. Insofar as they correlate, the crisis persists because of his refusal to accept this, to accept that he lacks what the other desires. His response was not acceptance, but rather a "radical aggression" against the other: "each time we get close, in a given subject, to this primitive alienation, the most radical aggression arises—the desire for the disappearance of the other insofar as he supports the subject's desire" (*S,* 1:170).

Lacan gives a striking example of this sort of violence which shows that this conception is not simply a theoretical construct for him, but a conception with an empirical basis in his own clinical experience; he spoke of a little girl who became "very peaceably absorbed, at an age when she was scarcely walking on her feet, in the application of a good-sized stone to the skull of a little playmate from next door, who was the person around whom she constructed her first identifications." Similarly, the violence of Shahriyar is not fundamentally about "patriarchal rage"[29] or even gender. Rather, what Lacan says of the little girl holds for him as well: he displays "the most fundamental structure of the human being on the imaginary plane—to destroy the person who is the site of alienation" (*S,* 1:172). It is insofar as the wife, the other here, is the site of Shahriyar's alienation that he kills her. Thus, Shahriyar's rage, I would argue, is fundamentally due to his "primitive alienation."

And yet Shahriyar does not simply kill each wife. Before he does that, we are told quite precisely what he does to each virgin: *ya'khudhu wajhahâ,* that is, literally, "he takes her face." If love, as imaginary passion, as infatuation with the image, is one pole of the imaginary relation, hate is the other pole. But hate, as we know, is not simply satisfied with the disappearance of the other. As Lacan says: "If love aspires to the unfolding of the being of the other, hate wishes its opposite, namely its abasement, its deranging, its deviation, its delirium, its detailed denial, its subversion. That is what makes hate a career with no limit, just as love is" (*S,* 1:277). *Ya'-khudhu wajhahâ* is Shahriyar's "detailed denial" of each virgin in her particularity—as is often the case in *The Thousand and One Nights*, the literal Arabic text pulls no punches.

How is Shahriyar's imaginary impasse to be broken? A number of analyses have already told us that Shahrazad will show Shahriyar the "metonymy of his desire," to use Lacan's phrase—his desire in its displacements, that is. Nevertheless, all of the readings influenced to one degree or another by psychoanalytic notions seem to overlook something revealing about Shahriyar's method at this point: I mean the grim and uncanny similarity between Shahriyar's method and the game of *Fort/Da* that Freud analyzed in *Beyond the Pleasure Principle*.

There Freud describes how his grandson makes a wooden spool with a piece of string attached to it disappear and reappear, exclaiming "O!" and "Da!"—which Freud and his daughter understood to mean "*Fort*" and "*Da*" ("Gone!" and "There!"). Freud linked this game to the child's "great cultural achievement . . . allowing his mother to go away without protesting. He compensated himself for this, as it were, by himself staging the disappearance and return of the object within his reach" (*SE,* 18:15).

In response to his crisis, Shahriyar has invented his own version of *Fort/Da*. But we should note that for Lacan, the significance of this game in which the child mimes its mother's disappearance and reappearance with a spool attached to a thread is not that by this game the child somehow "masters" his mother's disappearances. That, he says, is a "phenomenon of secondary importance" (*FFC,* 62). Rather, its importance is that in this game the child makes use of the symbol. The play of difference in the opposition absence/presence reflects the play of difference in language between absence and presence. Lacan, following Hegel, speaks of this initial symbolization, which comes to pass through making the object disappear, as being the "original murder of the thing" (*S,* 2:174). Thus, we can see that Shahriyar, in the very manner in which he proceeds is, nevertheless, on the threshold of being "cured." What is needed is for someone to teach him a less bloody version of *Fort/Da*.

The Vizier's Daughter

It is the vizier's gloomy job to find a new bride for Shahriyar each day, but the day comes when he can find no more virgins in the kingdom, and he returns home, dreading the anger of the king. Then we learn that he has two daughters—the situation at the story's beginning is now transposed, a father with two daughters instead of two sons. The older daughter is Shahrazad; the younger is Dunyazad. The older, Shahrazad, is distinguished from the younger, rather as Shahriyar is from his younger brother, by being *more* of something; Shahrazad is more learned. She has read a "thousand books" from the present and previous ages, and knows well all the lessons that they offer. Seeing her father's gloom, she asks her father about its cause, and he tells her of his predicament. She then proposes that he marry her to the king and, being resourceful, perhaps she will find a way to stop the slaughter. In this we see that death figures as a stake in a wager, even as it is in the master-slave dialectic, and the relevance of that dialectic will also be seen in the case of Shahrazad.

Her father is dismayed. To dissuade her, he tells her a cautionary tale, the story of "The Merchant, the Ox and the Donkey." He means it to be a cautionary story about power relations, rather like the story of "The Lion and the Bull" from *Kalilah wa Dimnah*, and a central issue in this second part of the tale is the meaning of his story. The vizier's story also has two parts, and the vizier pauses between to see if Shahrazad has "gotten the point."

A rich merchant, who knows the language of birds and animals (going Solomon one better), owns an ox and a donkey. At day's end the ox always finds the donkey well fed, well watered, and resting in a clean place, while the ox is tired from his drudgery of pulling a plow or turning a millstone. One day he remarks to the donkey how lucky he is. The donkey's response is that the ox should pretend to be sick. This is overheard by the merchant, and the next day when his plowman tells him that the ox is ill, the merchant tells him to use the donkey instead.

After two days of hard labor, the donkey, needless to say, sorely regrets his advice to the ox. So now he tells the ox that the merchant has instructed his plowman to have him slaughtered if he has not recovered the next day. The ox, no surprise, "recovers."

And at this point, the vizier breaks off, stops his tale and asks Shahrazad if she is still determined to marry Shahriyar. Yes, she tells him.

The vizier wishes Shahrazad to identify with the donkey, to realize the dangers of intervention, of trying to help another. But this she refuses to do. We will say more about her refusal shortly; all that need be said for the moment is that the fact that Shahrazad is not deterred does not mean that she does not understand the tale to this point. Well, then, her father says, he will do to her what the merchant did to his wife, and he goes on with the story.

Now the merchant has again overheard the donkey's latest advice to the ox, and the next day, with his wife, he visits the ox in his stall. The ox "farts and frisks about" to show how healthy he is. The merchant laughs at this, and his wife asks him why he laughs. He explains to her that God has given him the gift of understanding the language of birds and animals but that he may not disclose what they say to anyone else or else he will die. She insists that he tell her however—or else she will know that he is really laughing at her instead. They argue until he gives in and agrees to tell her. Since he is about to die, the merchant makes out his will and goes to the stable to perform his ablutions. In the stable are a rooster and a dog, and the dog asks the rooster, who is enjoying himself with one of his fifty wives, how he can be happy when their master is about to die. The rooster replies that the master is a fool. He, the rooster, manages fifty wives, while the merchant cannot even manage one. If the merchant had any sense he would beat his wife until she repented of her desire to know what the animals say. The rooster, perhaps, has God's advice about disobedient women in mind: "As for those from whom you fear disobedience, admonish them and send them to their rooms and beat them" (Qurʾan 4:34).

When the merchant hears the rooster's words, he "recovers his reason" as the text has it. That is, he gets a stick and follows the rooster's advice with regard to disobedient wives, and he beats her until she repents. And they live happily until they die, the vizier concludes.

One cannot fail to notice a certain deflection in the narrative at the point at which the vizier first breaks off; what begins as a story about the donkey and the ox ends as a story about the merchant and his wife. The deflection is semantic. The first is a story about masters and slaves, while the second is a story about husbands and wives. In the first story the vizier wishes Shahrazad to identify herself with the donkey and Shahriyar with the merchant, while in the second he wishes her to identify herself with the stubborn wife who is beaten for her attitude and to identify himself with the merchant. Thus, it can be seen that Shahrazad's refusal in the first instance prompts him to propose another identification. With respect to our terms "master—slave" and "husband—wife," the vizier attempts to get Shahrazad to inscribe herself in yet another triangle, to see herself not as a wife to Shahriyar but as a slave.

But Shahrazad also refuses this identification. Her father's story has had no effect—or has not had the effect he intended. Shahrazad, in her refusal to make the identification, does not give us her interpretation, so we must infer it. The place to begin is to find the link between the two stories. Here, Muhsin Mahdi is surely right when he says that the link is the lie that the donkey tells the ox in order to extricate himself from the situation into which he has gotten himself. It is this lie that causes the merchant to laugh and that is the source of his problem with his wife—which shows him willing to die to satisfy her desire. The merchant sees the critical role of the lie, belatedly. After all, the merchant does not beat the donkey; he beats his wife. The lie is allowed to stand. And the new social order—domestic tranquility, we might call it—rests on it (along with the threat of violence, to be sure).

We must assume that Shahrazad sees the importance of the lie as well, for she rejects a simple imaginary identification with any of the characters. What she seems to take from the tale is the lesson it provides of the efficacy of the symbolic register, of language, in transforming the subject's relations to the imaginary register, the specular other, and to the real, the blows. Shahrazad's insistence, then, shows us two things. First, that she refuses the role of slave, because she is willing to die. She accepts the wager, with death as its stake. Second, that she will use symbolic means to change the subject's understanding of himself. So, we can see that Shahrazad is in a sense proposing a different sort of triangle now; husband, wife, and a symbolic pact.

At this point, a word of caution is perhaps called for. We should not overestimate what Shahrazad will achieve. Feminist readings, with some enthusiasm, tend to make Shahrazad the model of the independent woman, as a triumphant counter-example to the cultural ideal of a submissive woman that is rather prominent in Muslim and Arab cultures. But Shahrazad is not a feminist, and *The Thousand and One Nights* is no postmodern tract. If Shahrazad is successful, she will end up with a marriage, and in that marriage Shahriyar's position as husband and her position as wife will still correlate—to a degree—with that of master and slave. The story, like a Hollywood movie, despite certain "transgressive" moments, as they are often called now, will finally uphold the good old-fashioned way, the given order—though this does not entirely undo the ironies of its "critique," I would say. In any case, marriage will be far better for Shahrazad than the other alternatives, mere slavery or death.

What happens next bears this out. Her father does not beat her as he would if he took his own story seriously. Instead, he does what his daughter has asked him to do. He goes to King Shahriyar and tells him that, since he can find no other young woman, he will marry his own daughter to him. Shahriyar is impressed and the marriage is agreed upon. While her father is off at the palace arranging her marriage, Shahrazad goes to her younger sister Dunyazad and tells her of her plan. Dunyazad will accompany her to the palace and at the right moment Dunyazad is to propose that Shahrazad tell a story to entertain them. "Which if Allah wills it, shall be our deliverance" (1:10).

The next day Shahrazad is married to Shahriyar. As Shahriyar takes her into his bed, Shahrazad begins to weep. She wishes to see her younger sister once more, she explains, and in all the repetitions that various writers have noted in this story, I do not know if this one has been noted; Shahrazad at this point expresses a desire to *see* her sister that correlates with Shahriyar's desire to *see* his brother which set everything in motion in the first place. Whether she knows it or not, this is the sort of desire that Shahriyar has shown himself willing to accede to. So Dunyazad is led in and seated at the foot of the bed, and there she remains while Shahriyar deflowers her sister. Now, in light of what I said earlier about Shahriyar's reason for killing his wives, about his being in the thrall of the imaginary, this is significant. The dyadic relations of the "mirror stage" are giving way to the triadic of the symbolic.

When Shahriyar has deflowered Shahrazad, Dunyazad proposes to her sister that she tell a story to pass the time until dawn, and Shahrazad replies that she will gladly—if the king permits. Shahriyar assents, and Shahrazad begins "The Story of the Merchant and the Jinni."

Here we must again consider the fact of the wager seen in Shahrazad's words to her father: "Either I shall live, or I shall be a ransom and a deliverance for the children of the Muslims"(1:7). Thus, the first story told by Shahrazad begins the "play" whose outcome is unknown. Descriptions here of "ransom stories" and "time-gaining" frames tend to obscure the fact of the wager and the uncertainty of the outcome. For the story is not a "ransom" in the sense of a payment agreed to in advance by Shahriyar for a life, as in *diyah* or *Wergild*, but it is rather equivalent to the roll of the dice by which Shahrazad risks all, having wagered her life. It only becomes a ransom at the pleasure of the king. Narration as the relation between Shahrazad and Shahriyar is structured as a wager whose stakes are life and death, and this structure is fundamental to the structure of the book.

With the introduction of narration as a wager whose stakes are life and death, the frame story has now put forth the three principles that will order the various narratives for the rest of the book. The first was seen in the brothers' search for someone who has experienced what they have or worse. Henceforth, having heard an amazing story, someone poses the perhaps rhetorical question, "Has anyone ever heard a more amazing story?" and someone steps forward and tells one. This means of embedding is tied to the prominence of the amazing and the uncanny as topoi, as we shall see in later chapters. The second type—and the least important—is example in the form of analogy; the minister employs this when he tells his daughter Shahrazad "The Story of the Donkey and the Ox." As analogy it functions on the pattern of "the situation of you and me is as A is to B."[30] While the second relation, analogy, plays on similarity in *kind*, the first relation plays on difference in *magnitude*. The third is, as I have shown here, the wager. In this form, the embedded narrative constitutes the "play" whose stakes are life and death in the framing narrative. Now the three are by no means mutually exclusive. For the wager to be won, the story must seem more amazing than the story that preceded it. Yet it also happens that an amazing story is often told simply in response to the question, "Has anyone ever heard a more amazing story?" In the form of the wager, it also happens that the wager is "displaced" in many instances; that is to say, the life at stake is not always that of the person who narrates. Nevertheless, as wager, it is one of three principle means of structuring narration in the book, and, as we shall see, story cycles such as "The Merchant and the Jinni," "The Hunchback," and "The Porter and the Three Ladies of Baghdad" bear witness to this.

Of course, when dawn arrives Shahrazad has not finished "The Story of the Merchant and the Jinni." In the story of the first sheikh, she has reached the point at which the first sheikh is about to unwittingly kill his own son who has been "ensorcelled"—to use one of the Burtonisms that I like—that is, turned into a calf by his stepmother:

> "I advanced towards the calf, and I took the knife in my hand . . ." and then morning overtook Shahrazad and she fell silent from permitted speech, and then her sister said to her, "How excellent is your account" . . . And she [Shahrazad] said to her, "But what is this compared to what I shall tell tomorrow night should I live and should the king preserve me—" And the king said to himself, "By God, I shall not kill her until I hear the rest of her story." (1:14)

Shahrazad's ploy here conforms precisely to the "*fort*" stage of the game, and it is, I think, no coincidence that within the story that she tells, something is about to be made "*fort*" also; the first sheikh is about to kill his only son. A point not only of maximum suspense within the story but one also precisely analogous to that point which things have come to between Shahriyar and herself, since, according to his previous habit, Shahriyar could be expected to kill (or have someone else kill) Shahrazad now. But for the moment the killing of the son is, for Shahriyar who does not know the outcome, replaced with—an absence, the cessation of speech. Shahrazad has removed the object (narration). And on this account, and in the same way, Shahrazad's death is deferred for the balance of the story, as the king's words show. But it only comes about as a result of the cessation of narrative. It is not so much that she has substituted narration for her death; rather in a very specific way, the absence of something has been substituted for it.

It is perhaps noteworthy that Shahriyar does not respond in words to her question, "But what is this compared to what I shall tell tomorrow night should I live and should the king preserve me?" His response is only to be found in what he does (and in what he does not do):

> And they spent the rest of that night embracing each other until dawn. Then the king went off to his court, and the minister entered bearing the burial shroud under his arm. The king passed judgments and made appointments until the end of the day when he left without giving the minister any command having to do with that [burial shroud]. The minister was amazed in the extreme. Then the members of the court dispersed. And King Shahriyar went back to his palace. (1:14)

Then the second night begins, in which Shahriyar will hear the rest of "The Story of the First Sheikh," but at the end of this night he will find himself lacking something else. It is this structure, Shahrazad's *Fort/Da* method in narration, that accounts for the idiosyncrasy of the temporal scheme of *The Thousand and One Nights*, wherein the division into "nights" never coincides with the divisions between stories—or almost never. For were Shahrazad to finish a story at the end of the night, Shahriyar, not being left in suspense, might very well decide in the cold light of dawn to lop off her head. It is rather like a game of Russian roulette; as in that pastime the game only goes on if something is missing.

What Shahrazad has achieved is apparent in King Shahriyar's actions. She has transformed Shahriyar's bloody version of *Fort/Da* into a symbolic, bloodless one. Shahrazad, that is, destroys the object in order to create the symbol. The object has become symbol or language, and she makes it disappear and reappear. Why does Shahriyar accede to this new form of the game? It is a matter of transference. By the cessation of narration Shahrazad induces a "transference" in Shahriyar. What existed in the imaginary solely as object has been transformed into a symbol—into words, that is—by means of an absence. His desire is released from its imaginary impasse into the symbolic circuit. But only to speak of desire and narration or language is to overlook the place of death in Shahriyar's "cure." Shahrazad's substitution of her *Fort/Da* game of language for that of virgins bears witness to the relation of both desire and language to death. In language "the symbol manifests itself first of all as the murder of the thing, and this death constitutes in the subject the eternalization of his desire" (*E,* 104). By means of her version of *Fort/Da*—with its "occultation" of narration, "in which subjectivity brings together mastery of its dereliction and the birth of the symbol"—Shahrazad shows Shahriyar the nature of his desire. Of this *Fort/Da* game Lacan said, "These are the games of occultation which Freud, in a flash of genius, revealed to us so that we might recognize in them that the moment in which desire becomes human is also that in which the child is born into language" (*E,* 103).

4
The Mirror of Love

TO FALL IN LOVE IN *THE THOUSAND AND ONE NIGHTS* IS TO FALL IN LOVE at first sight. I know of only a few exceptions to this rule. Indeed, it is in its portrayal of the phenomena of romantic love that this diverse collection of tales may show its greatest consistency. No matter whether one is dealing with the stories that scholars have tagged as "early" or "late," the commonplaces of romantic love—love at first sight, "lovesickness," the delusions of the lover, and so on—recur again and again as seemingly uncontested truths about the human experience of love. The consistency and pervasiveness of these motifs in *The Thousand and One Nights* tell us that we are dealing with a stock of cultural "truths" that are part of an overarching psychology of love. That psychology is elaborated elsewhere in the considerable medieval Arabic literature of love in works such as Ibn Ḥazm's *The Dove's Necklace* and al-Sarrâj's *Deaths of Lovers*. And insofar as *The Thousand and One Nights* makes use of the conventions and clichés of that literature, it is in its love stories and in its depiction of love that this work, so often an exception with respect to medieval Arabic literature, is most in accord with it.[1]

More specifically, the proximity of *The Thousand and One Nights* in this regard to the rest of the medieval literature of love is shown by the use which the *Nights* makes of the so-called 'Udhrî love stories. Elsewhere in medieval Arabic literature these stories are found amidst a corpus of the love poetry that seems to have developed in the Umayyad era—that is, in the latter half of the seventh and the first half of the eighth centuries A.D. In these stories, Andras Hamori writes, "the lovers pine and pine, and in the end give up the rarefied ghost. Some go mad first . . . many of them are poets. The poet is still the tale's protagonist. Lovers from the Yemenite tribe of 'Udhrah were said to be particularly given to such gloomy attachments, which are therefore known as 'Udhrî love."[2]

Certain Udhri love stories develop, by and by, into long narratives in the later literature, but in their earlier versions and in *The*

Thousand and One Nights they usually do not surpass the extent of anecdote. A common plot of an Udhri love story goes like this: A man from the tribe of Udhrah falls in love at first sight with a woman. For some reason the love is impossible—perhaps she initially spurns his love or perhaps her father has promised her to another. In any event, the lover falls ill with lovesickness. Fearing for his life, his friends plead his case with her. She relents and visits him. When he sees her, tears flow from his eyes and he recites poetry. Now she falls in love with him, but it is too late. The disease has progressed too far, and he dies. Then, deprived of the object of her passion, she too dies from lovesickness. When Udhri love takes up a sedentary urban existence, the result is recognizable as courtly love in its medieval Arab-Islamic version, the subject of works by J. C. Vadet and Lois Giffen.[3] *The Thousand and One Nights* contains a few brief stories about lovers from the tribe of Udhrah, however, almost all the longer love stories in the *Nights* share themes with Udhri love stories.

With regard to the various motifs of these stories an obvious question arises: How are we to understand motifs such as love at first sight and lovesickness? Are they simply curious remnants of a more naive age? That is, are they merely elements in a kind of "Ptolemaic" psychology, which proved to be extremely useful tools for the medieval storyteller but whose value is now superseded by our own more sophisticated conceptions of love?[4] Or is it possible that these stories, coming to us from an alien culture and a distant time, still speak to us? Since love at first sight and lovesickness are the most prominent features of this psychology of love, they are the phenomena we will consider here.

To understand love, we must first fall in love. Hence, the obvious place to begin is with the phenomenon of love at first sight. This phenomenon receives its most elaborate treatment in *The Thousand and One Nights* in the story "Qamar al-Zamân"—Shahrazad's telling of the story extends her life by almost eighty nights. But the love of Qamar al-Zaman and Princess Budûr comes to an unhappy end; in the third part of the story Budur betrays Qamar al-Zaman. Critical opinion is divided about the merits of that ending, but for now we will set aside that question and consider the story's portrayal of love at first sight.

The story begins with the beautiful young prince Qamar al-Zaman rejecting his father's request that he marry. Qamar has been reading up on the extensive literature of misogyny in medieval Islam. To bring him around, King Shahrimân locks Qamar away in a tower. One night a female jinni named Maymûnah flies past the tower and spies him as he sleeps. She is astonished by his beauty, falls in love with him, and describes him to a male jinni named Dahnash. As it happens, Dahnash has been equally impressed by the beauty of the Princess Budur, who it must be said has also defied her father's desire for her to marry. The two jinnis argue about the physical merits of their favorites and make a wager. To settle their bet, they convey Budur from China to the Isles of Khâlidân and place her in the bed next to the young man. Seeing them side by side, they are astonished by the physical similarity between the two, but they are still unable to agree on whose favorite is more beautiful. So they summon a third party to arbitrate, a jinni named Qashqash. The latter says that the two seem to him equal in beauty, but if they must solve the matter, there is only one way to do it. Wake one youth and then the other and observe which one is most moved by passion, for the one who is more desirous thereby proves the other's superiority (and his or her inferiority). They first wake the young man and observe his reaction. Then they do the same with the young woman. The two beautiful youths both promptly fall in love. But while Qamar al-Zaman is able to resist the physical allure of Budur, Budur cannot resist Qamar's physical charm: "Her hand fell on his penis, and her heart quaked and desire washed over her, for the physical desire of women is stronger than that of men" (*shahwat al-nisâ' aqwâ min shahwat al-rijâl*, 1:837). In other words, Budur's inability to control herself bears out the view of female sexuality mentioned in the previous chapter in relation to the kidnapped lady. Part and parcel of that general view is the assumption that the sight of the object leaves the subject nearly helpless with respect to his desire (*hawâ* or *'ishq*)—a point on which, I might add, both decadent poets and austere jurisprudents in medieval Islam were in complete agreement.[5]

In any case, Budur's acquiescence to her desire for Qamar settles the bet in favor of Maymunah who had championed the young man's superior beauty. However, in the liberal spirit of a lover she "forgives" Dahnash's debt. Then they fly Budur back to China and themselves vanish from the tale.

When Qamar al-Zaman wakes up and tells of his love, he is taken for mad. He beats a servant who doubts his account of the previous night. Much the same happens to Budur, but she goes so far as to kill her chambermaid—is it again that the female's passion is stronger? Then both fall ill with lovesickness. Though they know not what ails them, their families begin to fear for their lives.

Two elements in the episode have special importance. The first is the striking similarity of Qamar al-Zaman and Budur, a fact remarked by everyone—except themselves. The second is the wager; the flame of love between Qamar al-Zaman and Budur is kindled in the context of a wager between jinn. It is interesting on both of these counts to compare "Qamar al-Zaman" with the story of "The Two Viziers" (1:148–99), which makes use of this same episode of the jinnis placing the young woman and man beside each other in bed. That story tells of two cousins pledged to one another in marriage by their fathers. Various peripeteia act to separate their fathers; the girl grows up in Cairo, while the boy grows up in Basra. Two jinnis bring the two together for one night in order to prevent the girl's marriage to a repulsive hunchback. Then they are separated again, and the rest of the story tells how they are finally reunited.

The plot of each story requires some means of causing the two people who are widely distant in space to fall in love, and the jinn serve this purpose in both stories. And what André Miquel says about the role of the jinn in "The Two Viziers" also holds true in the case of "Qamar al-Zaman"; once the jinn serve this purpose, they disappear from the story.[6] But a number of other possibilities exist in the *Nights* for achieving this end, and the soon-to-be lovers need not actually be in one another's presence. Hearing a description (à la "Ardashîr and Ḥayât al-Nufûs" or "Tâj al-Mulûk and Princess Dunyâ") or seeing a drawing (à la "The Goldsmith and the Singing Girl") would suffice.[7] However, by bringing the two young people into one another's presence the jinn may serve another function: they also act as *witnesses* to the striking similarity between the young man and woman. When Maymunah reveals Qamar al-Zaman to him, Dahnash says, "They have been poured from the same mold of beauty" (1:827). And when Budur is placed next to Qamar al-Zaman, we are told, "They were the most similar of people to each other" (1:828). The jinn in "The Two Viziers" also note the resemblance of the two lovers, but it is explained by their consanguinity (they are first cousins). In "Qamar al-Zaman," however, it is an uncanny effect given special emphasis through the reactions of the jinn. Since the story places such emphasis on their similarity—after all, they are both named after the same heavenly body—we might wonder if there is any significance beyond the suggestion that they are destined for each other.[8]

Some verses inserted into the narrative emphasize the uncanny resemblance nicely; for Budur, "Full Moons" is compared to *qamar* in them:

> A moon [*qamar*] she rises, willow limb she bends,
> She breathes ambergris, and gazes, a gazelle.

> It seems that sadness loves my heart and when
> She parts, finds a place therein to dwell.[9]

The result is that Qamar promptly falls in love with a being who is compared to *qamar*. The names of the two lovers, their uncanny physical similarity, the poetry—everything is designed to emphasize the mirror-like image that casts the spell of love on Qamar al-Zaman and Budur. The Freudian view of the phenomenon of "falling in love"—*Verliebtheit*—finds artistic confirmation here, as a glance at Freud's views on the relation between narcissism and *Verliebtheit* in his paper "On Narcissism: An Introduction" will show. Having postulated "a primary narcissism in everyone" (*SE*, 14:88), Freud goes on to say:

> As always where the libido is concerned, man has here again shown himself incapable of giving up a satisfaction he had once enjoyed. He is not willing to forgo the narcissistic perfection of his childhood; and when, as he grows up he is disturbed by the admonitions of others and by the awakening of his own critical judgement, so that he can no longer retain that perfection, he seeks to recover it in the new form of an ego ideal. (*SE*, 14:94)

Freud's view of narcissism requires a new distinction in his theory between "ego libido" and "object libido," and this distinction was used to explain *Verliebtheit*. What occurs when one falls in love is the "flowing over of ego libido" onto the object. But why does one fall in love? What causes the ego libido to be diverted to the object? Since we are dealing with "heavenly bodies," we may speak of coincidence, of conjunction. In the passage just cited, Freud speaks of both an "ideal ego" and an "ego ideal." The two terms are often conflated, but Lacan insists that they designate different phenomena. In Lacanian terminology, the "ideal ego" is an imaginary phenomenon, while the "ego ideal" is a symbolic one. The latter expresses itself in the expectations we have for ourselves, which must be reducible to symbolic expression, to language. The former is an image:

> The *Ichideal*, considered as speaking, can come to be placed in the world of objects on the level of the *Idealich*, that is, on the level where this narcissistic captation which Freud talks about over and over again throughout this text can take place. You can rest assured that when this confusion occurs, the apparatus can't be regulated any longer. In other words, when you're in love, you are mad, as ordinary language puts it. (*S*, 1:142)

Love as infatuation, or *Verliebtheit*, occurs when an external image coincides closely with the ego ideal. It is the "contours," so to speak, of the internal ideal that prevent us from falling in love with just anyone, for "it is not every day that one comes upon something which is so constructed as to give you the very image of your desire" (*S*, 1:142). One could compare it, as the storyteller does, to a mold—or as I like to think of it, to a silhouette. If the image of the other is close enough—then one falls. What one loves is an image fused and confused with all the trappings of one's own narcissistic ideal. The coincidence of the *Ichideal* and the *Idealich* completes a circuit and the "current"—ego libido that would otherwise be distributed and dispersed in various byways of the ego—flows through. "Love," Lacan says in one of his more baroque phrases, "is a phenomenon which takes place at the imaginary level, and which provokes a veritable subduction of the symbolic, a sort of annihilation, or perturbation of the function of the ego-ideal. Love reopens the door—as Freud puts it, not mincing his words—to perfection" (*S*, 1:142). For all these reasons, the Freudian explanation accounts for the long history of the lover being taken as "blind" and as "mad" and has, in this respect, an explanatory power that Aristophanes' myth lacks.

Freudian *Verliebtheit* then is the truth of love at first sight here and elsewhere in *The Thousand and One Nights*. Hence, the similarity between Qamar al-Zaman and Budur that the text insists upon again and again is not merely a sign that they are "fated" to fall in love with each other. It is also an explanation of *why* they fall in love with each other.

In the same way that the narcissism of *Verliebtheit* is given an objective expression in the story in the form of the lovers' uncanny similarity, other aspects of romantic love are also given objective representation. Here I mean the commonplace idea of the delusions of love—that is, "love is blind," the fact that lovers see something that no one else sees and do not see what others see. This delusory aspect is expressed in the story in two ways. On the one hand, the lovers are blind to their remarkable similarity; the jinnis see the similarity, but Qamar and Budur never do. On the other hand, the other humans simply do not see the other lover at all. Hence, common reactions of third parties as "What does he see in her?" or "I cannot see in her what he sees in her," here become "I cannot see her, because she doesn't exist." Only the fact that each possesses a ring marks their experience as real, but for the lovers' parents the rings are simply an enigma. Hence, with one exception, Budur's brother Marzubân, friends and family regard the two lovers as mad—which they are, though not for the reason their families think they are. That is, their friends and families mistakenly diagnose the sort of madness they suffer from. It is the sort of madness to which we are all susceptible—love. Only Marzuban sees this.

The jinnis' wager and the test that settles it also distinguish "Qamar al-Zaman" from "The Two Viziers." In the latter story, the two jinnis argue the physical merits of the young man and woman, but they never make a wager, whereas in "Qamar al-Zaman" the wager is a highly developed part of the scene. The stakes of the wager are the freedom or enslavement of Dahnash.[10] And we may look at the means of settling this wager more closely, for the third jinni, Qashqash, devises a means that is a marvelous mixture of naiveté and cunning.

Beauty will be measured by the desire it arouses: the one who desires more shows thereby that he or she is less beautiful. Qashqash's test assumes that the quantity of desire aroused is directly proportional to beauty—which might seem reasonable in general terms, though one might not want to be "mathematical" about it. Yet on this account the test seems "objective," since the opinions of the jinn do not seem to enter into the calculations of the result; instead the result depends entirely on the two subjects who serve as both the object to be measured and the standard of measurement. Thus, the lovers form a closed circuit of desire and beauty that excludes all else. Nothing else is needed to demonstrate their beauty and desire, even as narcissism is a circle. Of course, the relation of subject and object here is somewhat complicated—dialectical, one would have to say. Even if one is skeptical about "measuring" desire by means of Qashqash's test, one will nevertheless recognize in it, I think, a simple truth, a truth that most of us have probably experienced at one time or another. That is, if one lover desires the other more than the other desires him, then he finds himself in the weaker position and at the mercy of the other. How many love affairs begin to sour with the realization that there is a "quantitative" difference of this sort between the lovers? "I love her more than she loves me (that's why I let her get away with those things!)." In any event, it is now apparent that the basis of Qashqash's test is the same dialectic of desire played out in the master-slave relation that structures the frame story. For the lover who is inferior in beauty is analogous to the slave; he reveals his inferiority by desiring more, even as the one who will be enslaved reveals his inferiority by his greater attachment to life—which suggests no romantic relation is wholly free of the effects of the master-slave dialectic. This suggests the pervasive significance of the master-slave relation in *The Thou-*

sand and One Nights—indeed, I do not think it is an exaggeration to say that it is the paradigm form of human relations throughout the book, a claim for which other stories will be seen to provide more evidence. While the wager in "Qamar al-Zaman" is made by the jinnis, given the demise of love at the story's end it may be that its use here is to emphasize the risks of romantic love—as the song says, "Love is a gamble." Both the contestant in the fight for pure prestige and the lover seek recognition of their own desire. As in the wager of life and death in the frame story, Qashqash's test reveals again the twofold nature of human desire: I want you, but—and what is more important—I want you to want me. For this reason, his test also shows how human desire divides the subject into an "I" and a "me." If this weren't the case, then Qashqash's test could not work, for in that test each lover, Qamar al-Zaman and Budur, functions both as that which is to be measured and as the standard of measurement.

Yet the neat circuit of Qashqash's test should not lead us to overlook an asymmetry. As the story tells us, there is male desire and then there is female desire; and whether one conceives of the female as weaker in relation to her desire than the male is in relation to his, or her desire as stronger than his hardly matters. The conclusion that must be drawn is the same: women are not to be trusted. For this reason, I would argue that Budur's weakness, as shown in the test, is proleptic; it is intended to prepare us for her ultimate betrayal of Qamar al-Zaman by her desire for his son by his second wife Ḥayât al-Nufûs. For despite all the mirror images involved, this asymmetry ultimately will upset the whole apple cart—or shatter the mirror.

The same asymmetry can also be seen in their defiance of their fathers prior to their meeting. Qamar al-Zaman's defiance of his father, while wrong, nevertheless proceeds from what he considers to be the faithlessness of women—a position, after all, that the story itself will, by and by, confirm. On the other hand, Budur's defiance of her father, her refusal to marry, is a refusal to submit to what has been divinely ordained, the rule of the male in marriage. Qamar al-Zaman's position then has what might be called an "ethical" basis, whereas Budur's position simply concerns power. It is pure selfishness, "pathological" in the Kantian sense.

The wager thus reveals Budur's weakness, which—in conjunction with her unwillingness to submit to male authority—will reappear in the third part of the story. But our consideration of the demise of love in "Qamar al-Zaman" will benefit if we first consider the nature of lovesickness.

Lovesick

Love at first sight is also found in the story " 'Alî ibn Bakkâr and Shams al-Nahâr," but more important for our purposes is the fact that the story is the most detailed exploration of the disease of lovesickness in *The Thousand and One Nights*. Which is as much as saying that in this story, as indeed in many other medieval texts, there is hardly any distinction between love and lovesickness, and it was on this question, on the pathology of love, that various ethical positions were staked out by medieval writers. For if there was in the medieval Muslim world some consensus as to the psychology of love—how it comes into being and the paths of its expression—there was not a consensus as to its ethical dimensions. On that question there was a range of opinion. There were those who regarded it as a dangerous passion, a disease to be avoided, and there were those who thought it permissible and celebrated it, and then there were those for whom love was a disease, yet a strangely honored one. While we are mostly concerned with the psychology of love here, the very notion of love as "pathological" poses provocative questions for us, living as we do in a culture that celebrates romantic love in a rather naïve way.

The idea of love as a disease is closely linked with so-called Udhri love mentioned earlier, and "Ali ibn Bakkar and Shams al-Nahar" of all the love stories in *The Thousand and One Nights* adheres most closely to the classic plot of an Udhri anecdote. Indeed, it could be seen as simply an Udhri anecdote expanded into a story-length narrative. Its elaborate description of lovesickness involves a déclassé Persian, Ali ibn Bakkar, and a concubine of the caliph Harun al-Rashid, Shams al-Nahar. The lovers are only together three times during the course of their love affair, including the occasion when they meet and fall in love, and, as in the classic Udhri plot, their love is never sexually consummated.

One day while Ali is in the shop of a wealthy merchant friend, Abû 'l-Ḥasan, Shams al-Nahar, in the company of ten lady attendants, enters. Ali falls in love with her at once; in the Arabic, "she stole his reason" (*salabat ʿaqlahu*, 1:761). In a daze, he tries to leave the shop, but she asks him to stay, for she too has become instantly enamored of him. He sits down and utters two lines of poetry that compare her beauty to the sun; her name *Shams al-Nahâr* means "Sun of the Day." The merchant Abu 'l-Hasan, who is a frequent visitor to the palace, tells Shams about Ali, and she tells him that she will send a slave girl for him, and he should come to the palace and bring Ali with him.[11]

Later that same day, Shams al-Nahar's girl takes Ali and the merchant to "the house of Harun al-Rashid." There they are taken to a chamber that is compared to one of the "chambers of Paradise," and are lavished with food and drink by beautiful young women who are compared to the so-called *houris* of Paradise, the dark-eyed beauties provided for the pleasure of the male believers in heaven. The narcissistic dimension of *Verliebtheit* finds perhaps a displaced expression in the description of Shams al-Nahar's chambers and gardens. Bencheikh emphasizes how the images in the vault of one chamber seem to be mirrored by the images of the carpet, and the garden is repeated in the motifs in the chamber as though spaces mirror each other: "Thus the perspective oversteps the limits and gives the recluses the impression of being able to go beyond themselves."[12] But of course, they cannot "go beyond themselves"—except, as we shall see, through death.

After some entertainment by more such beauties, they are taken to a room where Shams al-Nahar appears, somehow more beautiful still than all the others. Ali and Shams cry and embrace; they drink and listen to love poetry until their tryst is interrupted by the arrival of Harun. Shams hides her lover and his friend, but on hearing some sad verses of love poetry, she faints. Meanwhile, the slave girls help Abu 'l-Hasan and Ali ibn Bakkar to escape in a boat.

There follows an interval in which the two lovers pine for each other and exchange love letters through the intermediaries of the merchant and the slave girl. Then the merchant, who is well-known at the palace, fears that his complicity in the love affair will be discovered, and he turns the matter over to a friend who is a jeweler.

The third and final meeting of the lovers comes when the jeweler and the slave girl arrange a rendezvous in a house the jeweler owns. Again, an intrusion ruins the party. A gang of robbers loots the house and kidnaps them, while the jeweler, thinking it is Harun's guards, flees. When the robbers learn the identities of their captives, they release them to the jeweler, apparently out of fear of the caliph or sheer deference to his concubine.

After the lovers return to their respective homes, rumors of their love reach the caliph. When the jeweler hears of this, he rushes to Ali ibn Bakkar, and they flee the city. Ali, weakened by lovesickness, is further drained of strength by arduous travel. To make matters worse, they are again set upon by robbers who steal their clothes and leave them naked. An old gentleman finds them in a mosque where they have taken refuge, and he takes them home. He clothes them and feeds them, but for Ali it is too late. Hearing a slave girl sing some plaintive verses about the parting of lovers, he dies.

The jeweler entrusts the old man with Ali's body and returns to Baghdad, where Shams al-Nahar's slave girl tells him of Shams al-Nahar's death. While Shams was in the company of Harun, a slave girl sang verses whose pathetic meaning was simply too affecting, and Shams likewise died on the spot. The girl shows the jeweler the tomb of Shams al-Nahar. Finally we hear of the funeral of Ali ibn Bakkar, which was attended by throngs of people, and how the tombs of the lovers have become shrines. After many tears and sighs and swoons, all is over.

The symptoms of lovesickness are well known. Physical wasting away is one of them, as Ali ibn Bakkar himself tells us in some poetry he utters:

> Source of mine evils, she alone's,
> Of long love-longing and my groans and moans;
> Near her I see my soul in melting mood,
> For love of her and wasting of bones.
>
> (2:763)[13]

The Arabic terms in these lines are common throughout the literature. Burton's "evils" in the first line is *saqâm* or "growing thin"; "love-longing" is *wajd*, which means "strong passion"; *gharâm* is "infatuation" or *Verliebtheit*; and *walû*ʿ is "craving." Other stories describe the same physical symptoms of lovesickness, most prominently insomnia, loss of appetite with consequent weight loss and, as we shall see, catatonia:

> And due to the severity of his passion he became sleepless, his thoughts preoccupied with her. His pallor became yellow, and his body wasted away. (1:850, "Qamar al-Zaman")

> And when he woke up, passion and the pain of separation fell upon him, and he became gravely ill. For a whole year he did not leave his house. (2:246, " ʿAlî Shâr and Zumurrud")

> But she continued to shun him and repulse his advances until, from his love, his passion and his burning thirst for her, he fell very ill and took to his bed where he could not sleep. (2:382, "The Lover of the Banu Udhrah")

If some of my readers still entertain doubts about the reality of love at first sight, most, I think, will grant that there is some reality to lovesickness, even if the medieval prognosis in a case like Ali ibn Bakkar seems overstated. In fact, the symptoms are those that

Freud sees as shared by mourning and melancholia in his essay of that same title, or depression as it is more commonly called now. And as to the cause of lovesickness, the medieval Arab experts agreed with Freud. Lovesickness is caused by separation from the beloved, hence the cure is usually taken to be "union" (*wiṣâl*).

But the cure of *wisal* is impossible in the cases of Ali ibn Bakkar and Shams al-Nahar, for their union is blocked by a seemingly insurmountable obstacle. Shams al-Nahar is the property of the caliph. It is true that in another story, "Ghânim ibn Ayyûb, the Slave of Love," Harun gives his slave girl Qût al-Qulûb to her lover Ghanim. Here, however, such a solution is most unlikely if not impossible, because in this story Harun is not merely the representative of the Law that forbids this love, he is also another lover, and a deluded one at that. When Shams's servant tells the jeweler of her death, she also says, regarding the rumors of Shams's love for Ali, that "Harun would not accept the word of anyone against her due to the severity of his love for her" (1:809). In laying such emphasis on the strength of Harun's passion for Shams, the storyteller rules out a solution like that of "Ghanim, the Slave of Love."

So, on the face of it, Harun is the insurmountable barrier that dooms the love of Ali and Shams, sending them into a downward spiral in the narcissistic circuits of *Verliebtheit*. Love as a pact for Ali and Shams can only take the form of choosing death.

Yet there are indications in the story that Harun is not the only problem here, and on this point Lacan's discussion of troubadour poetry in his seventh seminar on "The Ethics of Psychoanalysis" may be relevant. For, setting to one side the whole question of whether the troubadour poets were influenced by Spanish Arab love poetry, there is no doubt that medieval Arabic love literature and European troubadour poetry share many common themes and topoi. What Lacan says of troubadour poetry certainly holds for Arabic love poetry: "The object involved, the feminine object, is introduced oddly enough through the door of privation or of inaccessibility" (*S*, 7:149). Lacan's discussion of courtly love begins with the woman as desired object and ends with positing her as the "traumatic thing." The field of *das Ding*, Lacan contends, indicates in Freud's later theory that space beyond the pleasure principle where Freud suggests "that which in life might prefer death" (*S*, 7:104).

We have already seen in the frame tale in the case of the kidnapped woman how woman is conceived as *fitnah*, a source of discord—one might as well say "trauma"—and as pure lack. And Lacan also uses the term "vacuole" to describe the "thing." More evidence of the beloved experienced as a traumatic thing is found in the love poetry in "Ali ibn Bakkar." Consider the lines he sings when he first sees her:

> She is the sun dwelling in the sky
> Give your heart this lovely solace:
> You can never rise to her,
> And she can never descend to you.
> (1:761)[14]

Thus, from the very outset, before Ali knows her identity (and so before he can know that she is property of the caliph), she is already described as inaccessible to him. And that inaccessibility is linked to loss and to death. In the Arabic hemistych *fa-ʿazzi ʾl-fuʾâda ʿazâʾa jamîlâ*, the word *ʿazzi* is the imperative form of a verb that means to console the bereaved; *ʿazâʾa*, "consolation," is its gerund. Here it is the absolute object of the verb, but *ʿazâʾa* can simply mean "the ceremony of mourning." Lovesickness is, thus, a form of mourning. And, given the narcissistic aspect of *Verliebtheit*, it means that Ali ibn Bakkar (and Shams al-Nahar) in some way mourns himself (and she, herself). As soon as he falls in love, he is dead.

Furthermore, Ali himself rejects the cure of *wisal* or union. When Shams tells him that they have no course except to bear patiently what has happened to them, he says:

> My reunion with you shall not content [me], nor will looking at you put out the fire in me, nor will the mastery that love has over my heart go away except with the departure of my spirit. (1:765)

Indeed, he also says, "You should know that everything has an end, and the end of love is either death or union [of the lovers]. And I am very close to death" (1:804). Chasteness, as I have said, is another commonplace of Udhri love, and Ali's view seems to reflect the idea, common though by no means universal, that sexual union "kills" love.[15] By that view, however, one can see that by choosing to keep love alive, Ali chooses death for himself and thus becomes a so-called "martyr of love," a prominent idea first formulated by the jurist Ibn Dâʾûd (d. 910). In this view, one who kept himself chaste and thereby died of lovesickness was as much a martyr as the soldier who died in battle fighting for Islam. Certainly the ending with the two lovers' tombs visited as shrines is consonant with this. Since death from lovesickness was taken quite seriously by all the parties to the debate, certain ironic and playful clichés that commonly depict the beloved as a killer may nevertheless have another sort of resonance in light of these theories:

> Oh Swordsman sound, when she gazes
> At you with a shattering blow of her eyelids.
>
> (1:778)

Other examples in "Ali ibn Bakkar and Shams al-Nahar," which also deploy stock images of medieval Arabic love poetry, depict the "menace" posed by the beloved in other ways. The comparison of the beloved's glance to an unerring and fatal arrow is a common cliché in this regard:

> She blocked my escape with the sword of her glance
> And split my strength to endure with the lance of her shape.
>
> (1:778)

> Fate struck me with an arrow of her glance
> A fatal blow and I have left my friends
> Fate opposed me and my forbearance waned
> Yet before I reckoned it would be so.
>
> (1:773)

A line in the *Dîwân* of Jamîl, a famous Udhri lover, though ironic, nevertheless is explicit in calling the beloved a killer:

> I want her well and she wants to kill me
> Quite a difference between my murder and well being![16]

It is interesting to consider these light, ironic verses in relation to that wholly negative view of love mentioned earlier. As Lois Giffen writes:

> Ibn al-Jawzî or Ibn Qayyim . . . could point to the damning evidence offered by popular theory which described *ishq* and *hawâ* (love) as humbling the lover before the beloved and causing "enslavement" (*taʿabbud* or *tatayyam*) and bondage of the will. Since Islam by definition is spiritual submission (*islâm*) to God, it was wrong, they argued, to be the spiritual slave or servant of a human being.[17]

On this point, a line of poetry that Ali says makes it quite clear that the beloved is his ultimate master:

> Master, dear heart
> and precious life . . .
>
> (1:764)

The demand that one die as proof of one's love, while it is jest in Jamil, is treated seriously in the *Nights* in the anecdotal story "Three Unhappy Lovers." In this story a man tells the story of his daughter who loves a youth who loves a singing girl who, in turn, loves the man's daughter. The tale is brief enough that it may be translated in full here:

> And among the things told [Shahrazad said] is that al-ʿUtbî[18] said: I was sitting one day with a group of educated people, and we were exchanging anecdotes about people and the conversation led us to anecdotes about lovers. Each one of us said something about that, but among us was one man who was silent until he said, "Shall I tell you a story the likes of which you have never heard?" We said yes, and he said: "I had a daughter who was in love with a young man though we did not know about it. The young man, however, was in love with a singing girl—who in turn was in love with my daughter.
>
> One day I was at a gathering and the young man and the singing girl were also there, and the girl sang these lines:
>
> > Among the signs of how love humiliates the lover is crying,
> > Especially of a lover when he finds no pity.
>
> "Excellent, my mistress," the young man said, "are you goading me to die?" The singing girl replied from behind the curtain, "Yes. If you really are a lover, die." So the young man put his head down on a cushion and closed his eyes. When the cup came round to him, we shook him and, behold, he was dead. We gathered around him, but our pleasure was ruined and we left at once.
>
> When I got home my family wondered why I had come home early. I told them what had happened with the youth, thinking that this would astonish them. But when my daughter heard what I said, she left the sitting room we were in and went to another room. I followed her and I found her stretched out on a cushion in the way the young man had been. I shook her, and, behold, she was dead.
>
> So we prepared her for burial, and the next morning we set out for her funeral while the young man's family set out for his, and while we were on our way to the graveyard, we met a third funeral party. We asked them whose funeral it was, and they told us it was the funeral of the singing girl. For when news of my daughter's death reached her, she had died just as my daughter did. We buried the three on the same day. And this is the most astonishing thing ever heard of lovers. (2:439–40)

Although the triad of lovers is structured differently, the anecdote, like "Ali ibn Bakkar," depicts the lover as willing his own death in love.

Giffen notes that it may have been the influence of Islam that transformed passionate pagan love among the Arabs into the chaste Udhri love that, paradoxically, then becomes a quasi-religion with writers like Ibn Daʾud who hold that there are "martyrs of love," which, again, in its turn is condemned once more as a form of blasphemy by stern spirits such as Ibn al-Jawzi and Ibn Qayyim.[19] In other words, passion even in a "sublimated" form is still a sin and a temptation to blasphemy. In this view God is a "jealous lover" in absolute terms who allows no other passionate attachments between his slaves. While Ali ibn Bakkar's gloomy rejection of union or *wisal* and the enshrinement of love at story's end reflect Ibn Da'ud's "religion of love," as Giffen calls it, insofar as all the earthly lovers are defeated here, since Harun is denied Shams al-Nahar also, the second, gloomier view of love may also exert some influence.

For all the sentimentality involved, the story and poetry and the anecdote finally deliver a very gloomy view of love in relation to a terrifying beyond. To submit to it is to die. We might now consider the end of "Qamar al-Zaman," where it is love that dies.

The Vicissitudes of Love

The second part of "Qamar al-Zaman" describes how he and Budur are separated after their marriage and then reunited again. Camped one day while en route to see his father, King Shahriman, Qamar finds Budur sleeping in their tent and, his desire for her aroused, he undoes her trousers. He finds a red jewel engraved with a script that he cannot read, and he says to himself, "If this jewel were not something very important to her, she would not have tied it to her belt or hidden it in the most precious place" (1:874). He takes it outside to examine it, and at once a bird swoops down and snatches it from his grasp. The bird leads him on a strange chase; it flies fast enough to elude him, but never so fast as to leave him behind. Eventually it leads him to a city full of hostile Magians, where he finds shelter with the only Muslim in the city and pursues a career as an apprentice gardener.

When Budur wakes up and finds that she is missing her husband and the jewel, she fears that the men in their party would have designs on her if they learn of her husband's absence. So she dons his clothes and disguises herself as him—a ruse that is easily carried off due to their amazing resemblance. She now travels to the City of Ebony, where King Armanus marries her to his daughter Hayat al-Nufus and cedes his throne to her. Budur confides her secret to

us, who, sympathetic to her plight, agrees to help her
erade.

, we are told of Shahriman searching for his son and, ng no success, returning home to build a "House of Sorrow" in his memory.

All the while Qamar al-Zaman plies his menial trade and waits for the one ship a year that sails from the city of Magians to the land of the Muslims. As that time draws near, he witnesses a strange battle between some birds, and in the entrails of the vanquished bird he discovers Budur's red jewel. Obviously, this is a good omen, and the next day he discovers a treasure of gold in a subterranean chamber. He gives half of the treasure to the gardener and keeps half for himself, making arrangements to ship both the gold and the jewel hidden amongst a cargo of olives home. But the day he is to leave, the gardener dies and Qamar al-Zaman misses the boat while attending to his burial. Nevertheless, the jewel still reaches Budur, and she sends the ship back to retrieve him. Still disguised as king, Budur has Qamar al-Zaman brought to her chambers, where she plays a joke on him. She cajoles him into submitting to what he thinks will be sodomy (though submitting causes him some discomfiture). Then, when they climb into bed—lo! Budur reveals herself to him.

The loss of the jewel is the peripeteia that sets all of these events in motion, and its rediscovery brings all to an end by reuniting husband and wife. The "secret" of its inscription we never learn; we only witness the uncanny behavior of the bird and the uncanny effect of the jewel on the fate of Qamar al-Zaman and Budur. Some of the readers puzzle over the meaning of the jewel and the bird.[20] First, let us note that in medieval thought the jewel or gem was equated with the notion of "essence." Had Qamar al-Zaman, then, lost the essence of his desire? Is the jewel Lacan's *objet a*?

The *objet a* is "a privileged object, which has emerged from some primal separation, from some self-mutilation induced by the very approach of the real . . ." (*FFC*, 83). As such, it is the object as the traumatic cause from which the subject emerges. Žižek says of *objet a* in Lacan's theory of the subject:

> . . . if the subject is to emerge, he must set himself against a paradoxical object that is real, that cannot be subjectivized. Such an object remains an 'absolute non-subject' whose very presence involves *aphanisis*, the erasure of the subject; yet as such this presence is the subject himself in his oppositional determination, the negative of the subject, a piece of flesh the subject has to lose if he is to emerge as the void of the distance

towards every objectivity. This uncanny object is the subject itself in the mode of objectivity. . . .[21]

By this reading, the inscrutable writing on the jewel, which is the first hint at its uncanny nature, is not then the mark of this narrative's imperfect assimilation of an anterior narrative (à la Gerhardt) but is itself the message: the lack that sustains desire. It is this very enigma that provokes him to cut the jewel off her belt and take it outside—where he promptly loses it to a bird. The negativity of desire is represented by this means, and *objet a* represents in Lacan's "algebra" the lack that sustains desire. Thus, when Qamar al-Zaman removes it from Budur, he effectively removes his desire from her also, and the entire time that the jewel is missing, lodged in the entrails of the "bad bird," his desire is effectively "elsewhere." It is missing in action, so to speak. While he is in the city of the Magians, Qamar al-Zaman doesn't know where it is, and, denied his object, he too is effectively lost. For if *objet a* is the object as traumatic cause of the subject, then, when it is swallowed by the bird who disappears, Qamar al-Zaman is effectively "erased." He is transformed into a kind of pale shadow, and the significance of the city of Magians seems linked to this transformation of Qamar. After all, the plot would only seem to require a separation of the lovers, not Qamar's exile among pagans. But such an exile amongst hostile non-Muslims requires him to conceal the primary sign of his social identity in order to survive, his being a Muslim. His state, deprived of *objet a*, is a form of living death. And though he waits for the one ship a year that sails from the city of the Magians to the lands of the Muslims, it is only his rediscovery of the jewel that ends his exile. This is accomplished through the birds. They fill the role of the jinnis in the first part of the story, as agents of the separation of the lovers, but there is a difference. What was supernatural has now become uncanny.

The effect of the jewel's disappearance on Budur must not be neglected either. In fact, it is Budur who dominates the second part of the story, and it is precisely the disappearance of the jewel that brings this about. When she no longer possesses *objet a* for Qamar, that is the object of his fantasy, she is free. And her freedom consists in pursuing her own fantasy, not that of being a man, but of occupying the man's place of power, of being the master. And most of the second part of the story describes her successful attempt to masquerade as a man, which allows her to be what she wanted to be from the very beginning, a king.

There is a certain similarity here with an episode in a novel called

Fragoletta that Lacan discusses in his fourth seminar, *La relation d'objet*. In the end, the hero of the novel kills his love interest, a girl named Fragoletta. The girl, Lacan says, "has presented herself to him as a young man without his realizing it, which shows the equivalence of a certain feminine object of *Verliebtheit* with the other as rival."[22]

The displacement of the object of fantasy, *objet a*, entails a displacement of master and slave. The different roles of Budur and Qamar al-Zaman in this second part of the story again reflect the asymmetry of their desire present from the beginning, as it was revealed in the wager. Budur, who showed female weakness and who rebelled against male sovereignty, now freed of male domination, tries to assume the role of man or, perhaps more to the point, the role of the master, while Qamar al-Zaman is reduced to virtually a slave-like existence. But with respect to gender, it is not a matter of simply switching roles, for the order of power (master-slave) and the order of sexuality (male-female) are skewed in relation to each other; Budur masquerades as a man and even "marries" a woman, Hayat al-Nufus; but Qamar al-Zaman does not masquerade as a woman. Instead, he is asked to be a homosexual object for the master. Although homosexual desire is often attributed to evil characters in *The Thousand and One Nights*, here it is treated with a comic touch; the "sexual carnival," as Hamori calls it, is played for laughs. There is perhaps an ironic look back at Qamar's aversion to females at the outset. When he now shows himself to be averse to men, it is as though the storyteller says, "Oh, you don't like that! Well, how about some of this?"

Budur's willingness to give free rein to her desire, her attitude towards her father, and the relish with which she assumes the role of the king—all of these things bode ill for her marriage to Qamar al-Zaman, and point towards the third part of the story wherein she betrays Qamar. As noted before, Gerhardt considers it of little merit; she speaks of its "plain lack of any logic whatever."[23] But Hamori and Bencheikh disagree. While the story of Amjad and Asʿad is peripheral to the issue of love at first sight here, I should say that—as may be inferred from the preceding discussion of Budur—I agree with Hamori and Bencheikh as to its merits. Both writers show that many features in "Amjad and Asʿad" betray a conscious effort to relate the third part to the preceding story. And since the third part of the story undoes all that has preceded it in the first two parts, both address that relation as a thematic contradiction. Bencheikh speaks of a "*dialectic du sens*," while Hamori speaks of an "antinomy." "Antinomy," with its Kantian echo, perhaps better expresses the unresolvable conflict in the story between romantic love and family structure. Qamar only escapes it when he abandons his two wives and returns to his father. The story develops the theme of love at first sight in great detail, and the events that follow must be seen as a cautionary tale about the delusory and narcissistic aspects of love. As we have noted, the two lovers never notice the thing about each other that all the other characters in the story notice first, their uncanny resemblance to each other. Qamar's inability to even recognize Budur in the sexual masquerade further emphasizes the point in relation to him. While he loves her does he ever truly see her as she is? Or is he simply captured by his own image in the mirror of *Verliebtheit*?

Taken together, "Ali ibn Bakkar" and "Qamar al-Zaman" offer two gloomy alternatives: either the lover or love must die. To regard love as pathological in some degree is not a new idea, but it is an idea largely forgotten in our own culture with its rather facile understanding of this human passion. On this account, the fear and suspicion of the beloved expressed in fiction and poetry are an acknowledgment of what could be called the pathology of *Verliebtheit*, a pathology that includes both its narcissistic structure and the traumatic thing that lies beyond the desired object.

Giffen argues that the conflicts between the demands of Islam and those of Arab customs created a certain class of discontents, some of whom, like Ali ibn Bakkar, by and by find their way into the *Nights*. And Lacan says much the same thing about courtly love poetry:

> The poetry of courtly love, in effect, tends to locate in the place of the Thing certain discontents of the culture. And it does so at a time when the historical circumstances bear witness to a disparity between the especially harsh conditions of life and certain fundamental demands. By means of a sublimation specific to art, poetic creation consists in positing an object I can only describe as terrifying, an inhuman partner. (*S*, 7:150).

In the work of al-Sarrâj (d. 1106), *The Deaths of Lovers*, Abû Zuhayr al-Madînî says of passionate love (*ʿishq*), "It is derangement, abasement, and it is the disease of the people of elegance."[24]

5
Double Trouble

THE THEME OF THE DOUBLE, AS WE HAVE SEEN, IS A PROMINENT ONE IN *The Thousand and One Nights*, figuring in the tale of the two brothers Shahriyar and Shahzaman and their mirror-like relations, and in the story of "Qamar al-Zaman" with its lookalike lovers. As important as the theme is in those stories, three stories of the Harun al-Rashid cycle develop it in even greater depth and detail, and deserve separate analysis. In their different ways, they all explore various dimensions of a crisis first seen in the frame story, the imaginary crisis of the ego, to put it in Lacanian terms.[1]

The story of "The False Caliph," which Shahrazad begins on the 285th Night (2:157–176), promises initially to be an intriguing treatment of the theme. The story opens, as Harun stories often do, with the caliph Harun al-Rashid suffering from insomnia. He summons his minister Jaʿfar the Barmecid and his executioner Masrûr, and, disguised as merchants, they wander the streets of Baghdad to divert themselves. By the Tigris they come upon an old man with a boat, and they offer him money to take them out on the river. He replies that he would be happy to do so, but, as they must know, the caliph Harun al-Rashid goes out on a pleasure boat each night, and he has forbidden anyone else to be on the river at the same time on pain of death. Needless to say, Harun and his companions are astonished to hear this. Eager to see this pretender, they claim to be foreign merchants who are ignorant of the caliph's command, and they offer the old man yet more money to take them to a place where, unobserved, they may watch the pleasure boat of the false caliph go by.

The boatman accepts their offer, and soon the pleasure boat drifts by. Harun is still more astonished to see a man who resembles himself in his dress and behavior. What is more, the false caliph is accompanied by men resembling Jaʿfar and Masrur as well as numerous attendants, musicians, singing girls, and slaves. Harun says to Jaʿfar, "I am baffled!" The next night they go out with the old boatman again, and again they observe the false caliph's pleasure boat. But this time they follow it until it docks beside a garden. They order the old man to dock their boat and they go ashore to mix with the garden party.

They simply observe matters until the false caliph, upon hearing verses lamenting a lost love, rips his garments and falls into a swoon. His torn garments reveal the scars of a flogging. When the false caliph comes out of his swoon and Ja'far asks him how he got such scars, he replies with a story that is essentially that of the second lady in "The Porter and the Three Ladies of Baghdad," though, of course, with the genders of the two lovers switched. The man is Muhammad ibn Ali, son of the richest jeweler in Baghdad, and he tells how he fell in love with Ja'far's own sister, and how she grew jealous and punished him when he answered a summons by Harun's wife Zubaydah. And even as Harun reconciles the second lady in "The Porter and the Three Ladies of Baghdad" to the husband who beat her and abandoned her, his own son Amin, here too he reconciles the estranged couple.

But after a most intriguing beginning, this explanation of the false caliph's masquerade disappoints us. The disappointment may be due in part, as Mia Gerhardt says, to the fact that the false caliph's impersonation of Harun is so weakly motivated. Chauvin can only explain it thus: "He plays the role of the caliph in the hope that Harun will reconcile him with his spouse."[2] But this presumably did not require his elaborate year-long masquerade. But I would claim the disappointment stems rather more from the fact that the man's explanation of his masquerade abandons the theme of the double. Indeed, the story initially promises to depict not only the double of a character but that of a whole sphere of reality, as though it will reveal to us a strange mirror-like world worthy of Borges, but here the storyteller's imagination is not up to the task. Perhaps it would require the imagination of a Borges to make good on the initial promise of the story, to devise a second half which would develop the possibilities of the first half, most prominently an exploration of the relation of illusion and reality that is so much a part of the theme of the double.

With these remarks in mind, we might examine two other Harun stories that also explore the theme, though more successfully as I will show. And insofar as these stories are more successful explorations of the theme, they not only possess more interest in their own right but they will also show us how "The False Caliph" goes wrong, and will suggest in a general way where the storyteller ought to have taken his story. The first story is "Khalîfah the Fisherman."

KHALIFAH THE FISHERMAN

Khalifah belongs to a recurring character type in *The Thousand and One Nights,* of whom other examples are Aladdin and Muhammad the Lazy-Bones. Through no fault of their own, they end up wealthy. Their comedies reflect the view from below, the view of the slave who looks at the foibles of the master and says to himself, "He's just an idiot like me who got lucky!" This no doubt is a view, as Nietzsche would tell us, which betrays the *ressentiment* of the slave, but it is one that nevertheless may be a tonic for a culture like our own that takes the hagiographic style as the most appropriate idiom for discussion of the wealthy.

Khalifah's story begins with one of those astonishing events that are recounted in the *Nights* in a most matter-of-fact way. Khalifah, a poor fisherman, casts his net into the Tigris three times, and with each cast he brings forth from its waters a talking ape. The first two apes are unlucky creatures, but the last ape is a lucky one. He tells Khalifah that he brings his master ten gold dinars each day, and he orders him to cast his net into the Tigris one more time. Khalifah does so, and catches a large fish. The lucky ape tells Khalifah to take the fish to a certain Jewish moneychanger who is in fact his master. Khalifah is to give the Jew the fish only on the condition that he in turn gives Khalifah the rights to his ape, the lucky ape, in exchange for the first unlucky ape. Khalifah does so, although he has some difficulty remembering the ape's precise instructions—he is, if not absentminded, a little slow on the uptake. No matter, he is now master of the lucky ape, though his luck will still swing back and forth from good to bad a number of times.

For the next ten days it improves. He sells his catch each day for ten dinars, earning exactly the reward that the ape promised him. Then, one evening while befuddled with hashish, Khalifah's imagination gets the best of him, and he begins to fret that his "fortune" is threatened by the caliph Harun al-Rashid, who will demand to borrow all of his money. To steel himself for the beating he expects the caliph to use to extract his money, Khalifah beats himself. But his cries awaken his neighbors. Then he hits upon the expedient of sewing the money into his cloak. But having done this, he forgets that he has put the money in his cloak—again he is a little absentminded. Khalifah, it becomes clear, is an example of a medieval character type, the *mughaffal*, someone who is characterized by heedlessness, inattention, and gullibility. The result is that he jumps into the river with his cloak on and loses it. Then, while diving to recover the money, someone takes his clothes too. He ends up naked, entangled in his own net, and we leave him in this condition for the time being while we are told of Harun al-Rashid's infatuation with a beautiful slave girl.

A jeweler, Ibn al-Qirnâṣ, purchases a beautiful young slave girl named Qût al-Qulûb (or "Nourishment of the Hearts") for Harun, and the caliph falls madly in love with her. He spends all of his time with her, and the members of his court become worried about his obsession with the girl. Rather as Shahriyar thinks to distract Shahzaman from his woes with a hunting trip, Jaʿfar proposes a hunting party to Harun, hoping thereby to distract him from Qut al-Qulub. While hunting they come upon Khalifah in the situation just described—at which point we must note that the fisherman's name *khalîfah* is the very word for "caliph" in Arabic.

When Harun advances to meet Khalifah alone, Khalifah mistakes Harun for the thief who stole his clothes and threatens him with a stick: "Give me back my clothes or I will beat you with this stick until you pee on yourself or dirty your robe!" And Harun says to himself, "By God, I couldn't bear half a blow from this tramp!" (4:166). So he gives Khalifah his own cloak to cover his naked body. Then Khalifah offers to take him on as a helper, and Harun helps him cast his net. They haul in a large catch of fish, and Khalifah sends Harun back to town to fetch two baskets in which to carry their catch. But Harun goes back to Jaʿfar and his slaves and, as a prank, offers a gold dinar to anyone who brings him a fish from Khalifah. The slaves fall upon Khalifah and steal all but two of his fish. However Ṣandal, Harun's chief eunuch, takes pity on the fisherman; he offers to buy his last two fish, telling him to come to the palace the next day and he shall pay him handsomely. Khalifah wanders back to town, penniless again but not entirely hopeless.

Meanwhile, Lady Zubaydah, jealous of her husband's passion for Qut al-Qulub, has seized the opportunity of Harun's absence to get rid of the girl. Qut is drugged, locked in a trunk, and the trunk taken to the market to be sold, unopened, to the highest bidder. Then Zubaydah spreads rumors of Qut's death throughout the palace. When Harun returns and hears of this, he is plunged into grief.

The next day Khalifah goes to the palace to seek payment from Sandal, and Jaʿfar recognizes him. Hoping now to distract the caliph from his grief, he tells Harun of the presence of his odd "master," and indeed Harun is somewhat cheered by this news. To amuse himself, he arranges a sort of lottery for Khalifah whose prizes range from wealthy reward to death. Khalifah's luck is poor to middling; in three draws, he first earns one hundred blows, then nothing, and on the third, one dinar. Though he escapes death,

Khalifah leaves, seemingly down on his luck again and disgruntled until Sandal again takes pity on him and gives him one hundred dinars.

Once again flush, Khalifah happens to walk through the market just as a chest from the harem of Lady Zubaydah comes up for auction. On an impulse, he bids one hundred and one dinars and the chest is sold to him. He hauls the heavy trunk home, but finds himself unable to open it. Exhausted and once again bemoaning his ill luck, he falls asleep on it. Soon, however, he is awakened by sounds from within the trunk. Thinking them to be the sounds of a jinni, he rouses his neighbors. They lend him a lamp and a hammer, and he succeeds in breaking open the lock. He is astonished to find a beautiful young woman.

Qut al-Qulub climbs out of the trunk. Being hungry and thirsty, she sends him out for food and drink, and once again Khalifah's neighbors donate the necessaries. When she feels better, Qut al-Qulub reveals her identity to Khalifah and promises him that if he returns her safe and sound to Harun al-Rashid, he will be very handsomely rewarded. Hearing the caliph's name, Khalifah expresses his doubts about the stingy rascal who helped him fish. But Qut al-Qulub mollifies him, and convinces him to carry a letter to Ibn al-Qirnas. Ibn al-Qirnas then arranges for Qut al-Qulub to be returned to Harun. And now Harun does indeed reward Khalifah very handsomely.

Like "The False Caliph," "Khalifah the Fisherman" also makes use of a piece of an earlier story; in "Ghanim the Slave of Love," Lady Zubaydah locks a slave girl also named Qut-al-Qulub in a chest. There, however, Qut al-Qulub ends up—after many adventures and misadventures—married to Ghanim. Here her story is joined to that of the rude and somewhat obtuse fisherman who becomes the unwitting agent of her deliverance.

The character of Khalifah, impoverished, truculent, and a little slow-witted—even when people spell something out for him, it takes him a while to get it—these qualities limn some of the essential characteristics of the Lacanian ego. And indeed there is an almost perfect image of this in the story. By this I mean the scene on the bank of the Tigris when Khalifah, who has once again lost everything, and, caught in *his own net*, sees Harun approach; it is one of those marvelous, suggestive images that typify *The Thousand and One Nights*. The scene can be read as the comedy of the Lacanian ego, the ego as a kind of trap in which the subject, due to his own incompleteness, is caught, fascinated by the image of the other, who, as an imaginary whole, holds out the promise of supplying what the subject lacks. But the other cannot give back what he does not have to give; the promise of "wholeness" is an illusion of the ego that can never be fulfilled. In our comedy beside the Tigris, this is seen in the fact that Khalifah wants from Harun something—his clothes—that Harun cannot give him. Clothes, we might remark, are, like the ego, the garb of the subject; they hide more than they reveal. When Harun gives him his own much finer cloak, this cannot satisfy Khalifah; he wants his own rags. The *meconnaisance* of Khalifah is like that of the ego; he cannot recognize the riches offered him and wants his rags instead.

In this, we must say, Khalifah behaves like a master. His dissatisfaction recalls a remark of Kierkegaard in *Either/Or* apropos the master and his desire; that is, if he asked a servant for a glass of water and the servant brought him the finest wine in the world, he would dismiss him.[3] For his pleasure consists not in drinking the finest wine in the world but in having his way. Khalifah's solution is different but still emblematic of the master's desire: he cuts off the lower portion of Harun's cloak. The cutting off of the hem—a *circumcision* after all—may be taken as the sign of the pact that makes Harun ostensibly his servant. When the cloak is ruined, when it is *missing* something—then it is Khalifah's. It's a comedy of riches to rags.

The striking image of Khalifah caught in his own net is also worth considering in relation to his poverty—his "net worth," that is, which is just about nil—and to his bachelorhood. The Arabic word for net, *shabakah,* derives from the root *sh-b-k,* whose fundamental sense is "to be connected, linked." Another derivation of the same triliteral root is *shabkah* (which looks identical to *shabakah* in an Arabic text written, as it customarily is, without the short vowels marked), and *shabkah* means the bridal fee a man must pay for his bride. The nature of the Arabic system of radicals and derivatives can make it easy sometimes to produce such "resonances" where perhaps none may exist. However, Lacan's essay "The Agency of the Letter in the Unconscious" offers us warrant enough to speculate in this instance on the basis of the "materiality of the signifier." Hence, in view of what Khalifah will eventually catch, I think his *shabakah* may have a further symbolic function. After all, the analogy between courtship and hunting—or fishing in this case (a single Arabic word denotes both hunting and fishing)—is age-old in Arabic literature as it is in other literatures. As the pre-Islamic poet al-Muthaqqib al- ʿAbdî sings:

> Would that she were still the object of desire
> As when she hunted while I was hunting her.[4]

Furthermore, this same connection of *shabakah* and *shabkah* occurs in a story told by the author Tanukhi, whose work has been previously mentioned in connection with the *Nights*. In a story in *Happiness After Hardship,* a bedouin must steal a horse named Shabkah as the price for his bride, his pretty cousin.[5]

At the outset of "Khalifah the Fisherman" we are told that Khalifah is too poor to get married, a fact that in itself would set him off as an oddball in a culture where almost everyone, no matter how poor, manages somehow to get married and where to remain single is almost an affront to society—"No monkery in Islam!" is a famous saying of the Prophet. But Khalifah cannot afford a *shabkah* until the story's end when, having returned Qut al-Qulub to Harun, he is richly rewarded. Then, when he has transformed his *shabakah* into a *shabkah,* Khalifah buys a house and marries "a girl who was daughter of one of the notables of the city . . ." (4:190). Unlike "Ghanim the Slave of Love," where the slave gets back the woman that he has returned to the master, in "Khalifah the Fisherman" the master keeps that girl and gives another girl to the slave. An exchange that recalls the medieval writer al-Jâḥiẓ's comparison of women to bouquets and apples: he says that, except for the issues of paternity and law, they would belong to the same category of object, that which men may offer one another. If a man has several, he keeps one and gives the rest to his fellows.[6] In any case, the result is the usual finale of comedy, marriage; Khalifah the oddball is "assimilated"—or as the anthropologist might put it, the exchange of women between men sustains the social order. Through marriage, a pact between male lineages, Khalifah emerges from the imaginary relation of the ego and its double and submits to the symbolic order.

The meeting of the caliph—or *al-khalîfah*—and Khalifah the fisherman also illustrates an important aspect of the theme of the double, the reversal of master and slave. When Khalifah, mistaking Harun for the thief who has stolen his clothes, threatens him, the "real" master, Harun, submits and for a time becomes a servant. His submission is playful and, yet, not wholly playful, for he submits on account of real fear. Nevertheless, Harun is able to quickly seize the upper hand again, and henceforth Khalifah's fortune, for better or worse, remains dependent on Harun who, when he is not distracted by his passion for Qut al-Qulub, manipulates Khalifah in various ways, most of which escape Khalifah's notice.

Still, for all that, Harun is never quite the perfect master, a fact that is seen in his moment of fear by the Tigris and made even more evident in his passion for Qut al-Qulub and in Zubaydah's ability to deceive him. And as a result of this deception, Harun must depend on Khalifah to get Qut al-Qulub back, a twist that may be seen as another reversal of the master and slave positions. His dependency on Khalifah in these two instances, first on the river bank and later when Khalifah comes into possession of Qut al-Qulub, makes his position analogous to that of the lucky ape; as the lucky ape is both servant to Khalifah and the agent of the fisherman's good fortune, so too Harun is at times both servant and agent of Khalifah's good fortune.

The master-slave relation, an essential component of the theme of the double, figures even more prominently in another Harun story, "The Sleeper Awakened." Indeed, the manipulations of the master are still more calculating and more provocative than those in "Khalifah."

The Arch-deceiver

Harun's double here is a character named Abu 'l-Hasan *al-khalī*ʿ.[7] Lane and Burton translate *al-khalīʿ* as "wag," and while this serves the story, other meanings of *khalīʿ* might be kept in mind. The verb form *khalaʿ* has a wide variety of senses, but the ones that are linked to the adjectival form of *khalīʿ* have meanings like "to throw off all restraint, to act profligately," and "to disown, repudiate a son."[8] Thus, a *khalīʿ* can be a "repudiated son, a profligate, a dissolute man." At this point, let us just say that the tag tells us that, rather in the same way as Khalifah the fisherman, Abu 'l-Hasan is a *khârij* or "outsider."

The story begins with mention of the death of a father, and tells us of the son who inherits his fortune. It is a common opening in *The Thousand and One Nights*, and such stories usually proceed to tell us how the young man wastes his fortune and then makes another. "The Sleeper Awakened" will also tell us that story, but by means of an unusual path, a path that begins with the odd behavior of Abu 'l-Hasan. After receiving his inheritance, Abu 'l-Hasan divides it into two parts. He sets one half aside as a form of insurance, and then proceeds to spend the other half on wine, women, and song. When it is gone and he stops his lavish entertainments, his so-called friends desert him. He finds out that, as the old song says, "nobody knows you when you're down and out." Except, of course, Abu 'l-Hasan is not truly down and out, for he still has the other half of his inheritance. Nevertheless, he is chastened and even somewhat embittered by this experience, and with the rest of his money he pursues an entirely different course of action. Henceforth, he will entertain only complete strangers, and each stranger for only one night. To this end, he goes to a bridge over the Tigris every evening and picks out a stranger whom he takes home. He feeds the man, entertains him, and puts him up for the night, but in the morning he abruptly turns him out. Thereafter, if he sees the man, he simply refuses to greet him and treats him once again as an utter stranger.

One evening he happens to extend an invitation of this sort to Harun who again is promenading in disguise. Abu 'l-Hasan plies him with food and drink, and Harun, astonished at his generosity with a total stranger, suggests that he would like to return his hospitality on another occasion. Abu 'l-Hasan replies, "How impossible it is that what has passed should ever return, and that I should ever spend another evening with you besides this one" (*B*, 137). Harun, now even more curious, asks him to explain this strange habit.

As prologue to explaining his odd life style, Abu 'l-Hasan tells Harun a brief tale about a beggar who cheats a cafe owner out of paying for his meal, and then discovers that the man defrauds his customers by mixing horse meat with his beef. Abu 'l-Hasan no doubt means to equate the fraudulent butcher with his erstwhile fair-weather friends, and so represent himself as the one who sees through the other's disguise. Yet at the moment he tells the tale we cannot fail to notice that he is the one who *does not know* the identity of the other. And it is precisely Abu 'l-Hasan's ignorance of Harun's real identity that gives Harun the extraordinary power over him required for his ruse.

After this prologue, Abu 'l-Hasan tells him how he spent the first half of his inheritance, and thus the reason why he pursues his unusual lifestyle. They drink a good deal of wine, and Harun persists in seeking a way to return Abu 'l-Hasan's hospitality, asking him if he doesn't after all have one desire (*shahwah*) that he might fulfill for him. Perhaps under the influence of the wine Abu 'l-Hasan admits that he does have one particularly keen desire. He would like to take revenge on some neighbors, four sheikhs and an imam in a nearby mosque, who have embarrassed him in front of his guests and threatened to complain to the caliph about him:

> They have oppressed me greatly. I wish God would grant me the power for one day to give each one of them four hundred lashes in front of the mosque and discredit them publicly in the city of Baghdad, saying, "This is the punishment for someone who stirs up trouble." This is the only thing I want. (*B*, 146)

Harun replies, "May God grant what you desire." Then Harun pours a cup of wine for his host laced with "Cretan henbane," a potent soporific apparently used to make a medieval "mickey finn"—it is used elsewhere in the *Nights*. Abu 'l-Hasan drinks it and keels over.

Masrur carries Abu 'l-Hasan to the palace and puts him in Harun's bed. Harun instructs all of the court officials and the palace servants that when Abu 'l-Hasan wakes up they are to carry out his orders and treat him just as though he were the caliph Harun al-Rashid himself. In his private chambers, Harun gives his female slaves similar instructions. Then he hides behind a curtain to watch the fun.

When Abu 'l-Hasan is awakened by a female slave the next morning and sees the opulent surroundings of the palace and the assembled servants, he is bewildered and says to himself, "Either I'm still asleep, or this is Paradise." He tries to sleep again, but is awakened by a eunuch, who says to him, "This is not your usual habit, Prince of the Faithful." Abu 'l-Hasan bites his finger to make sure that he is not dreaming. He questions some of the slaves and they all insist that he is indeed the caliph. Then a slave brings him a pair of fancy slippers. Abu 'l-Hasan tucks them into his sleeves, not realizing they are merely to be worn to the commode. All the while, Harun watches and laughs.

After using the commode, Abu 'l-Hasan begins to perform his prayers, and now a critical point is reached; while praying he convinces himself that he is after all the caliph:

> He said [to himself], "By God, I am in reality none other than the Prince of the Faithful! This is certainly no dream, for all of these things do not happen in a dream." And so he became convinced in himself that he was the Prince of the Faithful. (*B*, 152)

Then he proceeds to his court where, warming to his role, he addresses Jaʿfar as a "Barmecid dog" and orders him to give one hundred gold dinars to his mother, and then to have the four sheikhs and the imam whipped and paraded through the city in disgrace. After dealing with other matters of state, Abu 'l-Hasan repairs to the caliph's private apartments where he whiles away the afternoon eating and drinking and flirting with the slave girls. All the while Harun secretly looks on, taking immense pleasure in his ruse, until, when night falls, he has a slave girl drop another lump of henbane in Abu 'l-Hasan's wine. Again he passes out on the spot, and Harun has Masrur convey Abu 'l-Hasan back to his house.

Abu ʾl-Hasan wakes the next morning and calls for the slave girls, but it is his mother who comes. When he insists that he is the caliph, she tells him he has been dreaming. Doubts seize him, yet he is unable to dismiss his experience as simply having been a dream. Hoping to cheer him, his mother inadvertently worsens things; she mentions that Jaʿfar the Barmecid had the imam and the sheikhs beaten and paraded in disgrace the day before. Hearing this, Abu ʾl-Hasan insists that he is the Prince of the Faithful and, convinced now that his mother is deceiving him, he beats her with a stick until the neighbors hear her cries. They pull him off her and haul him away to a hospital. There he is stripped of his clothes and beaten every day until, after ten days, he gives up his story.

Released to his mother, Abu ʾl-Hasan returns home and soon he takes up his old habit of waiting for a stranger by the bridge over the Tigris. Once again he meets Harun, who will not be turned away. Against his better judgment, Abu ʾl-Hasan takes him home again, and once again Harun drugs Abu ʾl-Hasan and has him carried to the caliph's palace. Again Abu ʾl-Hasan wakes to find himself in the palace of the caliph, and again a eunuch assures him that he is the Prince of the Faithful. This time, however, Abu ʾl-Hasan is more wary. He still carries the scars left by the beating in the hospital. Here as elsewhere in the *Nights*, the wound is the sign of an encounter with the Lacanian real. And as with the Lacanian real, the encounter in the *Nights* is enigmatic for the character. The stories of the three Qalandars, as we shall see, exemplify this also; the real *qua* enigma is precisely the reason why Abuʾl-Hasan never "learns" from his bumps and bruises.

To convince himself he is awake, he first has a young girl bite him on his finger, then he has a little Turkish slave boy bite him on his ear. "Enough!" Abu ʾl-Hasan cries, but the young boy does not understand Arabic and persists in biting him. Again Harun, who watches secretly, can hardly contain his mirth. Thinking now that it is all an elaborate deception played upon him by malicious jinn, Abu ʾl-Hasan casts off all restraint, along with his clothes—the sense of *khalîʿ* or "dissolute" is seen here also—and dances naked among the slaves.

And now finally Harun, still beside himself with laughter, reveals himself to Abu ʾl-Hasan as the perpetrator of the deception. To reward Abu ʾl-Hasan, he gives him a wife, one Nuzhat al-Fuʾâd ("Heart's Delight"), who is Zubaydah's treasuress. He also gives him a pension and lodgings, and invites him to be one of his boon companions. So ends the first part of the story. A second part follows in which Abu ʾl-Hasan turns the tables on Harun.

Abu 'l-Hasan and Nuzhat al-Fu'ad exhaust their money, and he conceives a trick to win two hundred dinars and some silk. They fake their deaths, Abu 'l-Hasan first. Nuzhat al-Fu'ad, feigning grief, tells Lady Zubaydah that her husband has died, and Zubaydah gives her one hundred dinars and some silk for a burial shroud. Then Nuzhat al-Fu'ad feigns death and Abu 'l-Hasan, tearing his beard out and rending his shirt, tells Harun that his wife has died. Harun gives him one hundred dinars and some silk for a burial shroud. Abu 'l-Hasan returns with the money and the gift to his wife and the two celebrate their success.

Meanwhile Harun goes to his wife to console her over the loss of her handmaid. However, he finds her ready to console him over the loss of his dear companion Abu 'l-Hasan. Initial confusion is followed by a dispute about who has really died. Harun and his wife make a wager and send servants to find out the facts, and the servants return with conflicting stories. Finally Harun proposes that they all go to Abu 'l-Hasan's house to settle the question once and for all. When Abu 'l-Hasan sees them approach, both he and Nuzhat play dead. Harun and Zubaydah, finding both seemingly dead, begin to argue again as to which one must have died first, and more wagers are made, until Harun says, "I will give a thousand dinars to the person who can tell which of them died first!" At this, Abu 'l-Hasan springs up and says, "Oh Prince of the Faithful, I claim the money, for I will tell you that I am the one who died first!"

When Abu 'l-Hasan explains why he devised the trick, Harun and Zubaydah are too amused to be angry. Harun gives him the thousand dinars, and all live happily until "there came to them the Destroyer of Delights and Severer of Societies, the Plunderer of Palaces, and the Garnerer of Graves."[9]

Certain features in "The Sleeper Awakened" provide evidence of conscious patterning after other stories in *The Thousand and One Nights*. Most prominent in this respect is the resemblance between Abu 'l-Hasan's behavior and that of Shahriyar.[10] Even as Shahriyar only keeps each wife for one night, so Abu 'l-Hasan restricts his relations to one night. Where Shahriyar then kills his wife in the morning, Abu 'l-Hasan rudely turns his guest out, henceforth never again to acknowledge that person—in a sense it is also as though the person has ceased to exist for him.

There are similarities as well with "Khalifah the Fisherman."[11] As noted above, both Khalifah and Abu 'l-Hasan are eccentrics, living on the margin of society. Each is the unwitting subject of various manipulations by Harun; each is given a wife by Harun, and each tale features a ruse involving the presumed death of someone dear to Harun. But more important for this discussion is the difference that the figure of the double exists on different planes in each story. In "Khalifah the Fisherman" the double has an uncanny quality, arising from the mere coincidence of the name and the chance involvement of Harun and Khalifah. Moreover, Khalifah and Harun are unwitting doubles; that is, neither sees the other as a double in any sense. In contrast, in "The Sleeper Awakened" Abu 'l-Hasan exists as Harun's double as the result of Harun al-Rashid's own manipulations of him—manipulations, as we said, that are far more extensive than those in "Khalifah the Fisherman." Furthermore, in "The Sleeper Awakened" each character is aware of the resemblance between them. Indeed, for Abu 'l-Hasan that awareness creates the uncertainty about his real identity that lands him in the madhouse.

Numerous analogues of "The Sleeper Awakened" exist, at least one of them in another medieval Islamic version. In the twelfth-century mystical allegory *The Conference of the Birds* by the Persian poet Farîd al-Dîn ʿAṭṭâr (d. 1190?), a story is told of a princess who falls in love with a beautiful slave, and has him drugged and brought to her bed. When he wakes up, they make love. Then, while he sleeps again, he is transported back to his slave quarters, only to awaken and question whether what happened was illusion or reality. The poem was probably completed in the last quarter of the twelfth century, but again it would be difficult to say who is borrowing from whom; perhaps the most likely possibility is that both borrow from an unknown third source.

In European literature, as Gerhardt notes, themes of illusion and disillusionment are particular favorites of Spanish literature; the affinity of the story with many episodes in *Don Quixote* is obvious, and the close relation of the story to Calderón's play *Life is a Dream* (*La vida es sueño*) has also been remarked.[12] We will look at the theme of the double in Calderón's play later. First I would like to consider "The Sleeper Awakened" against a different sort of text altogether, Descartes's *Meditations on First Philosophy*. In that work, too, the themes of illusion and disillusionment are important; indeed, the *Meditations* begins on a note of disillusionment:

> It is now some years since I detected how many were the false beliefs that I had from my earliest youth admitted as true, and how doubtful was everything I had since constructed on this basis; and from that time I was convinced that I must once and for all seriously undertake to rid myself of all the opinions which I had formerly accepted, and com-

mence to build a new foundation, if I wanted to establish any firm and permanent structure in the sciences.[13]

The progress of Descartes's thought in the First Meditation suggests why this text is apposite here. There is first his mention of "certain persons, whose cerebella are so troubled and clouded by violent vapors of black bile, that they constantly assure us that they think they are kings when they are really quite poor . . . or who imagine that they have an earthenware head or are nothing but pumpkins or are made of glass."[14] Though he quickly distances himself: "But they are quite mad, and I should be not any the less insane were I to follow examples so extravagant." Immediately after this Descartes takes up the instance of dreams: "In dwelling carefully on this reflection I see so manifestly that there are no certain indications by which we may clearly distinguish wakefulness from sleep that I am lost in astonishment."[15]

In the first and second meditations of that work, Descartes introduces the hypothesis of the evil genius. First Descartes rejects the possibility that he is mad; then he accepts the possibility that he is dreaming. The third stage of Descartes's doubt is his hypothesis of the "evil genius," his means of introducing even more widespread doubts than those offered by the hypothesis of the dream—what the commentators often call "hyperbolic doubt." In the end, Descartes will argue that the notion of a deceiving god is self-defeating as a hypothesis. For "any meditator who supposes that there might be a malignant deceiver has a criterion by which he identifies dubitable ideas."[16]

If we consider Abu 'l-Hasan's story against the progression of doubt in Descartes's text, we find that much of what happens to Abu 'l-Hasan may be described by words found in the *Meditations*. His predicament begins when a being, who, while not omnipotent, is nevertheless "extremely powerful," "employs all his energies in deceiving" him.[17] His first reaction, when he wakes up in the caliph's bedroom, is to doubt the reality of what is happening to him. Two possibilities offer themselves: either he has died and gone to heaven, or he is still asleep and merely dreaming that he is the caliph—and naturally enough, we might say, since he finds himself in a bed. So he closes his eyes, and like the narrator of the *Meditations* he can say at this moment that he "is almost capable of persuading himself that he now dreams."[18] The emphasis in this stage then is for Abu 'l-Hasan to pose the possibilities of waking or dreaming to explain his predicament: " 'By God I am in reality none other than the Prince of the Faithful! This is certainly no dream, for all of these things do not happen in a dream.' And so he became convinced in himself that he was the Prince of the Faithful" (*B,* 152). Yet if he sometimes thinks that he is the caliph, he still has not entirely forgotten his identity as Abu 'l-Hasan, for if he had, he would not have ordered the sheikhs and the imam to be whipped, nor would he have ordered Jaʿfar to give his mother one hundred dinars. Insofar as these acts show that Abu 'l-Hasan retains part of his identity as Abu 'l-Hasan even as he assumes a new identity as Harun al-Rashid, they are perhaps the correlate of that "criterion" that Descartes argues his subject must retain in order to even identify "dubitable ideas." Even so, Abu 'l-Hasan is still confused, and there is some irony it seems in his use of the title assumed by the Abbasids, "the Prince of the Believers" (*amîr al-mu'minîn*), if we consider his confusion as to what he really *believes*.

His confusion reaches a new level when Harun drugs him again and has him transported back to his house. When his mother tries to cheer him with the news of the money Jaʿfar gave her and how his enemies have been punished, she not only strengthens him in his delusion but propels his doubts to a new level. Henceforth, he no longer tries to understand his predicament in terms of waking or dreaming but rather in terms of madness or sanity. Thus, two of the stages of doubt in Descartes's *Meditations* are found in Abu 'l-Hasan's story as well: the possibility that he is dreaming and the possibility that he is mad.

But Abu 'l-Hasan is drugged yet a third time and carried back to the palace. What of this episode? His reaction at this point is simply to give up trying to understand. That is what I take to be the meaning of his doffing his clothes and dancing naked. This act, I would contend, constitutes a kind of *epoche*, a term taken from Stoic philosophy that means a suspension of judgment. And here too we see a parallel in Descartes's work. For that term is used in reference to Descartes's meditator whose response to the manipulations of the evil genius at the end of the First Meditation runs thus: "If by this means it is not within my power to arrive at the knowledge of any truth, I may at least do what is within my power, and with firm purpose avoid giving credence to any false thing, or being imposed upon by this arch-deceiver, however powerful and deceptive he may be."[19] I would argue that Abu 'l-Hasan's response when he casts off his clothes and dances naked among Harun's courtesans can be understood as a form of *epoche*. For by doing so he tells us that, like Descartes, although he cannot explain what is happening, he is no longer being taken in. What is more, as a gesture of defiance it is aimed at *someone*, and so we may say that at this point Abu 'l-Hasan has in effect posited his own "arch-deceiver." For both Descartes's meditator and Abu 'l-Hasan, the only response to their predicament that is not complete submission to the mastery of the arch-deceiver is *epoche*. To put it in somewhat different terms, this *epoche* is objectified in Abu 'l-Hasan's nakedness, and we may see a curious correspondence between his nakedness and the bareness of the Cartesian *cogito*, who by means of doubts produced by the evil deceiver is similarly stripped bare of physical attributes.

This point for Abu 'l-Hasan might well be an impasse, were it not for the fact that the arch-deceiver Harun is not truly an evil deceiver—though to be sure a sadistic streak is evident in his voyeurism. For now Harun steps out from behind the veil and reveals his ruse to Abu 'l-Hasan. Similarly, in the Cartesian "narrative" the *cogito* is faced with an aporia unless Descartes can prove that God cannot be a deceiver.[20]

Michael Williams argues that Descartes develops a "stratification of doubt," and so too we can detect a stratification in doubt as Abu 'l-Hasan progresses (or regresses?) through his doubts.[21] Yet for all the correspondences between the predicaments of Abu 'l-Hasan and Descartes's meditator, we should not overlook one element found in "The Sleeper Awakened" that is not found in the "narrative" of the *Meditations*. It is a critical element in the story in that it gives Harun the idea for his elaborate deception; by this I mean the *shahwah* or "desire" that Abu 'l-Hasan reveals to him, his fantasy of revenge against the sheikhs and the imam in his local mosque. The double in this plot makes its appearance first as an instance of *imaginary* rivalry in the Lacanian sense, the slave's fantasy of revenge against the master. It is Abu 'l-Hasan's revelation of this desire that gives Harun the idea for his deception, and thus that allows him to be manipulated and exploited by Harun.

Abu 'l-Hasan does not at first reveal much about the source of his hatred for these men. But when he gives Jaʿfar the order to punish them, he says that it is the punishment of one who "talks too much and disturbs his neighbors and ruins his pleasure and his eating and drinking" (*B*, 154). In other words, it is the rivalry of competing desires that yields Kojève's "fight for pure prestige," the master-slave competition, and Lacan's description of it, cited before, holds for Abu 'l-Hasan's desire: his desire is projected and alienated in the other on the imaginary plane, and as a result the subject seeks the destruction of the other. The double in "The Sleeper Awakened" shows us that the ego as a form of alienation "always finds its reflection confronting it, which dispossesses it of all it wishes to attain" (*S*, 2:266).

The association of the "Sleeper Awakened" plot with a revenge fantasy, it should be said, is not peculiar to the story in *The Thousand and One Nights*; it is also seen in Calderón's play *Life is a Dream.* When a son, Segismundo, is born to Basilio, the king of Poland, dire astrological calculations predict that his son will turn out to be a tyrant. To forestall this event, Basilio has him imprisoned in a tower.[22] There he is raised and educated by a single keeper, who tells the boy nothing of his identity. When Segismundo comes of age, Basilio thinks to allow him an opportunity to rule for one day, to see if, perchance, his education may have overcome the fateful influence of the stars. To do so, however, he devises a plan to soften the blow for Segismundo should he fail this test. He has Segismundo drugged and placed on the throne in precisely the same way as Abu 'l-Hasan, and even as the latter's first thoughts are of revenge, so too Segismundo's first thought is to revenge himself on whoever imprisoned him for his whole life.[23] Basilio watches in dismay as his son "flunks" the test, and he has him drugged again and locked up in the tower again where his keeper Clotaldo tells him it was only a dream.

If the fantasy of revenge is integral to the plot of "The Sleeper Awakened" in more than one instance, only a moment's reflection is required to understand why this should be so. The essential element of the plot is the transformation of the slave into the master, and it should be no surprise if the first thought of a slave become master is to revenge himself on the master become slave.

The story of Amphitryon, best known in the comedies of Plautus and Molière, parallels this. Amphitryon is a victorious general returning home from war and expecting to be welcomed by his wife Alcmene. He sends his slave Sosia ahead to inform her of his imminent arrival. However, at this point Zeus, infatuated by Alcmene, has assumed the shape of her husband and is in his house making love to her, with Mercury in the form of Sosia posted outside as lookout. Sosia, on reaching the house, is thus confronted with his double. Sosia and Amphitryon find their very identities called into question by their doubles Mercury and Zeus, and all is confusion until play's end. Then Alcmene bears twins, one son by Amphitryon and the other, Hercules, by Zeus, who then reveals his ruse to Amphitryon and exonerates Alcmene of the charge of adultery.

The deceiving gods of the Amphitryon story find their equivalents in Descartes's hypothesis of a deceiving God and in the human master in the sleeper awakened plot, whether in Calderón or *The Thousand and One Nights*. Similar, too, is the reaction of the slave/dupe who is shaken, if not wholly dispossessed of his identity—a crisis that in each case involves the same elements: the question "If I am not me, who am I?", and then a progression of doubts. The perplexities are first posed in the question of whether he is awake or dreaming, then mad or sane, and finally alive or dead. The dupe's confusion always manifests itself under the gaze of the real master, the arch-deceiver, who, whether divine or human, stands back and observes. He may watch the confusion of the slave with horror as Basilio does in *Life is a Dream* or with amusement as do Mercury in "Amphitryon" and Harun in "The Sleeper Awakened," yet the master deceiver is at the same time himself always unseen, even if he is not invisible, in that he is never recognized for who he truly is. Thus the themes of illusion and disillusion closely bound to the theme of the double almost necessarily involve mastery and servitude.

With respect to the gaze of the master, the moment in "The Sleeper Awakened" when Harun observes Abu 'l-Hasan throw off his clothes and caper about naked among the slave girls stands in contrast with the moment when Shahriyar observes the orgy in the garden involving his wife and her slaves. Shahriyar is "unmastered" by what he sees, whereas Harun's position as master remains secure. Indeed, he "cuckolds" Abu 'l-Hasan insofar as he takes something that belongs to him—his ego, that is. Moreover, Abu 'l-Hasan does not partake of sex with any of the caliph's concubines. He casts off restraint—but not entirely so. And luckily for him, because when the master steps out from behind the curtain and reveals how he has cuckolded you, you are expected to take it in good humor—which is quite different from the reaction of Shahriyar and Shahzaman. Whether the arch-deceiver is a deity or a human master, in the ruse he plays the stake is always placed on the level of being, since it is the very identity of the subject/dupe that is called into question, and only when the arch-deceiver removes his veil is the subject granted his being again. In other words, the revelation of the ruse makes it clear that the subject's identity is, nevertheless, still something granted him by the master.

But "The Sleeper Awakened" does not end with the epiphany of the arch-deceiver; it goes on to tell us of the "undressing" of the master. That second part of the story reveals the master's dependency on the slave and the inherent deception involved in being a master. This dependency is apparent in the way that Harun seeks Masrur's opinion to strengthen his argument against his wife Zubaydah. But the master's dependency is revealed in a more profound fashion by Abu 'l-Hasan's "death." For the death of the slave does not simply deprive the master of a possession; more to the point, it reveals his impotence in the face of the Absolute Master. As Žižek puts it, mastery is "of a strictly *metonymical* nature: a Master never fully 'measures up to its notion,' to Death qua 'Absolute Master.' " For which reason, the master is "by definition, an impostor—i.e. somebody who illegitimately occupies the place of the lack in the Other (the Symbolic Order)."[24] Thus, when Abu 'l-Hasan springs up to claim the stake of the game, Harun's pretensions to mastery are revealed. But this is not to say the story radically subverts the master or the notion of mastery. As Žižek says, "It would be wrong to conclude—from the fact that anyone who occupies the place of the Master is an impostor and clown—that the perceived imperfections of the Master subvert his authority. The whole artifice of 'playing a Master' consists in knowing how to use this very gap (between the 'notion' of the Master and its empirical bearer) to our advantage: the way for a Master to strengthen his authority is precisely to present himself as 'human like the rest of us,' 'full of little weaknesses' . . ."[25] Note that when Abu 'l-Hasan turns the tables on Harun, despite all the reversals involved, one element remains the same; it is still the being of the slave that is called into question. Harun does not ask, "Am I alive or dead?" but rather "Is he alive or dead?" Thus, the spectacle of Harun as dupe helps to accommodate Abu 'l-Hasan—and us—to the master as impostor, as arch-deceiver, that is.

With these things in mind, we might reconsider the disappointment of "The False Caliph." I think it should be clear now that the problem is not simply that Muhammad ibn ʿAli's masquerade is poorly motivated by the story of his love for Jaʿfar's sister but rather that, after the garden party, the story itself has nothing to do with the themes of the double. "Khalifah the Fisherman" and "The Sleeper Awakened" suggest various themes that "The False Caliph" might have explored, but all would require the involvement of Harun with Muhammad ibn ʿAli. The story begins with Harun's disorienting confrontation with his double, but then this is simply laid aside and never picked up again. For the story to succeed, it ought to have maintained the focus on Harun and his reaction to his uncanny double.

For that is how "Khalifah" and "The Sleeper" succeed. Each explores the double in terms of a game between master and slave, which reflects the fact that "From the beginning, between the master and the slave, there's the rule of the game" (S, 1:223)—a game we play while we wait for the arrival of the Absolute Master.

6
The Circuit of Desire

THE GEOGRAPHY IS WHIMSICAL—AS BEFITS A STORY THAT IN THE END goes nowhere. The story begins in "China," but soon enough we find ourselves in Basra, the port on the Persian Gulf. Baghdad, Cairo, Damascus, and Mosul are later points on the itinerary. As is often the case in the *Nights*, time is also scrambled in a way that yields amusing anachronisms. One man's story takes place in the palace of Harun al-Rashid who reigned from 786–809 A.D., while a contemporary tells his stories to a caliph who reigned from 1226–1242 A.D. But particulars of space and time are trivial matters that the storyteller ignores while pursuing larger themes: the vicissitudes of desire in the social circuits of power; the relation of language and death. The story of "The Hunchback" is often cited by theorists of narrative like Todorov and Genette for its formal brilliance; no other story group in the *Nights* joins so many different narratives in a complex artistic whole. But it is not merely a formal tour de force. The formal and the thematic combine in "The Hunchback" to chart, in greater detail than any other story in the *Nights*, the paths of desire within the social circuits of power.

Our story begins when a tailor and his wife, returning home after a day given to diversions, come upon a hunchback brimming with drink. They invite him home, and the tailor purchases a fish, lemons, honey, and bread for a banquet. When the mood grows gay and lively, the tailor's wife stuffs a piece of fish in the hunchback's mouth. The piece of fish, however, conceals a bone, and the hunchback chokes on it and—apparently—dies. I hedge on this point, though the Arabic text does not: "he died at that very moment" (*mâta li-sâʿatihi*). The tailor panics, but his wife hatches a plan.

They wrap the body in a shawl and set out, the tailor carrying the body while the wife cries out for a doctor to treat her "sick child." They are directed to the house of a Jewish physician. A black slave girl answers the door, and they give her a piece of silver for her master. While she goes to fetch the physician, the tailor props the body at the bottom of the staircase. Then he and his wife flee.

The Jewish physician, seeing the piece of silver, hurries to his patient. But in his haste, he stumbles and falls down the stairs, knocking over the body of the hunchback. Seeing the inert body, he concludes that he has killed him. Now he too panics, and he too turns to his wife for calm thinking. This woman too has no difficulty in conceiving some ploy. Here also the popular prejudice, evident in *The Thousand and One Nights* and elsewhere in medieval Arabic literature, prevails; woman is a schemer. The physician's wife proposes that they take the body up on their terrace and lower it into the house of their neighbor, and this they do.

The neighbor is a steward in the royal kitchen who, we are told, seldom leaves the kitchen without filling his pockets. Now he returns home and, seeing the shadowy form leaning against the wall outside his kitchen, takes it to be a thief. He strikes him with a mallet on the head and, when he falls to the ground, again on his chest for good measure. Then, discovering that the man is apparently dead, he too is seized with fear. The steward however consults no woman (because he is a Muslim?). He hoists the body of the hunchback on his shoulder and deposits the body near the market—where, of course, the tailor purchased the fatal fish. We sense a circuit is being closed.

A Christian, a broker to the king, passes through the lane tipsy with wine and muttering to himself, "Doomsday has come! The Last Judgment has come!" And, in his case, it *is* almost at hand. We are told that he is wearing a new turban, his old one having been stolen earlier that day. Thus, when he stops to empty his bladder and notices the shadowy form of the hunchback, he takes him for another thief intent on stealing his new turban. He snatches him by the throat and knocks him down with a powerful blow.

It is now dawn. The license that darkness gives to desire in *The Thousand and One Nights* is being withdrawn as the law reasserts itself with the light of day. While the broker pummels the body of the hunchback, a watchman comes upon him, and arrests him for killing a Muslim. The hapless broker is dragged off to the governor's house. The governor orders that the broker be hanged in the morning, and the execution is announced throughout the city.

When the rope is placed around the broker's neck, the Muslim steward, overcome by guilt, comes forward to claim responsibility. The governor orders the steward to be executed, and now the Jewish doctor, feeling the pangs of conscience, steps forward to claim responsibility. When the rope is placed around the physician's neck, the tailor steps forth and confesses.

In the reactions of each character to the corpse one senses a taboo looming; shock is followed by panic and guilt. As Bataille wrote, "In the presence of a corpse horror is immediate and inevitable and practically impossible to resist."[1] Bataille mentions the primitive notion that death is never simply "natural," but rather is always the result of an evil done by some being, whether human or supernatural. In this view, he writes, "someone is always responsible, someone is always a murderer." And the physician's reaction could be seen as bearing this out. He is no more detached in the presence of the corpse than is the tailor. An attitude of detachment requires mental preparation, which in turn requires some foreknowledge that one is to be in the presence of death. But the physician is caught unawares.

Yet it would be misleading to say that the breaking of a taboo is the cause of their guilt. For their guilt is not in having broken a taboo with respect to the corpse, but rather it is the taboo-like power of the corpse that compels each man to recognize his guilt with regard to something else, with respect to his desire. For although no one is truly guilty of the hunchback's death, nevertheless the body of the hunchback in some way reveals to each man his guilt regarding his other desire. Each man gropes his way in the dark trying to satisfy some desire—greed, larceny, and drunkenness are the names the moralist would give them—until whoa! he bumps into death.

In other words, there is no need for recourse to a "primitive notion" of taboo here (with its problematic distinction between our thoughts and "primitive" thoughts). The corpse of the hunchback in these effects is better conceived as the "traumatic thing" in the Lacanian sense. This sort of object is, Žižek says, the "point of the Real in the very heart of the subject which cannot be symbolized, which is produced as a residue, a remnant, a leftover of every signifying operation, a hard core embodying horrifying *jouissance*, enjoyment, and as such, an object which simultaneously attracts and repels us."[2] It is on this account that the corpse reveals to each man his desire and his guilt.

As the tailor awaits his death, we learn more of the hunchback's identity; the king's chamberlain arrives on the scene and tells us that the hunchback is the king's favorite jester. Having heard of his death, the king orders the governor to come to the palace and to bring all the parties to the affair with him, including the body of the hunchback. Thus the tailor wins a temporary reprieve.

At the palace each man repeats for the king his story of how he came into contact with the hunchback, and, amazed by this chain of events, the king has them recorded. Then he wonders aloud if anyone has ever heard a more amazing tale—as we have seen, one of three stock means in the *Nights* of introducing a new narrative.

Each of the four men responds to the king's question by telling another story unrelated to the events of the hunchback; each is a story about a young man in love. The last of these four stories, "The Story of the Tailor," tells of a banquet the tailor attended earlier the previous day where he met a lame young man and a barber. The tailor's story encompasses the stories of "The Lame Young Man and the Barber" and "The Barber," which in turn contains the stories of his six brothers. There is a sort of pyramid of stories then having three tiers: the first of these being the story of the hunchback himself; the second tier containing the four stories told by the broker, steward, physician, and tailor; and the third containing the stories told by the lame young man and barber. As we will see within each of these groups of tales, there are great similarities among the stories, and there are thematic similarities between the various levels also. In dealing with so many narratives and narrators, it will be useful here to consult the "directory" or "tree" showing their relations.

---

1. The Story of Shahriyar and Shahrazad, wherein Shahrazad tells:
    2. The Story of the Hunchback: wherein
        3. The Christian Broker tells: The Story of the Christian Broker
        4. The Muslim Steward tells: The Story of the Muslim Steward
        5. The Jewish Physician tells: The Story of the Jewish Physician
        6. The Tailor tells: The Story of the Tailor, wherein The Tailor also tells:
            7. The Story of the Lame Young Man and The Barber
            8. The Story of the Barber, wherein the Barber also tells:
                9. The Story of the Barber's First Brother
                10. The Story of the Barber's Second Brother
                11. The Story of the Barber's Third Brother
                12. The Story of the Barber's Fourth Brother
                13. The Story of the Barber's Fifth Brother
                14. The Story of the Barber's Sixth Brother

In all, Shahrazad tells thirteen stories. By the time we have gotten as far as the stories of the barber's brothers, we receive these stories at the end of a chain of narrators that consists of the barber narrating to the tailor who narrates to the king, who, as we have noted, has ordered the stories recorded, which record Shahrazad has presumably read ("She had read books, chronicles and biographies of kings and accounts of bygone nations, and it was said she had collected a thousand books . . ."), and which she finally narrates to Shahriyar—and to us.[3] With so many narrators and narratives, the question of the effect of each narrator on the story may arise in the minds of some readers. But in fact no narrator here acts as "subjective filter"; modern notions of the distortion and resistance inherent in language are not found. No doubt in this instance *The Thousand and One Nights* reflects what may seem to some of us a naive view of language; language, that is, as a perfectly transparent medium coextensive with a world itself composed of signs (*âyât*). Such a conception of language, though not particular to medieval Islamic culture, was nevertheless characteristic of it. Nevertheless, the story still raises the question of language, but it does so on another plane, through the displacements of the corpse.

The first thing to be said about those displacements is that, like Shahrazad's narration each night, they are intended to ward off death. Thus, the shuttling of the hunchback's body through the night runs parallel to the movement of Shahrazad's desire in narrative; the displacements continue in each case all night long, but cease in the morning when the rule of the king asserts itself. Even as Shahrazad through her narration seeks to control the displacements of Shahriyar's desire, the movement of the hunchback traces the path of the king of China's desire. All of which points to the fact that the corpse is not only an image; it is also a signifier. The meaning of that signifier may seem obvious, but, I think, it is nevertheless worth considering for a moment. "A dead body," Bataille writes,

> . . . cannot be called nothing at all, but that object, that corpse, is stamped straight off with the sign "nothing at all." For us survivors, the corpse . . . is no answer to any expectation like the one we nourished while that now prostrate man was still alive; it is the answer to a fear. This object, then, is less than nothing and worse than nothing.[4]

"Less than nothing and worse than nothing"—here Bataille (dispensing with the notion of taboo) comes to grips with the truly traumatic nature of the corpse, the absolute otherness of death. The very corporeality of a dead body makes us feel that otherness as an uncanny absence of an ineffable something—life. But in the real, as Lacan emphasizes time and again, everything is always in its place and nothing is missing. Lack and absence can only be construed in terms of a symbolic system that attempts to impose an order on the real. And indeed, the muteness of the signifier in question here, its evocation of the real of death in language, lays bare the function of the signifier. In his "Seminar on 'The Purloined Letter,' " Lacan poses the question of "what remains of a signifier when it has no more signification."[5] He answers with reference to the scheming minister in that story, a man who is, we are told, a "gambler." The gambler's passion, Lacan says,

> is nothing but that question asked of the signifier, figured by the automaton of chance.
>
> "What are you, figure of the die I turn over in your encounter [*tuche*] with my fortune. Nothing, if not that presence of death which makes of human life a reprieve obtained from morning to morning in the name of meanings whose sign is your crook. Thus did Scheherazade for a thousand and one nights. . . ."

As the displacements of the letter in Poe's "Purloined Letter" determine the subject, so here the displacements of the body, this sign of "nothing at all," determine the fates of our four principals: the tailor, the doctor, the steward, and the broker. For the king is of a mind to have all who touched the hunchback put to death. In this we may remark in passing a piece of wit characteristic of *The Thousand and One Nights*; that this ugly little misshapen fellow should be the object of the king's desire. From the point of view of the slave, it seems the master might have anything he wants, but in "The Hunchback" he wants his deformed little man, and those who interpose themselves between the master and his possession are sentenced to die. Needless to say, the king does not act in accord with Islamic law in sentencing all four men to death for their involvement with the hunchback. Despite the general imprint of medieval Islamic culture on *The Thousand and One Nights*, one can overestimate its effects. Some narrative strata simply lie below the stratum where its impress is visible. In this instance, in ordering the deaths of all four men, there is no question of the king following Islamic law—though the operation of that law code will be seen elsewhere within the hunchback cycle. Rather, it is again the master-slave dialectic that operates here. The king is a master, and the other four men find themselves to be, willy-nilly, his rivals. And insofar as the relation of master and slave is defined by the differing relations of the two rivals to death, the body of the hunchback as signifier means two different things to the king and his subjects. To the master, the hunchback signifies his pleasure, but to the slave, who lives at the pleasure of the king, it signifies his own death.

In the context of this relation, the displacements of the hunchback's body trace a circuit of power. The story opens with the hunchback already displaced, detached from the king—though we only understand this retrospectively since we do not know the relation of the hunchback to the king until his body has come to rest. Nevertheless, as the guarantor and embodiment of the law, the king's presence is felt in each instance, insofar as each of the four men fears the punishment of the law. The displacements of the hunchback reveal the effects of power to be inescapable. As the hunchback's corpse is relayed from one man to the next, the new man's situation replicates that of the previous one—again, much as the displacements of the purloined letter determine the characters in Poe's story. As I suggested before, it seems from the distribution of sectarian and professional labels among the characters that we are to understand its itinerary as somehow having traversed an entire society. As a sign of "nothing at all," the corpse operates without any regard to such roles.

Yet if the corpse is a sign, it is also, as Bataille says, an image. This dual aspect is seen in two ways in the story. First, for each of the four hapless men the body of the hunchback provides the "image of his destiny"—that is, the image of his biological death. At the same time, as a sign the corpse registers biological death in a particular place in a symbolic system; here it makes it an instance of punishment at the hands of the law. It offers, we may say, an interpretation of biological death. The dual aspect of image and sign is also seen in the way in which the initial path of the corpse is retraced in the telling as each man tries to explain himself before the law. In the initial trajectory, the emphasis falls on the corpse as image, as an imaginary other. As image of death, the corpse confronts each man as the uncanny other in the imaginary order. Yet again, there is an instance of *meconnaisance* of the image, and it is this *meconnaisance* that causes the panic and that, therefore, propels the narrative. In the retelling, on the other hand, the emphasis falls on the corpse as a sign. The path of the corpse is shown to be also the path of the signifier, as each man tries to account for himself before the king, and it is the meaning of that sign which orders their relations as instances of the master–slave relation.

A hint of all that is to come is found when the steward is introduced. Then we learn of a sequence of thefts that likewise take place within a symbolic order, a hierarchy of power relations:

> Their neighbor was a steward who managed the king's kitchen, and often he used to bring butter home which the cats and the mice ate. And when the night carried some pleasant smell, the dogs used to descend on his kitchen from the rooftops and cause him mischief, often

> consuming everything that he had taken from the king's kitchen. (1:201)

On the other hand, the corpse as imaginary other is seen in the steward's reaction when he sees the body of the hunchback propped against the wall of his kitchen:

> Carrying a candle the steward entered his house, and there he found one of Adam's sons, a stranger that is, standing in the corner beneath the ventilation shaft. The steward thought, "By God, this is a fine thing! The one who steals our things is a man!" and he said to the hunchback, "So, you're the one who steals my meat and butter! I thought it was the cats and dogs, and I've killed almost all of them unjustly when it's you who comes down from the roof!" He grabbed a big mallet and hit him with it, and he beat him with it until he found he was dead. (1:201)

The steward looks at the other but sees only his own reflection; that is, he sees another thief. In fact, it is the cats and dogs who steal from him even as he steals from the king, and whom he has punished even as the king would punish him if he were caught, which furnishes a nice example of *meconnaisance* typical of the imaginary relations of the Lacanian ego. The hunchback, precisely because he is mute, functions as a kind of mirror for the steward—and for the other men as well; his muteness assures that the imaginary relation will not be altered, which is to say corrected, by speech.

Another element in this scene provides a segue to the next stratum of stories; here I mean the stolen food. In "The Hunchback" everything is set in motion by a mishap at a meal, and in the stories that will be told by the broker, the physician, the steward, and the tailor, a discovery made at a meal is crucial. Those stories begin when the broker steps forward to reply to the king's question, "Has anyone ever heard a more amazing story?"

Unlucky in Love

The broker, who is a Coptic Christian from Egypt, meets an elegant young man in the marketplace in Cairo. (The marketplace was also where we first found the hunchback, of course.) After mutually profitable dealings, they share a meal at which the broker is shocked to see the young man eat with his left hand, a serious breach of etiquette in Muslim culture where that hand is reserved for certain acts of hygiene. When the broker asks why he does so, the young man thrusts his right arm out of his sleeve to reveal a stump at his wrist. Then he tells the tale of how he lost his hand.

The young man, a merchant from Baghdad, comes to Cairo on business and in the market meets a beautiful young woman. They fall in love at once, and the young man lavishes his money on her until one day he finds himself penniless. Poverty means not only ignominy in itself but also, he fears, the end of his love affair, since he will no longer be able to support the lady in the manner to which she is accustomed. Walking through the market in despair, he brushes against a soldier and feels a fat purse in his pocket. In a rash moment, he takes the soldier's purse. But the soldier catches him and takes him before the governor. When the purse is found on the young man, the Islamic sentence is imposed; the executioner lops off his right hand. However, when the soldier hears the young man's motive, he feels pity for him; he persuades the governor to spare his life and gives the young man the purse and the twenty gold coins it held. The young man purchases food and drink for another feast with his lover. When he lifts his cup of wine with his left hand, she asks why he cannot use his right. He tells her he has a boil on it. At length he falls asleep and she takes the opportunity to look at his right hand. Seeing it has been cut off, she guesses the meaning of its loss. When he wakes up, she learns that he has spent all his wealth on her. Taken by his sacrifice, she has a marriage contract drawn up on the spot. They get married and all her wealth is now his also. But soon his wife falls ill and within a month's time dies.

Life goes on, however. The young man, minus his hand and his wife but with his fortune replenished, settles his affairs in Cairo where he meets the Christian broker. The broker then accompanies him to China where he came upon the hunchback on his way home.

The broker's story does not satisfy the king, however, and he still insists that all four men be hanged. Now the steward steps forth to tell his tale.

The steward's tale begins at a dinner party where he meets a handsome young man. When a dish called a *zirbajah* is served, the young man recoils. Urged to eat some of the dish, he replies that such an act would require him to wash his hands forty times with soap, forty times with potash, and forty times with a preparation of a root called galingale. Forty, we should note, is a number associated with purification in Islamic culture: the dead are mourned for forty days, and the *ʿiddah* (or period of time that must pass before a woman may remarry) is forty days. Three times forty we may take as suggesting neurotic insistence on perfection. After he performs these acts and begins to eat some of the *zirbajah*, the guests notice that he is missing his thumbs. When they remark this, he reveals that he is also missing his big toes. Then he tells the astonished party the story of his love affair with a slave girl who belonged to Harun al-Rashid's wife Zubaydah.

His story also begins when they fall in love in the marketplace. Then she arranges to have him smuggled into the palace, where she is secretly married to him. But on his wedding night he forgets to wash his hands thoroughly after eating some *zirbajah*. When he embraces his refined wife, she cries out in disgust and has him whipped by palace guards. She thinks then to have the offending hand cut off, but she relents, and settles on merely having his thumbs and big toes cut off. Then he promises her that he will never eat *zirbajah* again without washing his hands one hundred and twenty times.[6]

However, this story does not satisfy the king either, and he again orders all four men to be hanged. Now the Jewish physician tells his tale.

In a public bath in Damascus, the physician meets a handsome young man who is missing his right hand. The young man tells him how he came to Damascus with his uncles on a business trip, and how he became infatuated there with a beautiful young woman. They spend the night together and the young woman promises to bring another beautiful girl along with her the next evening. But the next evening when the young man caresses the new girl, the first girl kills her in a fit of jealousy and runs off. The young man buries the second girl's corpse and in a panic flees to Cairo, where his uncles have gone.

After three years he runs out of money in Cairo and returns to Damascus. When he tries to sell a necklace that belonged to the dead girl he is accused of theft, and his hand is amputated for the crime. It emerges that the necklace belonged to a daughter of the governor who has been missing for three years, and he is hauled before the governor to explain himself. After he hears the young man's story, the governor explains that the two girls were his daughters. The eldest, who killed the younger, was a profligate who tried to corrupt her younger sister. The governor pardons him and marries him to his third and youngest daughter.

The king, still not satisfied, again orders their hanging, and now the tailor steps forward and tells the story of "The Lame Young Man and the Barber." That story will carry us to the third tier of stories, and before examining them, we might consider elements common to the three stories of the physician, steward, and broker.

In each story a young man reveals a missing limb, and the story that follows tells how the limb was lost. Each is a story of love, and the same imaginary and symbolic phenomena found in other love stories in *The Thousand and One Nights* are found in these stories also. Foremost among the imaginary phenomena is love at first sight. As elsewhere in the *Nights*, each man falls in love at first sight, and there are also the usual symptoms in each case of lovesickness—"can't eat, can't sleep," and so forth. On the other hand, love in its symbolic aspect, as the pact or vow in which the lover stakes his own life, is represented here by the loss of limb. By showing himself willing to sacrifice limb and even life—to reverse the usual order—the lover transcends purely imaginary love, *Verliebtheit*, and signals his willingness to submit his desire to the law of the symbolic order. In each case the loss of limb signals the end of love madness for the young man; with that loss, the symptoms of lovesickness abate, and love as symbolic pact comes into play. The young woman, on some level, can be said to recognize this in each of the three stories. As a woman, she is already caught up in the symbolic network as an object of exchange, and she sees—somehow—the logic of the amputation. That is, she understands that the young man is willing to pay the necessary price to possess her. Indeed, the story of the steward makes the woman's assenting role explicit, for in this story she herself carries out the mutilation.

Thereafter, the stories describe various vicissitudes of love. In all three stories, the young man ends up married, but in the story of the broker, after ceding her wealth to her husband, the young woman herself wastes away from something like lovesickness. When she cedes her wealth to her husband, she falls ill; in her case, the loss of her independent wealth means the loss of her life. Marriage isn't for everybody, one is tempted to say. In marriage one publicly submits to a law; one bears witness to accepting a limit on one's desire. And though there are many limits, in some way they all recall *the* limit, death. Thus, by this act alone one acknowledges one's own death. The story of the broker seems to place special emphasis on this, on submission to the law as a form of death.

At first glance, the story of the tailor seems similar to the other three stories. At a breakfast that same morning, the tailor sees a lame young man who refuses to eat when a barber is introduced. Asked to explain his rude behavior, the young man tells another story of thwarted love. He tells the guests how the barber, through his ceaseless chatter, delays and disrupts the young man's rendezvous with the daughter of the *qâḍî* or judge of Baghdad. The result is a mêlée in which the barber inadvertently breaks the young man's leg while trying to help him escape. In other words, as in the previous three stories, a young man is wounded while in pursuit of love. There are, however, significant differences, and consideration of those and other details will show how the story of "The Lame Young Man and the Barber" furnishes a key to "The Hunchback" as a whole.

The Silent One

The lame young man begins by saying that for a long time "God had made women despicable to me" (1:236). Then one day he finds his way in the street blocked by a crowd of women. In a near-panic, he runs away and finds himself in a dead end—which is as much as saying that he discovers he must go "through" women to attain his desire. Hence, he falls in love with the next woman he sees. He sits down in the alley and, glancing upwards, sees a girl's face in a window, and he falls in love with her at once. Enthralled, he lingers until sunset, when the girl's father returns, and he learns that he is the *qadi* of Baghdad. An old lady in his own household acts as go-between and arranges a rendezvous for Friday while the girl's father is at the mosque for midday prayers. Friday morning the young man summons a barber to groom him for his rendezvous, but with the arrival of the barber things begin to go awry.

The barber begins by producing an astrolabe and consulting the stars. His calculations, he says, "inform me that you seek union with a certain person, but after this something will happen that I will not speak of." When admonished to get on with the task at hand, he defends his character by mentioning his service to the young man's father, a man who loved him for his discretion. Indeed, on account of his gravity and reserve the barber says that he is known as "the Silent One." He goes on to say that he feels it is his duty to look after the young man in place of his dead father. His nickname "the Silent One" must be reconsidered in light of this last remark, for, apart from the obvious comic reversal of a chatterbox being called "the Silent One," there seems a more profound irony here. The barber speaks for the dead father, who, like the hunchback after all, truly is a "silent one." That his nickname "the Silent One" must be understood as an allusion to death is evidenced by the words that the young man utters in despair at the barber's continued prattle: "You will surely slay me today!" (1:239). Since the death of the father, whether symbolic or real, marks the institution of the law, the barber, we may say, speaks for the law. And indeed, if "Khalifah the Fisherman" is a comedy of the ego, the barber's discourse is a comedy of the superego. For, like the discourse of the superego, the barber is that voice which one cannot escape, which one must listen to even if—and especially if—one is bent on disobeying it. Some of Lacan's remarks on this discourse deserve to be quoted in full in this context:

> This discourse of the other is not the discourse of the abstract other, of the other in the dyad, of my correspondent, nor even of my slave, it is the discourse of the circuit in which I am integrated. I am one of its links. It is the discourse of my father for instance, insofar as my father made mistakes which I am absolutely condemned to reproduce—that's what we call the *super-ego*. I am condemned to reproduce them because I am obliged to pick up again the discourse he bequeathed to me, not simply because I am his son, but because one can't stop the chain of discourse, and it is precisely my duty to transmit it in its aberrant form to someone else. I have to put to someone else the problem of a situation of life or death in which the chances are that it is just as likely that he will falter, in such a way that this discourse produces a small circuit in which an entire family, an entire coterie, an entire camp, an entire nation or half the world will be caught. The circular form of a speech which is just at the limit between sense and non-sense, which is problematic. That's what the need for repetition is, as we see it emerge beyond the pleasure principle. (*S*, 2:89–90).

Which might be a gloss on "The Story of the Hunchback." For here and elsewhere in *The Thousand and One Nights* the repetitions result from such a circuit of speech. The barber's speech carries us to that limit of "sense and non-sense," and the young man's attempt to shut off this discourse must fail. His angry outburst simply causes the barber to recall an occasion when he was to bleed the young man's father, and hearing this story, the young man loses patience and curses his father, "May Allah show no mercy to my father who knew the likes of you!" (1:241). But even this extreme measure fails. The barber remembers that he has invited a group of friends to his house but has forgotten to purchase food for the meal. The young man tries another tack, supplication; he offers to purchase all the food for the barber's banquet, if only the barber will finish shaving his head. The barber thanks him by inviting him to join his friends: "Zantût the bath-keeper and Ṣalî‘ the corn-chandler and Sîlat the bean-seller and ‘Ikrishah the green-grocer and Ḥamîd the street-sweeper and Sa‘îd the camel-driver and Suwayd the porter and Abû Makârish the bath attendant and Qasîm the watchman and Karîm the groom. . . ." He then launches into praises of their various virtues. Hamid, the garbage man who sweeps dung from the streets (which is burned to heat the baths), is the subject of some wonderful doggerel:

> Forfeit is my life for the garbage man!
>   A waving bough, he kindled my desire
> Fate joined us one night and I said,
>   as I grew weak and the flame went higher,
> "Thy love burns my heart!" and he replied,
>   "And no wonder that the dungsweeper lights a fire!"
>
> (1:244)

When the young man still refuses the invitation, the barber insists that in that case he must accompany him instead. This causes the desperate young fellow to say that no one may go with him, and at once the barber understands the situation: an unmarried woman is involved. "This is the city of Baghdad and no one can do such a thing—especially on a day like this—when our governor is so ruthless!" (1:245).

The rest of the story unfolds as summarized before. The barber accompanies the young man, and mistaking the cries of a slave being beaten by the *qadi* for the cries of the young man, he unwittingly reveals the presence of the young man to the *qadi*—even though *his* father is dead, there are still too many fathers about. The young man tries to hide in a box from both the barber and the *qadi*, but the barber learns where he is. While trying to get the box out of the house, the barber drops it, and the young man's leg is broken. With an angry mob in pursuit, the young man takes refuge in a shop where, in despair, he makes out his will.

While there are obvious similarities between this story and the stories of the three young men in the stories of the steward, the physician, and the broker, I believe the differences are more significant. The principle difference between the lame young man and the other three young lovers is that he, unlike the other three young men, never enjoys *wisal* or sexual union with his beloved. The entire affair goes wrong from the start, with the barber acting as both the prophet and the agent of bad fortune. Another difference seems significant on this account, the fact that the lame young man does not have a limb *cut off*. In the stories of the physician, steward, and broker, as in the stories of the three qalandars in "The Porter and the Three Ladies of Baghdad," it is the *absence* of a limb that signifies the narrative that is to follow. Their stories, we might say, "stack up" paradigmatically as examples of the same sort of tale—and, we might note, do not please the king. The tailor's story, on the other hand, involves a lame limb that leads to a great deal more narration, for it introduces the barber who tells seven more stories, his own story and the stories of his six brothers. Thus, we might say the broken limb is "syntagmatic" in contrast with the "paradigmatic" missing limbs, and the crook in the young man's leg is correlate with the deflection in the narrative at this point towards the barber—and also perhaps with the curvature in the hunchback's spine. In the stories of the barber's six brothers, amputation and crippling continue as themes, though with a difference. The young men in the stories of the physician, the steward, and the broker succeed however briefly in their love affairs, but the lame young man, with the barber's help, fails miserably. And since each of the barber's brothers will also fail, the lame young man's story provides a fitting transition to them.

When the lame young man finishes his story and departs the breakfast, the barber gives his side of the story. In fact, the barber claims it would have all gone much worse had he not involved himself. The young man would not merely have broken his leg; likely he would have lost his life. Then in further defense of his character, the barber tells the guests how he himself almost lost his life when he mistook a boat full of ten condemned criminals for a party of picnickers. He joins them and ends up before the caliph al-Mustanṣir awaiting a death sentence.[7] To save his head, he tells the caliph the stories of his six brothers, stories that lay emphasis on the wiles of women and involve a number of sadistic tricks played on the barber's hapless brothers.

The barber's first brother fuses the two principal characters of "The Hunchback"; he is a hunchback tailor. In his story, his infatuation with a married woman is exploited mercilessly by the woman and her husband until they finally trap him in a compromising situation. Then they drag him before the governor, who orders him whipped and paraded around the city before being expelled. Later he breaks his leg—like the lame young man. The second brother is also tricked by a beautiful young woman, the daughter of a vizier. He allows his beard and eyebrows to be shaved and his naked body painted red for the purposes of what she describes as an erotic game that will be prelude to lovemaking. Then, in this state, he chases the vizier's daughter through the house. But she leads him over a trap door, which drops him in this state into the marketplace below. He is beaten by an outraged mob and taken to the governor, who has him lashed for his folly, and he ends up a paralytic. The third brother, a blind beggar, is made the fall guy for a group of thieves, and he too is whipped and exiled. The fourth brother, a butcher, loses an eye when a sorcerer tricks a crowd into thinking that he sells human flesh for mutton. Driven from that town, he takes up life as a cobbler in another town, but the king sees him while hunting and has him beaten, for he abhors the sight of men missing their left eye. Indeed, the brother is informed that such men are usually put to death, so he flees to another land where he is taken for a robber. The fifth brother sells glassware in the street. One day while daydreaming of a wealthy life, he imagines himself kicking his mother-in-law, and he inadvertently kicks over his stack of glassware and destroys it all. He is then robbed by two different groups of thieves; the second group, not content with robbery, also cut off his ears. The sixth brother, a beggar, is first the victim of an elaborate joke played on him by a wealthy descendant of the Barmecid family. The latter invites him to a banquet, but no food is served; the dishes are only described in words. After he goodnaturedly goes along with this joke, the old man takes him in. But soon his patron dies, and the sixth brother, in search of another home, is captured by a band of robbers. The wife of the robber chieftain tries to seduce him, but her husband catches them together and cuts off his lips and—his penis.

Where the second tier of stories depicts a prosperous middle-class milieu, here in the third tier, in the company of the barber's brothers, we are on the lowest rung of the social ladder. Unlike the wealthy young men, the barber's brothers pursue the humblest of trades—indeed, all of them are reduced to begging at some point or another—and, in contrast with the well-to-do young men of the previous stories, their utter failure in pursuit of their desires is the result of their lowly station.

The first brother's story shows this most clearly. Because of his infatuation with his landlord's wife, the brother makes many pieces of clothing that he gives her and her husband for free, hoping by this to further the cause of his love. Laboring without pay, he is thus reduced by his desire to slavery. After he takes to begging to gain a few crusts, the lady and her husband marry him to the slave girl who had served as go-between. On the wedding night they tell him to go down in the basement by the mill to wait for his bride. However, the miller comes, ties him to the mill, and forces him to turn the mill stone under his lashes. Instead of the pleasurable rhythms of sex, he finds himself engaged in the sort of exhausting, repetitive labor usually performed by a beast.

And in all of the succeeding five stories the barber's brothers are similarly the dupes of those more powerful than they are. Their gullibility is ascribed to their ignorance of the "wiles of women," but this should not mislead us. Their stories, as I said, have taken us to the very bottom of the society, thus completing a descent through the social hierarchy, a trajectory foreseen in the steward's theft of butter from the king's larder, and in turn its theft from his kitchen by stray cats and dogs. And as the stories carry us down the tiers of the social pyramid, desire is mapped against power, and we find the topography is structured by the same relation that dominates the frame story: the master-slave relation. With respect to this depiction of the power structure of society, a glance at historical evidence from the late medieval, that is to say Ottoman, period is interesting.

Marshall Hodgson describes the Ottoman system of authority as one in which a single absolute authority is *personally* vested in the Ottoman Sultan. The result, as Walter Andrews says, is "a system where all elements are in a master-slave relation, [and] all patronage and preferment ultimately proceed downward in a cascade from the person of the monarch."[8] Our story depicts the hierarchy of power in a similar way, but here it is a matter of punishments that "cascade" downward.

"The Hunchback" is not the only story to depict power relations in this way, though it is the most elaborate. A rather similar depiction of this hierarchy of power is found in "The Young Woman and Her Five Lovers" (3:153–66), though in this story the hierarchy is stood on its head for comic effect. A young married woman, whose husband travels a lot, takes a handsome young lover. When the young man runs afoul of the law and is jailed, the young woman goes to the governor, who makes it clear that he will have the fellow released only in return for a sexual favor. The young woman tells him to come to her house that night. She then goes to the chief judge, the prime minister, and the king, complaining to each about the previous man's abuse of his power and receiving the same reply from each, that he will only help her in return for a sexual favor. Each time she agrees and tells the man to come to her house. Then she goes to a carpenter and asks him to make a cabinet with four compartments, each with its own sturdy door and lock. The carpenter also asks for a sexual favor, and she tells him to make five compartments and to bring the cabinet to her house. That evening the judge arrives and begins to woo her, but a knock on the door is heard. "It's my husband!" she says, and hides him in the lowest compartment, locking the door. The man at the door proves to be the governor. He writes the order for her lover's release, and then he begins to make love to her, but his attempt is also interrupted by a knock on the door. She locks the governor in the compartment over the judge. The same sequence is repeated with the vizier, the king, and lastly the carpenter. When she has them all locked in the cabinet she takes the release order and gets her lover out of prison, and they leave town. Meanwhile the five men are locked in the cabinet, no one daring to utter a sound for three days until the carpenter is unable to hold his bladder any longer. As his urine leaks on the king, the king's bladder also gives way, and he urinates on the vizier, and the vizier on the governor, and the governor on the judge. At length, the embarrassed men are set free by neighbors. The lowliest man, the carpenter, is on top, but for the others the hierarchy of power holds and each man is pissed on by his superior and pisses on his inferior. Where in "The Story of the Steward" the power structure is represented as a series of thefts, here it is a series of polluting degradations.

What is at stake in such a pyramid is not, let us note, the attainment of one's desire—an impossibility from the Lacanian standpoint whether one is a king or a beggar—but rather the ability to pursue it. The stories—all of them from the story of the hunchback to the stories of the well-to-do young lovers to the barber's brothers—trace in one way or another the vicissitudes of desire within the hierarchies of power, and the utter failures of the barber's feckless brothers, who occupy the lowest rung of society, should come as no surprise, for they are utterly powerless.

The powerlessness of the barber's brothers is emphasized in another way also. They are the only characters in the cycle who do not tell their own stories. In Tzvetan Todorov's well-known formula for *The Thousand and One Nights*, "narrative equals life; the absence of narrative, death," and this is also seen here.[9] The barber tells the other dinner guests that the caliph Mustansir, though amused by his stories, banished him nevertheless, but when the caliph died he returned to Baghdad, "and I found that my brothers had died" (1:275). Yet even before that, his brothers were all but dead because they lived as total recluses in the shelter of his house. Thus, the barber must tell their stories for them, even as he set himself up as spokesman for the young man's dead father. Hence, there is beyond the obvious humor, a more profound irony to his nickname "the Silent One."

On this account, the contrast between the mute hunchback and the garrulous barber masks an affinity at another level. That affinity is suggested by a fact already noted, that the barber's first brother is both a tailor and a hunchback. In their own ways the hunchback and the barber both describe a relation between language and death. The hunchback is the silence of death, which nevertheless "speaks" in the story because all who encounter him inhabit a symbolic order that transforms everything, even *nothing*, into a sign. The barber presumes to speak for that same silence, but there is another aspect to his relation to death also. As the irresistible force of language, the barber opposes the libidinal desires of the young man. Why? Because language, the symbolic order of experience, disrupts one's imaginary experience: "If this speech received by the subject didn't exist, this speech which bears on the symbolic level, there would be no conflict with the imaginary, and each of us would purely and simply follow his inclination. Experience shows us that nothing of the sort happens" (*S,* 2:326). In other words, we would "purely and simply follow our inclinations"—the way our cats and dogs do. But in a human being, that presumably simple impulse is refracted in the prism of language, both bent and scattered. The "unbinding of energy" that Freud associates with trauma occurs also when the libido, which is imaginary, enters the network of language; there the impulse toward union—*wisal* is what the soon-to-be lame young man seeks—encounters a system built on difference and opposition and is scattered along the signifying chain.[10] "Life is caught up in the symbolic piece-meal, decomposed" (*S,* 2:90). One can see why Lacan associates Freud's problematic "death drive" with language; precisely insofar as the "death drive" in *Beyond the Pleasure Principle* is the principle of difference and fragmentation, it mimics the workings of language. For this reason:

> The symbolic order is rejected by the libidinal order, which includes the whole domain of the imaginary, including the structure of the ego. And the death instinct is only the mask of the symbolic order, insofar—this is what Freud writes—as it is dumb, that is to say insofar as it hasn't been realized. As long as the symbolic recognition hasn't been instituted, by definition, the symbolic order is dumb. (*S,* 2:326)

Thus, the hunchback and the barber both represent aspects of the relation between language and death; the hunchback as "the mask of death" is the muteness of the symbolic order insofar as for the tailor, the physician, the steward, and the broker—who are caught up in purely imaginary pursuits—that order is "in travail, in the process of coming, insisting on being realized." While for the lame young man the opposition of the symbolic order in the person of the barber is experienced as a force outside of and opposed to his imaginary libidinal impulse, to his conception of life. That is why he makes out his will. He does so, we may say, because in the person of the barber the lame young man is pursued by death. As the tailor, the physician, the steward, and the broker find in the hunchback the image of their own death, the barber's speech reveals to the lame young man his own death also.

On one level, then, "The Hunchback" can be read as a fable about the relation between language and death. For the tale shows us how the hunchback must "die" a little in order to function as a sign—a matter remarked by Nietzsche in the essay "On Truth and Falsity in the Extramoral Sense":

> Every word immediately becomes an idea when, rather than serving as a sort of unique, entirely individualized first experience to which it owes its origin, it instead simultaneously must fit innumerable, more or less similar (which really means never equal, therefore altogether unequal) cases. Every idea originates through equating the unequal. . . The disregarding of the individual and the real furnishes us with the idea, as it likewise also gives us the form. . .[11]

As the individual object must "die" a little, must cede some of its individuality, for the concept behind the sign to arise, so too language itself arises through a kind of death. Or as Lacan says, "The word is the murder of the thing."

Yet we ought to recall that this fable about language and death is also a comedy, which fact alone would suggest that the hunchback is not only "the mask of death." Indeed, I would say that the comedy is not complete until another identity of the hunchback is revealed. But this task will require the skills of the barber.

Our story begins, after all, with hunchback already separated from the king. He is an object that has already been lost—and is this not the most fundamental story that psychoanalysis tells us? That all of one's life is simply a search for a lost object? Is it mere coincidence that when we reach the furthest recess of all the levels of narratives in "The Hunchback," the story of the barber's sixth brother, Shaqâshiq, the final wound that is inflicted is castration? What is more, in this tale that ends with his castration, language again acts as a force of pure frustration, when invisible dishes and drinks are brought by servants and placed in front of the hungry Shaqashiq.

After abject Shaqashiq's final insult and injury, we are taken back to the level of the tailor who, over the prostrate body of the hunchback, has been recounting for the king the story of the barber telling the stories of his brothers to the caliph al-Mustansir. The tailor then tells the king that the guests at the breakfast party, having heard both the lame young man's and the barber's sides of the story, locked the barber in a room and enjoyed their meal. When he returned home, his wife scolded him for living it up all day while she languished in the house. And that was why he took his wife out on the town, during which excursion they met the hunchback.

And now—finally—the king is satisfied. He has heard a story even more amazing than that of the hunchback: "He shook his head in delight and astonishment, and he said, 'The story of the young man and the busybody barber is indeed more delightful and more excellent than the story of this lying hunchback!' " (1:276). He orders the barber to be retrieved from the room in which he is locked and brought before him. After the barber is produced and told of all that has happened, he examines the hunchback and says, "There is wonder in every death, but the death of this hunchback ought to be recorded in letters of gold." Asked to explain, the barber says, "I swear upon your blessings that there is still breath in this lying hunchback!" (1:277).

The barber rubs an ointment on the hunchback's throat, and extracts the bone from him. The hunchback sneezes and then springs to his feet—erect, we may say—and says, "I testify that there is no god but Allah and Muhammad is his prophet." The king has the incident recorded in letters of gold, and he bestows robes of honor on all the parties. He gives the tailor and the barber positions and salaries in the palace, while the hunchback resumes his career as the king's drinking crony. If the hunchback's spine may be taken as the graph of narrative—insofar as every narrative marks a departure from the usual course of affairs—when he springs up, a second image is unavoidable; the hunchback is also the phallus, whose separation from the king has set in motion all the narration that follows, the oedipal crisis as "shaggy dog story": "it just goes on and on." Now we can see why the ugly little fellow is so appropriate as an image of the king's desire, and when the hunchback springs erect, the comedy is complete. All has gone for naught, and yet—and yet the king gets it up one more time. Once more before he is visited by the Destroyer of Delights, the Severer of Unions.

7
The Sublime Wound

"THE STORY OF THE HUNCHBACK" MAY BE REMARKABLE IN *THE THOUsand and One Nights* for the sheer number of characters who stagger across its pages blinded, lamed, disfigured, and maimed, but it is not exceptional in the thematic emphasis given to such injuries. The number of wounded characters there and elsewhere in the *Nights* points to the presence of the fantasy Lacan called *le corps morcelé* or "the fragmented body." The prominence of such images is seen from the beginning in the beheading of adulterous queens and slaves in the frame story. And thereafter body parts accumulate in its pages in impressive numbers as characters lose heads, legs, hands, eyes, and other parts while pursuing their goals. In the third story Shahrazad tells, "The Fisherman and the Jinni," the unfaithful wife is dispatched by being cut in half—again the price for her illicit desire for a black man. In "The Porter and the Three Ladies of Baghdad" the three qalandars or dervishes all lose an eye, while one of the ladies reveals horrible scars resulting from a whipping. And if dismemberment is particularly prominent in the earliest stories found in the book (*pace* Mahdi), I would point out that it continues to play a role in some of the latest stories inserted into the collection. "ʿAlî Bâbâ and the Forty Thieves" is an example we shall soon examine, and castration is the wound in "ʿAzîz and ʿAzîzah," a story narrated in the course of the mini-*sîrah* or geste, "ʿUmar ibn Nuʿmân," a story everyone agrees is a very late addition to the collection.

Surprisingly enough, maiming and dismemberment are not dissociated from comedy in the *Nights*. Indeed, the disfigured and maimed characters who grope and limp their ways through the pages of *The Thousand and One Nights* have, at times, an almost Beckett-like quality. For example, castration itself receives comic treatment in three stories inserted in "The Story of Ghanim ibn Ayyub, The Slave of Love." There, three black eunuchs are overheard telling the stories of how and why they were castrated. The racism found in the frame story seems to operate here too; that is, the eunuchs' race is part of the recipe for comedy. But we will also examine a story about the grisly dismemberment of a beautiful Arab woman with possible comic overtones; Harun al-Rashid will fall on his backside from laughter when he learns the cause of the woman's death. And this is not to mention the various mutilations of the barber's brothers in "The Hunchback" that are treated as matters of comedy. Are we simply dealing with a streak of sadistic cruelty in the medieval sensibility?

To say the most obvious thing, the wound in *The Thousand and One Nights*—as in life!—results from an action, a plan gone awry. The wound marks something that escaped the subject's calculations. In these respects, it falls under Lacan's concept of *dustuchê* as a bad encounter with the real, an encounter that always defies the subject's ability to conceive it in signs. The real as "hard, impenetrable kernel resisting symbolization," to use Žižek's phrase, is one sense of Lacan's sibylline formulation: "the Real is the impossible."[1] In connection with this, we should not perhaps be surprised to find that wounds are frequently among the signs of the uncanny, as when characters who are all wounded in precisely the same way meet one another in a seemingly chance encounter. Again, the three dervishes in "The Porter and the Three Ladies of Baghdad" who all lose one eye are an example we will discuss at some length here.

If the fascination with the wound shows itself in the sheer number of instances of scarring, maiming, dismemberment, laming, blinding, and castration in *The Thousand and One Nights*, it will be useful to make a preliminary distinction between two sorts of stories. On the one hand, there are stories in which an instance of maiming or dismemberment is merely one element among many. In such stories the wound does not seem definitive to the narrative, and it is therefore no surprise that in these stories the dismemberment often happens to a secondary character. "Ali Baba and the Forty Thieves" offers an example of this sort of dismemberment. On the other hand, there are stories in which the instance of maiming is what the story is about. In the first sort of story, the narration is often done by a character outside the story—in the case of "Ali Baba and the Forty Thieves," for example, Shahrazad, who plays no role in the events of the story, narrates. In the second sort of story, the story is narrated almost always by the person wounded. Borrowing Genette's distinction, one can say that in the former sort of story a "heterodiegetic narrator" is the rule and in the latter a "homodiegetic narrator" is the rule. The distinction between these two sorts of stories sheds new light on a feature of the frame story also: Shahzaman's remark,

"There is a wound *inside* me."[2] Shahzaman's wound is internal precisely because it resists narration.

In "Ali Baba and the Forty Thieves," Ali Baba's older brother Qâsim, who is lazier but wilier, ends up in pieces—he is, it seems, not quite wily enough. Ignoring Ali Baba's warnings, Qasim finds himself trapped in the thieves' cave when he is unable to remember a single homely word, "sesame" (*simsim*), which nevertheless possesses the power to move giant boulders. When the thieves find him, they hack him into six parts—the tally resulting from his head, four limbs and torso. When Qasim's absence is noticed, Ali Baba goes to the cave and finds the parts heaped in front of the stone, and he takes them home. Ostensibly in order to keep the cave a secret, Ali Baba conceives it necessary to conceal the manner in which his brother died; and here Ali Baba's clever servant Marjanah steps into the breach and hires a cobbler to stitch the dismembered Qasim back together for a proper burial. The cobbler figures out the secret and, in turn, gives it away to the robber chief, and the clever Marjanah must find a way to dispatch the robber chief and his thieves also. The dismemberment of Qasim results from his unrestrained greed, which so possesses his mind that he cannot recall the single word "sesame" that he requires in order to escape the cave. In such a story, whatever the significance of the dismemberment in isolation, we can conceive of another sort of death for Qasim that would leave the rest of the narrative intact, if not Qasim.

In the second sort of story, however, the injury is suffered by a central character, usually the narrator. The path of the subject's desire leads to the wound, and we cannot conceive of a different fate for the character without conceiving of a different story. Thus the wound becomes both the terminus of the narrative and a sign that calls for narration. In these stories, the wound, the missing limb or eye, is what must be narrated; were there no dismemberment, there would be no story. It is this second sort of story that is the concern here, for if the sheer number of instances of dismemberment in *The Thousand and One Nights* suggests a general significance of the wound in the book, the stories that narrate the wound, so to speak, must offer the best avenue to examine that significance. Here I should make it clear that our concern is not solely with dismemberment and scarring—loss of limb(s), scars resulting from vicious beatings, nor only with non-fatal instances, castration, the loss of an eye, a hand, and so forth—no, those who lose their heads or are cut in half are not thereby excluded from consideration either. The dead shall also have their say in what follows.

In a discussion of maiming, castration, mutilation, and disfigurement in *The Thousand and One Nights,* "The Hunchback," discussed in the previous chapter, is prominent. Here let us just recall that every story except the story of the hunchback himself and that of the barber narrates a wound or injury—and though the barber escapes injury, ten other men are decapitated in his story. Only the story of the hunchback himself seems to lack some form of dismemberment or disfigurement, and yet the hunchback, congenitally disfigured, may be read as an inaugural form of disfigurement, a form of disfigurement that is "already there," and that constitutes the subject.

Along with "The Hunchback," "The Porter and the Three Ladies of Baghdad" probably contains the most prominent examples in *The Thousand and One Nights* of this second sort of wound, the wound that signifies a narrative. But "The Porter" links the wound with another element not found in "The Hunchback." In "The Porter," the wound results from the breaking of a prohibition.

Indeed, taking into account only the prohibition, "The Porter" among all the stories in the *Nights* distinguishes itself by the numerous and strange prohibitions placed on various characters. While perusal of Nikita Elisséef's *Thémes et motifs des Mille et une nuits* yields a number of other stories under the rubrics of *defenser* and *interdiction,* the prohibitions in those stories are neither as numerous nor as mysterious as those in "The Porter." A story like "The Man Who Never Laughed" from "The Tales of the Seven Viziers," which is built on only one such prohibition, is more typical.[3] The mysterious nature of the prohibitions in "The Porter" also distinguishes it from other stories that one might place under the same rubric. For example, Elisséef lists the story of "The Barber's Second Brother" under the "prohibition on asking a question" along with "The Porter," but the prohibition in the former is really quite different from that in the latter. For by the time the barber's second brother has shaved his hair and eyebrows and daubed his naked body with red paint we begin to surmise the purpose of the prohibition: simply to allow the vizier's beautiful daughter to make a fool of him. Whereas in "The Porter" the purposes of the various interdictions and prohibitions are never known by either the characters or by us the readers until they are broken. The prohibition the Moorish sorcerer gives Aladdin—namely, that he must not stop in any of the first three subterranean chambers of treasure, for if he does he will be turned to a block of black stone—is more typical of the prohibitions issued throughout the *Nights.* Here, even if the reason for the prohibition is obscure, nevertheless the consequences of breaking it are spelled out. But in the case of "The Porter," neither the reason for the prohibition nor the consequences of breaking it are ever known in advance.

In fact, the occlusion of those two things is fundamental to the narrative line of "The Porter and the Three Ladies of Baghdad," and from a purely formal perspective, the entire story may be said to be "about" the conjunction of the prohibition and the wound that appear at first as separate and unrelated elements.

The story begins when a woman hires a porter to carry her purchases home from the market. She and her two sisters admit the porter under one condition: he must not ask any questions about anything he sees. A wild party ensues. There is music, food, drinking, and finally a naked romp in the pool by all three ladies and the porter accompanied by lascivious banter. Soon three qalandars or dervishes, drawn by the sounds of the party, meet in the street outside the house. By uncanny coincidence (*aʿjab al-ittifâq*) each has somehow lost his left eye. They knock on the door, and they too are admitted under the same prohibition. Next, Harun, Jaʿfar, and Masrur, disguised as merchants, hear the party, and they are also admitted under the same condition. At this point the risqué gives way to the bizarre. Two black dogs are brought in, beaten, and then embraced by the mistress. The second girl sings a dolorous song that causes the third girl, the "doorkeeper," to break down in sobs and rend her garments, revealing on her back the scars of a whipping. The prohibition, merely odd at first, takes on a different coloring, a more ominous one, in light of these strange acts.

Finally Harun is unable to restrain his curiosity and after some discussion, the porter is chosen to ask what is going on. At once, seven black men rush into the room, each with sword in hand, ready to decapitate the seven male guests, and the link between the prohibition and dismemberment looms for the first time. Looms—for it is deferred as the porter pleads innocent of having broken the oath, and tells his story; that is, how he met the "shopper" in the market. The mistress forgives him. She then asks the dervishes to explain themselves, and they proceed to tell their stories.

The story of each qalandar is the story of how he lost his eye, and gross appearances would suggest their stories are about "the same thing." And indeed their three stories share a number of other features that relate the stories thematically: each qalandar begins as a prince or king; each enters a subterranean chamber; and each has a brush with death. Yet, as we shall see, the stories also seem carefully contrived, in their *differences*, to explore different aspects, different possibilities, different implications of the wound.

In the first instance, "The Story of the First Qalandar," the prohibition is absent. In this story, the first dervish, while visiting his uncle, unwittingly helps two cousins commit incest in a subterranean chamber. When he returns to his own city, he finds that his father, the king, has been overthrown by his minister. The latter holds a grudge against the young prince because years before he accidentally shot out his eye while hunting. The young man flees, returning to his uncle's city, where he shows his uncle the subterranean chamber. There they find the charred bodies of his cousins, and he learns of his cousins' incestuous love affair. Then the rebel minister arrives on the scene with an army. He conquers the city and kills the uncle. To avenge the loss of his eye, the minister has the eye of the young man plucked out. The young man shaves off his beard and eyebrows and takes up a life as a wandering qalandar until he reaches Baghdad, where he meets the other two dervishes.

While "The Story of the Second Qalandar" does not feature an overt prohibition either, it introduces what could be considered a virtual prohibition. As a young prince, the second dervish is sent on a mission to the king of India, but he is waylaid by robbers. Forced to work as a lowly woodcutter, he finds a beautiful young woman in a subterranean chamber. She tells the young prince that she has been imprisoned there by a jinni who kidnapped her on her wedding night. The jinni comes every tenth day, and if the young man can content himself with her company for nine out of ten days, they can live in happiness. But he cannot, and one day in drunken bravado he summons the jinni. The jinni dismembers the young woman. To save himself, the young man tells the jinni "The Story of the Envious and the Envied." Though he spares his life, the jinni turns him into an ape and exiles him to a desert island. The ape/prince is rescued by a passing ship and he astounds the passengers and crew of the ship with his ability to write. When they come to a port, his ability lands him the position of scribe with the king. The king's daughter recognizes that he has been enchanted by the jinni, and wages a furious battle with the latter. The princess and the jinni both die, though not before she frees the young prince from the spell. But during the battle a spark thrown off the jinni puts out the eye of the ape/prince. However, this is as nothing to the king, disconsolate at his daughter's death, and he sends the young prince away, warning him never to return. He shaves his beard and eyebrows and takes up life as a wandering dervish until he reaches Baghdad, where he meets the other two dervishes.

Here a condition is imposed upon the second qalandar in the form of a compulsory pattern: nine days of *jouissance* and one day of hiding and abstinence. This sort of periodic function (with the glimmer of astrology and numerology) could easily be cast in the form of a prohibition, and in that respect too it points towards a sort of prohibition based on some arithmetic calculation that will recur in the story of the third qalandar.

"The Third Qalandar" is more elaborate yet, with gnosticism and numerology in the air. The third dervish, a king at the outset, sets sail with a great fleet of ships on a voyage of trade. Soon, however, his ship is destroyed by a mountain whose mysterious force pulls the nails from his ship's hull. Fulfilling a prophecy, the young king destroys a bronze rider on the mountain's summit, thus somehow disabling the mountain's magnetic power. In a dream, his rescue is foretold, but a prohibition is placed upon his invoking the name of God—a nearly impossible demand for a Muslim, who is prone to utter the word "Allah" in scores of daily situations. When he is rescued by a boat rowed by a bronze oarsman, in his joy he forgets the prohibition and utters the name of God. The boat sinks, and he finds himself castaway on another desert island.

On the island he meets a boy living in a subterranean chamber. The boy tells him he has been hidden there by his father, who hopes that he may thus elude the fate foretold for him: that before fifty days have passed he will die at the hands of the man who destroyed a bronze rider. Forty days are left. The young king is astonished, but says nothing, and he and the boy live safely until the fortieth day when the young man stumbles inadvertently, stabbing and killing the boy.

Wandering in gloom, he comes upon a palace occupied by an old man and ten young men, each of whom has lost one eye.[4] They take him in on the condition that he will ask no questions about what he sees. But observing the young men rub ashes on their faces and bemoan the curiosity that brought them their misery, he breaks his oath and asks about the cause of their strange behavior. They summon a giant bird, the Rukh, which carries him to a palace on the mountaintop containing forty beautiful young women. For a year he sleeps with a different girl each night. Then the young women tell him they must leave for forty days; furthermore, they tell him that the palace has one hundred chambers of which he may open ninety-nine, but the one hundredth door is not to be opened. During the thirty-nine days he opens all ninety-nine doors, discovering various gardens and treasures, but then, on the fortieth day, he finds himself unable to resist opening the one hundredth door. He enters the chamber and finds a strange black horse, which he mounts. When the horse resists his commands, he whips it and the horse takes flight, dumping him on the roof of the palace, where the ten one-eyed young men reside; as it does so, the horse lashes him in the face so hard he loses his eye. The young men, having warned him of his curiosity, now have no sympathy for him and ask him to leave. He shaves his beard and eyebrows and takes up a life as a wandering dervish until he reaches Baghdad, where he meets the other two qalandars.

The third qalandar's story features three prohibitions: invoking God's name is forbidden to him; the one-eyed men forbid him from asking about the cause of their misfortune; and the forty beautiful women prohibit him from opening the one hundredth door. To these prohibitions are added other elements, some found in the previous stories, some not. There are the numerical *Fort/Da* patterns of coming and going: the jinni in the second qalandar's story and the forty beautiful women here who must absent themselves for forty days.

All three qalandars are victims of bad luck to differing degrees, and in differing degrees each is responsible for his fate. The first qalandar seems relatively innocent. He shoots out the vizier's eye by accident, and his complicity in his cousins' incestuous love is unwitting. The two events seem unrelated, yet there may be a link between them; the same word, *mûla'*, is used to describe the cousin's passion for his sister that was used to describe the young prince's devotion to hunting. And, like the incestuous marriage of Oedipus and Jocasta, the incestuous relation acts like a kind of curse, bringing ruin in its train, with the city under attack and the fall of the dynasty as its consequences. On the other hand, the second qalandar through his drunkenness seems to share more complicity in his fate. The third, however, bears the greatest degree of responsibility, for he breaks a series of prohibitions, although his experience with the young man seems to qualify his culpability. For, rather like Oedipus, he tries to avoid what is foretold, but finds it impossible despite his efforts. One thinks of the story "Appointment in Samarra" in which the hero tries to elude the grim reaper, and precisely by trying to elude him, meets him. As Žižek says, it is the same with Oedipus: "the prophecy becomes true by means of its being communicated to the person it affects and by means of his or her attempt to elude it."[5]

In any case, there still seems a progression in the three stories, from innocence in the first case to one of complicity and some degree of guilt in the third case. Yet we should also note that this progression is accompanied by another, a progression from ignorance to knowledge—seen first in the prohibition on asking a question. Yet, despite their differences, each man suffers the same punishment at the hands of obscurely grasped agents.

The reasons for this lie, I think, in the strange nature of the prohibitions. They are not prohibitions on acts forbidden in themselves—though several acts commonly linked with taboos are found in the stories, most obviously incest. Rather, the prohibitions are placed on learning why something happens. "Don't ask why we beat these hounds and then embrace them," "Don't ask why we rub our faces with ashes," and so forth. The law as a limit placed on one's desire here takes the form of a prohibition against knowing—knowing the basis of the law, that is. Hence, the prohibitions have an arbitrary and "empty" quality. This seems why numbers as such play an important role in them.

Certainly some of the numbers involved have a specific significance in Muslim culture, while others seem to derive their meaning from a broader Near Eastern cultural context. Most obviously, the numbers forty and one hundred have particular significance in Muslim culture, and also more general meanings deriving from a long Near Eastern cultural tradition. In Islam, forty is a number strongly associated with the notion of purification. The dead are mourned for forty days, and the *ʿiddah,* or period of time that must pass before a widow may remarry, is forty days.[6] The one hundred doors, of which ninety-nine are accessible to the qalandar, recall the one hundred names of Allah. There are said to be one hundred names denoting God's attributes of which ninety-nine are known to men, but the one hundredth name is a mystery known only to the camel.[7] Yet it seems the broader function of the numbers is to emphasize the purely arbitrary nature of the law. "Do this nine times, don't do it ten times."

As in the primordial garden, the forbidden fruit here is knowledge. But knowledge of what? Of why there is a law. The peculiar and capricious nature of such a law has not escaped notice, especially in the case of events in Eden. In *Letters from the Earth,* Twain's narrator Satan remarks on the strange situation in the Garden in a way that is relevant to our story also. Satan says of God: "And he added a most strange remark: he said that if they ate of it they should surely die. Strange, for the reason that inasmuch as they had never seen a sample of death they could not possibly know what he meant."[8] The law is void of content except for the punishment, and that punishment is inscrutable to those on whom the law is imposed unless and until they break the law.

Something else must be noted here. As a result of telling their stories, the three qalandars thereby ransom their lives, as do Harun, Jaʿfar, and Masrur by telling their stories (the lie that they are foreign merchants), but they still do not learn the reasons behind the strange behavior of the three ladies. In other words, knowledge, the very thing for which Harun broke the prohibition (and risked death), is still denied him. That knowledge he will only gain in his capacity as caliph the next day, when he has all the young ladies and the qalandars brought before him and he compels them to tell their stories.

The lady who whips the dogs tells the first story. She begins by explaining various familial relations; she has four sisters, two by the same mother and father as herself, and two others by her father and a different mother, these two half-sisters being the two young ladies with whom she lives. She and her two full sisters inherit their parents' wealth. The two sisters squander their portions in ill-advised investments and cajole her into lending them more money, which they also lose. Then they talk her into financing and embarking on a risky voyage of commerce. The ship strays off course, and the narrator finds a city whose inhabitants, except for a handsome prince, have been turned to stone, this being their punishment for refusing to heed God's commandment and become Muslims. She marries the prince and takes him back to the ship, but her sisters become jealous and throw them overboard. She swims to shore, but her husband drowns. On shore she witnesses a battle between a white serpent and a black serpent and comes to the aid of the white serpent. The latter reveals herself to be a Muslim jinniyah. She turns the wicked sisters into dogs and transports the narrator and her half-sisters back to Baghdad, where she compels the narrator to agree to whip the dogs nightly. If she fails to do so she too will be "ensorcelled" and turned into a dog.

The story is essentially that of the second sheikh in "The Merchant and the Jinni" and "Abdallah ibn Fadl and his Brothers."[9] Where stories thus far have begun with prohibitions that are in every case broken, this story concludes with a command that is observed. Nevertheless, the command resembles some of the previous prohibitions in that we only partially understand its "logic." There is an inscrutable "something more" seen here not only in the fact that the woman must punish her siblings even though she does not want to do so, but also in the fact that the jinniyah makes the threat of further punishment against the agent of her own salvation.

The second story belongs to the scarred lady. Lured by an old woman to a house, she meets a handsome young man and they become engaged. When the marriage contract is drawn up, the young man insists on a crucial condition: she must agree to never set eyes on another man again. She agrees and all goes well until the old woman reappears and convinces the young woman to allow a merchant an innocent kiss on her cheek as payment for some cloth she wishes to buy from him. The nasty merchant bites her on the cheek. Her husband, seeing the wound, guesses at what has happened and orders two slaves to cut her in half. Again the old woman intervenes, now to save the life of the young woman. The husband has her flogged instead and the slaves carry her unconscious back to her former residence. When she wakes up, she goes back to the street where she and her husband lived, but finds the house razed and her husband vanished. She then goes to live with the lady with the two dogs, who is her half-sister.

Again a prohibition is broken; the wife looks at another man, indeed she agrees to an "innocent" kiss, which then turns into a vicious bite—for which, barely escaping death, she receives her wound, the scars left by her husband's horrible flogging.

The third lady, full sister to the scarred lady and half-sister to the lady with the dogs, has no story—a significant omission, I think, which we will discuss later.

Both women seemed wronged, though again as with the qalandars, in different ways and to different degrees. The first young woman loses her husband to the iniquity of her sisters, whom she seems inclined to forgive. Yet the jinniyah will not allow her to forgive them—it is rather like a contemporary "domestic" dispute wherein the wife may wish to forgive her husband but the police and courts insist on setting in motion the machinery of law. Moreover, as already noted, with the threat to the first sister, there is a strange sense that she is being punished. In the second case, the wrong done the young woman is a matter of a wholly disproportionate punishment. True, she violates the jealous injunction of her husband. But her punishment, savage flogging and abandonment, seems more than simply excessive. There is as well the ambiguous, enigmatic role of the old woman. She both coaxes the young woman into breaking the prohibition, then saves her life. Her ambiguous actions can be seen as further manifestations of the inscrutable aspect of the law.

In a story where great attention has been paid to formal patterning, to symmetries of all sorts, one question remains: Why does the third lady have no story? I intend to offer an answer to that question which will take us back to the missing eyes of the qalandars. But there are two more stories involving dismemberments that we must consider before answering that question. The first of these is the story that immediately follows "The Porter and the Three Ladies of Baghdad": the story of "The Three Apples."

The Three Apples

The story of "The Three Apples" offers a provocative and grisly case of dismemberment. Harun al-Rashid, wandering the streets of Baghdad in disguise with Ja'far and Masrur, comes upon an old fisherman down on his luck. Harun offers him one hundred dinars for whatever his net brings forth from the Tigris. The old man casts his net and hauls up a chest that contains the dismembered body of a beautiful young woman. Harun, scandalized by such a crime, orders Ja'far to find the culprit in three days or he will execute him. When Ja'far is about to be executed, two men come forward, one young and one old, each claiming to have murdered the girl. But as the young man tells his story to the caliph we are soon convinced that he is telling the true story.

The young man is a merchant; the old man is his father-in-law, and the dismembered body is that of his wife. His wife, while recovering from an illness, expresses a desire for an apple. The young man tries to buy an apple in Baghdad, but is told that they are only to be found in a garden in Basra that belongs to the caliph. He travels all the way to Basra, where he purchases three from the gardener. But when he returns, his wife has lapsed into a fever once more and has no desire for the apples.

By and by she feels better, though she never does eat any of the apples. In the meantime, her husband returns to his shop, and one day he sees a black man walk past with an apple in his hand. Curious, he asks him where he got the apple. From his girlfriend, he says. She told him that her husband went all the way to Basra to obtain three of them. The slave sharpens the story by quoting the wife to the effect of calling her husband a *dayyûth*, a term that in modern Egyptian colloquial means a "wittol" according to *A Dictionary of Egyptian Arabic*.[10] A "wittol" is, according to the *O.E.D.*, "a man who is aware of and complaisant about the infidelity of his wife."[11]

The young man hurries home. Finding his wife has only two apples, he demands an explanation. When she tells him she does not know what happened to the third, he falls upon her with his knife and hacks her to pieces. He puts the pieces in the chest and throws it in the Tigris. Then he returns home and finds his son—who is still ignorant of his mother's death—crying. When he asks the reason for his tears, the boy tells him that he took an apple without his mother's knowledge and when he was out in the street a black man snatched it from him and asked him where he got it. He told him that his father went all the way to Basra to get three of them for his mother. The young man is staggered by this, realizing he has killed his innocent wife on account of a slave's lie. Disconsolate, he finishes his story by asking Harun to kill him. But the caliph says he will execute no one but the black slave, and now he orders Ja'far to find the man within three days—or else. Again Ja'far goes home in despair, and, feeling it was mere chance that saved him the first time, he prepares to die. On the fourth day he bids farewell to his family. When he hugs his little daughter he feels something round in her pocket. It is an apple. The girl tells him their black slave, Rayḥân ("Oregano"), sold it to her for two dinars. Ja'far has the slave arrested and goes to Harun to tell him what has happened. The caliph expresses his amazement at the tale—in fact, he laughs—and Ja'far tells him it is not so amazing as that of "The Two Viziers." Harun asks him to tell that story but Ja'far only agrees if Rayhan's life will be spared. Harun consents, and Ja'far tells the story—which is beyond the bounds of our subject here. In the end, Rayhan's life is spared and Harun gives the young man a beautiful young slave girl to replace his wife. Considering the horrible fate of the young wife, the ending seems rather facile, a matter we will discuss in relation to the ending of "The Porter and the Three Ladies of Baghdad."

The plot is that of a detective story, with Ja'far as the gumshoe, in which role he is a plodding Watson who must take the lead in the investigation because there is no Holmes—he has not yet been invented. This plot has similarities with two purportedly true stories. In the book *al-Adhkiyâ'* (or "Clever People") by Ibn al-Jawzî (d. 1200), a story is told of the Abbasid caliph al-Mu'taḍid and a fisherman who catches body parts in his net when he casts it in the Tigris; the caliph cleverly unmasks the perpetrator. The second story is found in the work of Tanukhi previously mentioned, *Happiness after Hardship*. In Tanukhi's story, however, the crime is not a killing but an act of domestic espionage in the household of the vizier al-Qâsim ibn 'Ubaydallâh, a historical figure known for his treachery and cruelty—some historians claim he poisoned the poet Ibn al-Rûmî. When the caliph embarrasses him one day with mention of certain piquant details from his private life—his drinking and dressing up in the gowns of a singing girl—al-Qasim realizes he has a spy in his household. As it happens, al-Qasim employs a man as a kind of "house dick" to spy on his employees, and he charges this man with finding the spy within three days on pain of being exiled to Oman. Like Ja'far, al-Qasim's house dick simply sits down in despair—and all the answers come to him.

Rather more important for this study, however, is the calculated way in which the story of "The Three Apples" repeats certain elements of the frame story; the husband imagines that his wife has betrayed him with a black slave, and indeed, some of the language used by the young man is very close to that of the frame story: "The world blackened in my face. I locked my shop, having lost my reason on account of my rage." In the frame story, too, "the world blackens in the face" of Shahzaman who also "loses his reason" on account of his rage. In both stories there is a beautiful woman in a chest, though here she is cut up into pieces, and in both stories, too, a seemingly chance event plays a crucial role in setting the terrible events in motion. Shahzaman forgets something and returns to the palace, while Rayhan happens to walk by the young man's shop.

Yet if the apple is for the young man the "proof" of his wife's infidelity, it may be worth considering if it means anything else to the husband. Consider that the picture of the young man to this point is of a husband perplexed by his wife's illnesses and by her desires, and before the apple is "proof" of her desire for the slave, it is a gift from him, for which he has undertaken a trip and, what is more, run a certain risk; for, as we are told, the apples really belong to the caliph—they are not really the gardener's to sell. A theft that will lead to two more such thefts. Yet, having gone to these lengths to procure his gift, he finds that she is manifestly indifferent to it. That indifference may be considered in light of a detail found in the Mardrus translation, though not found in the Second Calcutta or Bulaq editions. In the Arabic texts the young man says that after his wife recovered the first time he wished to take her to the public bath; then Mardrus adds a further remark attributed to the young man: "I had not lain with her since the beginning of her illness" (Mardrus, 124). Mardrus often annoys the Arabists with the liberties he takes, but in this instance his addition is, I think, plausible both in the context of this story and because such a sequence is common in other stories. Indeed, even if it is a gloss, it shows an insight into the story for it points to the real mystery, the mystery of the apples.

This becomes apparent when the husband sees the slave with the apple in his hand. Then Mardrus's garnish makes the husband's reaction to the words of the black slave all the more plausible: "She doesn't want my apples and she doesn't want me!" Now the apple represents her manifest indifference to her husband. Yet, it has an obverse side also. To her husband, paradoxically, it remains the emblem of her desire insofar it now represents the enigma of that desire. "What do you really want of me?"—*Che vuoi*? in Lacan's

Graph III (*E,* 313), which is the central question confronting the subject. The apple's itinerary represents the elusive quality of her desire, desire in Lacan's words that is "caught in the rails—eternally stretching forth towards the *desire for something else*—of metonymy" (*E,* 166–67). So, too, the wife's desire is always elsewhere. This is seen in the final moments of the young woman's life, when her husband bursts in on her and asks her, "Where is the third [apple]?" and she replies, "I don't know. I don't know where it's gone." For her, too, there is an enigma in the apple, an inexplicable absence. Neither her husband nor Jaʿfar ever catches up to her desire. In the beginning, the husband is sometimes too early and sometimes too late—when she wants the apples, he doesn't have them, and by the time he has them, she doesn't care for them anymore. Jaʿfar, as sleuth, is obviously too late—the sleuth is always too late; the crime has already been committed. So neither ever learns what the woman's real desire was. When the husband believes the black man's lie, he makes the same mistake he made with the apples. He thinks, "Aha, now I know!"—but, in fact, he does not know, and he never will. So, on a certain plane, the real mystery is not who is responsible for her death but what she really desired. The relation between her desire and the apple can also be seen in the way that her indifference seems to be transmitted along with the apple from her son to the black slave Rayhan. For the curious thing is that it is the same with everybody else and the apple. Her son, the black slave Rayhan, and Jaʿfar's little girl—they all think they want the apple, but nobody ever eats it.

Yet if it were only a matter of her husband's inability to know what she truly desires, the young woman would have lived. The marriage would not even be remarkable in that regard, a husband wondering, "What does she really want?" Something else is required; this is the encounter in the market between the black slave and the husband with its seemingly aleatory quality.

The ending of "The Three Apples" leaves us, I think, with a lingering ill ease. The ill ease is, no doubt, partly due to Harun's reaction, his laughter, when the terrible deed is finally explained. There are, to be sure, comic touches prior to this; Jaʿfar, here as elsewhere in the *Nights,* is a comic figure, a slavish subordinate who flies into a dither at a word from the Master. Yet, even so, there is something jarring in Harun's reaction, especially after the scene of horror when the husband hears his son, who does not yet know his mother's grisly fate, explain how he took the apple.

However, I do not think that the storyteller's turn to comedy explains all of our ill ease. We would still be uneasy with the ending even if Harun did not laugh, for some of our ill ease, perhaps the greater part, is due to the discrepancy between the sort of justice Harun dispenses and the horrible act with which the story began. Perhaps the husband is punished for his "theft" of the apples from the caliph—yet it is the wife who dies. No matter how one views the end, a disturbing disproportion remains.

Here I see a similarity with "The Porter and the Three Ladies of Baghdad." The caliph again tidies up the mess without in any way addressing the grievous wrong that has been perpetrated. For both the scarred lady in "The Porter" and the young wife in "The Three Apples," some trivial act triggers a vicious retributive reaction. The young man hacks his wife apart; al-Amîn flogs his wife, destroys her house, and abandons her. Now it has been noted by many readers that the emphasis in the stories Shahrazad tells often falls on forgiveness rather than retribution, but even so, Harun's responses in each case seem feeble and inadequate. It is a matter that Andras Hamori addresses in an essay on "The Porter."

Taking the three stories of the qalandars together, Hamori isolates a pattern of descent into the subterranean and confrontation with death, followed by loss of an eye. The pattern has two variations, voluntary descent to near-death and involuntary descent to near-death, and in these variations (and in the stories of the two ladies) are seen what he calls "two forms of justice." On the one hand, "a justice of structure," as he calls it, a purely formal sort of symmetry, is seen in the way that everyone is married off at the story's end. But Hamori does not think that this "justice of structure" is meant to be the storyteller's final word on the matter. As he notes, "the storyteller has made sure that we also think in terms of human justice, and the matter becomes much less neat than the structure would have it: the men are responsible for their mutilation in very different ways."[12] Indeed, the two notions of justice cannot be reconciled, and that conflict, in his view, is precisely where the storyteller wishes to leave us. As he says, the qalandars have already shown by their curiosity at the ladies' house that they have learned nothing from their misadventures: "Thus, all the characters are led back into normal life without a transition: there is no repentance for the bad and no wisdom for the blind." The question of justice is a question we will take up again after a final example of the wound.

That example is found in the story of "'Azîz and 'Azîzah," and the latter may illuminate "The Three Apples" for its plot transposes the situation of "The Three Apples." If in "The Three Apples" the young woman seems indifferent to her husband's desire, in "Aziz and Azizah" it is the young man Aziz who is indifferent to Azizah's desire. But due to the "dissymmetries" of man and woman, the plot that results differs decidedly from that of "The Three Apples."

Aziz and Azizah

First, a glance at the surrounding terrain: "Aziz and Azizah" is embedded in the story of "Tâj al-Mulûk and Dunyâ," which in turn is told within the long *geste* of "ʿUmar ibn Nuʿmân." In "Taj al-Muluk," Prince Taj al-Muluk, while hunting, meets Aziz, who is a merchant, and offers to buy some of his products, but Aziz says he has none worthy of the prince. Taj al-Muluk then sees two handkerchiefs embroidered with images of gazelles and tries to buy them, but Aziz says he cannot part with them. To explain why, he tells the story of how he came to possess them. This story differs, however, in one significant way from the stories we have discussed thus far. Only at the story's end is the wound revealed; only then is it known that it is the story of his castration.

Aziz and Azizah are cousins destined for marriage. An orphan, Azizah is raised by Aziz's father, and as children they are even allowed to sleep together. But on his wedding day, Aziz gets lost while making a detour to a friend's house to invite him to his wedding. He finds himself in a strange alley. There a silk handkerchief embroidered with a gazelle floats to the ground near him. He looks up and sees a beautiful young woman, and he at once falls madly in love with her. He also completely forgets about his wedding. Love and marriage, the story tells us, have nothing to do with each other; love is the reason why Aziz does *not* get married.

When he returns home many hours late, he tells Azizah that he is in love with another woman, and shows her the handkerchief. Azizah examines it and tells him what it means. She then generously guides Aziz through the steps of romance, interpreting a number of other tokens given him in subsequent meetings, until, finally, Aziz—after, it must be said, committing a number of faux pas—possesses the young lady. Azizah, jilted as she is, falls prey to lovesickness and dies, though not before giving Aziz verses that will protect him from his lady love's wicked plans. When Aziz recites these verses to the woman, the young woman tells him that Azizah has saved him from a wicked fate. Aziz, ever the innocent, is astonished. The young woman says that she will spare him on one condition, that he never speak to nor look at another woman—more or less the prohibition imposed on the second young lady in "The Porter and the Three Ladies of Baghdad." It is the first indication that

Aziz is assuming a role normally played by a woman. It is also at this point that his mistress undergoes a curious change. As Bencheikh notes in his essay on the story, from this point on she assumes some of Azizah's characteristics; in particular, she becomes protective of Aziz. But like Azizah, she will also fail at protecting Aziz from his own gullibility.

After fourteen months of living like a "kept man," Aziz allows an old woman to lead him to a strange house where he is attacked and "raped" by another beautiful young woman. The young woman then compels him to marry her. At the same time, she reveals to him that his first lover is Bint Dalîlah or "Daughter of Delilah," apparently a notorious femme fatale. After feeble protest, Aziz agrees to the marriage. An unusual custom prevails at his wife's house; it is locked for all but one day of the year when a sortie is made to replenish provisions. So it is a year before Aziz can leave. When that day comes, he escapes and heads for his parents' house, but the way leads him past the garden of his first love, Bint Dalilah, and he cannot resist going inside. He foolishly tells Bint Dalilah where he has been, and, furious, she decides to kill him. But once again the verses of Azizah save him. Bint Dalilah contents herself with castrating him. Then she throws him out.

Aziz returns to his wife, but now she no longer wants him either, and so he goes home to his mother (his father has since died). There he bewails his folly in leaving Azizah and causing her death. His mother then gives him another embroidered piece of silk similar to the one he received from Bint Dalilah. It contains a letter from Azizah telling him that the woman who embroidered them is one Princess Dunya, whom Aziz one day may seek out. Why should he do so? In the Arabic, Azizah does not suggest a reason for Aziz to do so—though one could say that it is implicit in *The Thousand and One Nights* that when one finds a beautiful and desirable object, one then seeks its master/maker who is sure to also be beautiful and desirable. Mardrus, however, adds to Azizah's letter that he may seek her for consolation.

Seeing the two embroidered gazelles Taj al-Muluk falls in love with Dunya and taking Aziz with him he sets out to find her, and the story of "Taj al-Muluk and Princess Dunya" is then narrated. Only at the end of that story do we learn of Aziz's final destiny, that he becomes the prime minister of Taj al-Muluk.

Although in "Aziz and Azizah" it is not the wound but the embroidered handkerchief that calls forth narration, in the end Aziz's story, like those of the three qalandars and the scarred lady, is also the story of a wound that has resulted from the breaking of a prohibition. And as in those other stories, this final revelation does not dispel all the enigmas of the story for some readers. Gerhardt and Bencheikh, in particular, puzzle over Aziz's passive character, the pale father figure, the motivation for Bint Dalilah's evil intentions towards Aziz from the very beginning.[13]

As Bencheikh says, the story traces a double course: "The story always unfolds on two levels: Azizah looks only at Aziz, and Aziz has eyes only for the unknown girl [Bint Dalilah]."[14] There is a similarity here with the brief story previously mentioned, "Three Unhappy Lovers," in which a young woman loves a youth who loves a singing girl who, in turn, loves the young woman. There the circle is closed: they all die. Here the circle is not closed; Bint Dalilah is not in love with Azizah. Nor for that matter is she in love with Aziz. Rather, she seems bent on his destruction—at least at first—in which respect she is also rather like the singing girl in "The Unhappy Lovers" with her icy scorn for the young man. As we have seen, in that story the singing girl calls upon her lover to die: "Yes, if you really are a lover, die." But here the desire of the femme fatale does not close a circle; the different geometry leads to different ends, Azizah's death and Aziz's castration.

However, the "dual course" of the narrative is not solely the result of Azizah's unrequited love. There is another difference between Aziz and Azizah that is also involved in the "dual course": the difference between Azizah's knowledge and Aziz's ignorance, her ability to read and write the "signs of love" and his illiteracy with respect to those signs. This difference also explains Aziz's "strange" passivity and Azizah's activity; for these are simply the effects of this difference. We learn of this difference when Aziz describes for Azizah his first encounter with Bint Dalilah. The signs of love that Bint Dalilah uses are physical gestures that make various parts of the body distinct as signs. To be "read," they must be dissociated from her body and reconstituted as separate signs. In these gestures, which Azizah must interpret for him, Aziz encounters *le corps morcelé*, the fragmented body, here fragmented for the purpose of signification. Bencheikh speaks of how the "body is written" in the poem that Aziz receives from Bint Dalilah after their first meeting; in fact, the body is written also in the physical gestures that Bint Dalilah makes to Aziz, which he cannot understand.

This difference between Aziz and Azizah also explains the strange interlude between Azizah's death and Aziz's castration. After Azizah dies, Aziz, who gets over his cousin's death a little too quickly, plunges into his affair with Bint Dalilah. But now he has lost his protectoress and his "translator," so to speak, and he is treated first by Bint Dalilah, and then by his wife, as we might expect a Muslim wife to be treated by her husband. As Bencheikh says:

> Aziz plays exactly the role of a Muslim woman, married by command and without consent, faced with the alternative of that constraint or of a symbolic death, a social disappearance. Once the marriage is accepted, the woman is cloistered, maintained and serves exclusively as a sexual object.[15]

"What is lacking in this portrait," Bencheikh asks, "for it to represent exactly a type very widely spread in medieval and contemporary Arab society?"[16] Perhaps. Yet, it also seems possible that this portrait of marriage is sketched not by a surreptitious feminist but rather by an unreconstructed chauvinist who means to say something like, "You see! They would do the same thing to us if they could!"

Whatever the case may be, this much is clear: once Azizah has died, Aziz effectively plays the role of the woman in his relations with both Bint Dalilah and his wife. And he occupies this position until he is . . . castrated. At which point, when his physical appearance as a female becomes apparent even to him—"And I became like a woman" (1:604)—he actually becomes a man. This suggests that Azizah's death is also a form of castration for Aziz, since afterwards he occupies the position of the woman with respect to the symbolic order of marriage and male–female relations. Thus, in a sense, Aziz is castrated twice. But only after his second, real castration does he become a man with respect to the symbolic order. And only then, belatedly, does he learn to read "the signs of love." After this, in the story of Taj al-Muluk's pursuit of Princess Dunya that follows, Aziz is able to compose poetry and give advice to Taj al-Muluk, benefit of the knowledge he has gained through his castration. Only then does "the privileged signifier," the phallus, function for him. Only then, when he realizes that he lacks what the other wants, is he initiated into the symbolic order. For again, to follow the Lacanian reading of the oedipal crisis, it is the realization by the subject that he lacks what the other desires (for a child, that he lacks what the mother desires) that compels him to resort to symbolic means to understand his predicament. And it is only when he is really castrated that Aziz bewails the loss of his cousin. At which point, we may say, the death of his cousin Azizah comes to retrospectively signify for him his own castration.

The story of "Aziz and Azizah" unfolds within a strange "Amazonian" atmosphere. As Bencheikh says, Bint Dalilah and Aziz's wife act "according to the law of a community of women of which we know nothing save one trait which characterizes them: Women possess a truly 'virile' energy."[17] If we ask how women come by this "virile" Amazonian energy in "Aziz and Azizah," Aziz's fate tells us it must be due to some knowledge they possess by birthright. For while Aziz must be castrated to understand the signs of love, women, it seems, are born with this knowledge; by their birthright they know things that men must learn painfully and at considerable cost. Their advantage in this regard is seen at the very beginning; when the two cousins sleep together as children, Aziz is innocent of what "sleeping together" might one day mean, whereas Azizah already has a very good idea of what it will mean. Possession of this knowledge makes women seem a species apart from a hapless soul like Aziz—one cannot say from 'men' because apart from his dimly perceived father, Aziz is the only male in the story. After the wedding fiasco, his father is only mentioned once and makes one very brief appearance until, at story's end, we learn with Aziz that his father has in the meantime died. We do not even learn of his father's reaction to the wedding disaster from himself; it comes through Azizah instead. Women are indeed much more powerful than men in this story—no wonder men lock them up. Were it not for Aziz's mother, one could well say by the end of the story that "the only good woman is a dead woman." Azizah, that is.

That she dies an innocent, a "martyr to love," is clear. To consider whether Aziz's punishment fits his misdeed, we must consider what—apart from being a feckless disappointment—he does wrong.

The Law and the Sublime

Aziz, as noted, breaks a prohibition in the story, the prohibition of Bint Dalilah that he never look at or speak to another woman. On this account she would kill him, but for the talismanic protection of the words Azizah has bequeathed him: "Fidelity is fair but treachery is foul." So she settles for castration.

But this breach of what seems an extreme prohibition should not distract us from his other seemingly more serious misdeed, his failure to show up at his wedding. In view of which, it is rather ironic that Aziz should speak of keeping one's pledge, and one is tempted to say to him, "Fidelity is beautiful, but absentmindedness is a rotten shame." Bencheikh calls Aziz's "no-show" a transgression of "the will of moral, juridical and social authority."[18] Being lovesick and led on by an archtemptress, undisciplined Aziz cannot, perhaps, be held wholly responsible, but much more curious is the fact that he is not punished for his more serious transgression, but for his less serious one—for his situation with first Bint Dalilah and then his wife are what we call in our day "entrapment." If our astonishment is limited when we hear of the police practicing it, this does not mitigate for us the injustice of it. Aziz's castration is, on this account, another instance of what Hamori calls "the justice of structure," and "Aziz and Azizah" seems to pose the same sort of troubling question about the operation of the law that is posed by "The Porter" and "The Three Apples." As we have seen, Hamori poses that question in terms of "the indifference of the universe" to human justice, a view that was not unknown in medieval Islamic culture.

A note of Burton to an animal fable in the *Nights* is apposite here. The fable features a cat that provokes Burton to comment (and it didn't take much to provoke him) on the medieval philosophical school known as the *dahrî* or "materialist" school:

> This apparently needless cruelty of all the feline race is a strong weapon in the hand of the Eastern "Dahrî", who holds that the world is God and is governed by its own laws, in opposition to the religionists believing in a Personal Deity whom, moreover, they style the Merciful, the Compassionate etc. Some Christians have opined that cruelty came into the world with "original Sin"; but how do they account for the hideous waste of life and the fearful destructiveness of the fishes which certainly never learned anything from man? The mystery of the cruelty of things can be explained only by a Law without a Law-giver.[19]

This seems one possible cause of our disquiet with the conclusions of these stories, but I wonder if there is not still another aspect to it.

Here we should consider again the curious asymmetry noted earlier in "The Porter and the Three Ladies of Baghdad," namely, that while the three qalandars tell three stories, the three ladies only tell two. The so-called "shopper" (*al-khushkâshah*) has no story to tell, and in the final scene she is the lady that Harun himself marries—"wisely," Hamori adds. In other instances we find that where a character in one manuscript lacks a story to tell, another manuscript gives that same character a story; that is to say, someone recognizes the demands of a purely formal structure.[20] But that is not the case here. Why? Is the missing story of the third girl merely a missing eye transposed to another level?

In a different essay, Hamori speaks of "Qamar al-Zaman" as embodying an "antinomy." I would take that Kantian term as a cue to suggest another explanation of the disquieting effect of these stories. In Kant, the Sublime is distinguished from the Beautiful in that a beautiful object is apprehended as a whole, but those phenomena that strike us as sublime—powerful storms, towering mountains, and thundering cataracts are common examples—elude our ability to apprehend them as wholes:

> The feeling of the sublime is, therefore, at once a feeling of displeasure arising from the inadequacy of imagination in the aesthetic estimation of magnitude to attain to its estimation by reason, and a simultaneously awakened pleasure, arising from this very judgment of the inadequacy of the greatest faculty of sense being in accord with the ideas of reason, so far as the effort to attain to these is for us a law.[21]

Formless and purposeless chaos characterize our experience of the sublime, for as Slavoj Žižek says, the Kantian Sublime is "the failed synthesis of Beauty and Purpose . . . a negative intersection, to be sure, i.e., an intersection containing elements which are neither beautiful nor purposeful."[22] On this basis, Žižek correlates the difference in Kant between the ethical dimensions of the sublime and the beautiful with two conceptions of law in Lacan. One conception, Žižek says, is "law qua symbolic Ego-Ideal—i.e. law, in its pacifying function, law qua guarantee of the social pact. . . ." The other conception is "law in its superego dimension—i.e., law qua 'irrational' pressure, the force of culpabilitization totally incommensurable with our actual responsibility. . ."[23] Again, consider the ferocious, retributive reactions of the husbands in "The Three Apples" and "The Tale of the Scarred Lady." By this logic, then, the wound, the dismembered body, the scars of the flogging, and the empty eye sockets are sublime images of the Law insofar as they evoke the incommensurate relation between punishment and culpability. Indeed, in some versions the frame story itself offers the first instance of the law in its sublime aspect; for in these versions Shahriyar swears an oath to marry a virgin each night and have her put to death in the morning, and that oath is a law, incomprehensible and sublime, which henceforth binds him to act as he does.

Moreover, insofar as the stories depict the Law as something that is essentially inscrutable, they give substance to Žižek's critique of Althusser's "Ideological State Machine." Žižek takes Althusser to task for never explaining how the ideology is internalized in the subject, and proposes his own explanation; the external ideology "exercizes its force only insofar as it is experienced, in the unconscious economy of the subject, as a traumatic, senseless injunction." However, "this 'internalization,' by a structural necessity, never fully succeeds . . . there is always a residue, a leftover, a stain of traumatic irrationality and senselessness sticking to it . . . it is precisely this non-integrated surplus of senseless traumatism which confers on the Law its unconditional authority."[24]

Hence, Harun simply ignores the incommensurate relation of punishment and guilt in "The Three Apples" and "The Porter and the Three Ladies of Baghdad." He acts simply "to pacify." In Žižek's terms, he is the beautiful object that embodies the Law in its pacifying aspect, while in contrast, the scarred body, the dismembered corpse, the gaping eye socket are the sublime objects that embody the Law in its terrifying superego aspect. This perhaps is why Harun takes the lady with no story as his wife. For, as caliph, Harun represents Lacan's *nom-du-père*, the master signifier that has no meaning in itself but simply represents the subject's integration into the symbolic order of language (and therefore the law, whose prohibitions are alluded to in the punning similarity to *non-du-père*), a relation perhaps also seen in the "stories" that introduce Harun, Jaʿfar, and Masrur into the party as "merchants." For these stories, slight as they are, are nevertheless of a different order than the stories of the qalandars and the young ladies. They are lies. In the structure of "The Porter and the Three Ladies of Baghdad" the missing story is a negative expression of the content of the Law; the empty signifier marries the girl who has nothing to say.

The wound in these stories from *The Thousand and One Nights* is the physical expression of the Law in its sublime form, the Law as trauma.

8

Peut-on tuer avec des noyaux de dattes?

THE RECURRENT THEMES AND MOTIFS THAT HAVE PROVIDED THE BASES for preceding chapters suggest the importance of various forms of repetition, recurrence, and return in *The Thousand and One Nights*. Purposeful repetitions begin of course in the frame story itself, where Shahzaman marks for the reader the first and most important one when he observes his brother's wife have sex with a black slave even as his own wife did. And thereafter the reader can hardly fail to notice various kinds of recurrences and repetitions on all levels of the text, from small individual motifs (e.g., missing eyes), to precise phrases that recur, to the reworking of the same plot line (e.g., the second sheikh's story in "The Merchant and the Jinni" and the first girl's story in "The Porter and the Three Ladies of Baghdad" use the same plot). Certain of these repetitions reflect a major theme of the book: even as the two kings search for other examples of humiliated husbands to confirm their own experiences, in subsequent stories the search for similar examples to confirm one's own experience will remain one of the most common ways of introducing a new narrative in *The Thousand and One Nights*. A story is concluded, and someone asks, "Has anyone ever heard a more amazing story?" Yet, the story thus introduced often contains many elements in common with the story that preceded, and, ironically, part of what qualifies it as "more amazing yet" are the uncanny recurrences of events found in the preceding story. For as the "same" confirms one's experiences, a fortiori, if someone has experienced the "same" strange thing, the less strange is affirmed, while at the same time the recurrence is rendered all the more amazing. "The Hunchback," as we have seen, provides one of the most elaborate examples of this phenomenon.

Yet the question remains whether repetition per se has a significance in *The Thousand and One Nights*. Sandra Naddaf compares narrative repetition to the decorative form of arabesque.[1] This suggests that repetition in the book is, like arabesque, purely formal, but Naddaf does not leave it at that. She argues that the goal of both arabesque and narrative repetition is to create a counter-realist realm beyond temporality and naïve representationalism.

Rather than a spatial form such as arabesque, here we will consider various forms of repetition and return in the *Nights* in relation to another narrative form, the dream. We will argue that the various forms of repetition and return bear directly on the question of the unity of *The Thousand and One Nights*. Our examples of repetition and return come from the first story that Shahrazad tells, "The Merchant and the Jinni."

"The Merchant and the Jinni" is the story of a hapless merchant who inadvertently kills the son of a jinni, and how his life is then ransomed by the stories that three sheikhs tell the jinni.[2] Indeed, the episode in which the merchant kills the jinni's son gives us warrant—were any needed—for comparison with a dream on account of its enigmatic quality, its strange juxtaposition of seemingly unrelated elements.

While on a trip the merchant sits down beneath a tree and begins to eat some bread and dates. When he finishes eating a date he throws the pit away, and suddenly a towering jinni confronts him and says he is going to kill him as he has killed his son (!). The merchant begs for a year's reprieve in order to settle his affairs, and the jinni grants this. A year later, having made provisions for his family, the merchant returns, as promised, to the same place to await his death. There, one by one, the three sheikhs come upon him and ask him why he is sitting in such a place, a "refuge of the jinn," as they call it (1:11).

By the innocent act of casting aside a date pit, the mundane world is invaded by death, the death of the jinni's son, and for the merchant, the imminent prospect of his own death. And what Freud says of the dream holds here too: "even if it is quite coherent . . . it confronts our mental life as something alien, for whose origin one cannot in anyway account" (*SE*, 7:160).

Freud explained dream-narrative by means of two basic mechanisms, condensation and displacement. He would extend their use later to explain not only dream-work, but also jokes and "the psychopathologies of everyday life"—forgetting, "slips of the tongue," and so forth. In every instance they are *intertextual* concepts, and we will use them to show how, in the story of "The Merchant and the Jinni," numerous other figures and pieces of narratives—some well-known, some rather more obscure—are "condensed" and "displaced."

The setting of the orgy in the frame story furnishes the first example. The author tells us that the orgy takes place in a garden with a tree in the middle. Beckoned by the queen, the black slave climbs down from the tree to couple with her. Later in the story, the two kings by the seashore are said to be in a meadow and they take refuge in a tree—from which they will climb down to couple with the kidnapped young woman. "The Merchant and the Jinni" begins with the merchant sitting down beneath a tree, and when he returns on the first day of the new year to suffer his fate, the writer adds "he traveled until he arrived at that *garden*" (*al-bustân*, 1:11). Hence, in this *garden* and this *tree* are condensed the gardens and the trees that have figured twice in the frame story; first as the scene of the scandal of Shahriyar's wife and the black slave, and second, as the place where Shahriyar and his brother Shahzaman hide from the jinni in a tree in a meadow (*marjah*) with a spring, and then have sex with the kidnapped young woman. Now, those gardens and trees inevitably recall the garden and tree in Genesis, and insofar as a third trauma occurs in this locale, the garden and the tree of Eden are also condensed in this tree and this garden. Here and in the frame story, as in Genesis 2:7–9, the tree in the garden marks a primal scene, a place where an originary violation occurs.

The question put to the merchant by the first sheikh and repeated by the second—"Why are you sitting here in this place which is a refuge of the jinn?"—also raises the notion of "return" here. The word "refuge" translates the Arabic word *ma'wâ*. The verbal form of the root *'awâ* means "to return" to a place such as one's house. The word *ma'wâ* in the phrase *ma'wâ 'l-jânn* is, in Arabic morphology, a noun form that designates the place where the action of the verb takes place. Hence, *ma'wâ* tells us that the location of the first episode in Shahrazad's first story is a "place to which one returns." What is more, the phrase *ma'wâ 'l-jânn* may also allude to another garden through this one, for it may involve a pun in inverted form on *jannat al-ma'wâ*, or "the garden of refuge," the place said to be "the paradise to which repair the souls of martyrs."[3]

With the arrival of the three sheikhs more repetitions accumulate; as we have seen, they repeat each other's words, and each sheikh inexplicably leads an animal or two on a rope. When the jinni arrives, each sheikh in his turn proposes to tell him a story that, if it pleases him, will win for the sheikh the right to one-third of the merchant's blood, which again brings death into play as a stake in a wager involving narration—as in the case of Shahrazad. The jinni agrees, and each sheikh tells a story haunted by the return of numerous other familiar plots and characters.

The first sheikh tells him that the gazelle he leads on a rope is, in fact, his wife: "This gazelle is my cousin, my own flesh and blood. I married her when she was young . . ." (1:12). The condensations and displacements of the first sheikh's story also involve people and events found in Genesis.

His story goes as follows: When, after thirty years of marriage, his wife has still not given him a son, the sheikh takes a mistress. Soon enough the mistress gives birth to a son. While the sheikh is away, the wife casts spells on the mistress and the son, turning the mistress into a cow and the son into a calf. When her husband returns, his wife tells him that the mistress has died and the son has run away. She then persuades him to have his herdsman slaughter the cow/mistress for a feast day, despite the husband's misgivings about the cow's mysterious behavior. He agrees, but this turns out to be a bad decision, for despite her healthy appearance, the cow mysteriously yields nothing but skin and bones. Thus, when his wife tries to convince him to kill the calf/son, the sheikh resists. Instead he tells his herdsman to take the calf home. The latter's daughter is also skilled in magic and sorcery. When she sees the calf, she hides her face, laughs, and then cries. She tells her father that the calf is his master's son whom the wife has bewitched. That was why she laughed. She cried because the wife has connived to get the mistress slaughtered. The herdsman takes his daughter to the sheikh, and the girl proposes to remove the spell, if she can take the son for her husband and be allowed to cast a spell on the wife. The sheikh agrees. The herdsman's daughter marries his son and turns his wife into a gazelle. Some years pass. The sheikh's daughter-in-law dies and then his son wanders off into a foreign land. The sheikh leaves home to find him and, in the course of his search for his son, he comes upon the merchant.

The jinni says this is a most amazing story and agrees to give the sheikh the right to one-third of the merchant's blood.

A glance at the story of Abraham and Sarah and Hagar reveals the condensations and displacements of the first sheikh's story. Two versions of the story concern us: the biblical version, told in Genesis, chapters 16–23, and its revision within the Islamic tradition as part of the so-called "stories of the prophets."

In Genesis we learn that when Sarah bears no children, Abraham takes her Egyptian slave Hagar as a concubine and she becomes pregnant. This arouses enmity between Sarah and Hagar, and Abraham tells Sarah to do as she wishes with Hagar. Sarah chases her slave off into the desert, where she is saved by an angel, who tells her that she shall bear a son named Ishmael. Next we learn that circumcision is established as the sign of the covenant between

God and Abraham. In the same passage we also learn that Sarah will bear a son named Isaac who, instead of Ishmael, will be heir to God's covenant—surely someone has noted the coincidence that in the same passage in which he gives up his son, Abraham also gives up his foreskin. Two intervening chapters, 19 and 20, relate the destruction of Sodom and Gomorrah and Abraham's "lapse" at Gerar in which, fearing for his life, he allows another man to take Sarah, telling him she is only his sister. Then, in chapter 21, Isaac is conceived and born, and Sarah prevails upon Abraham to send Hagar and Ishmael packing. They wander off into the wilderness of Paran, where Ishmael becomes father of the Arabs in a kind of biblical footnote, while Isaac becomes the father of the Jews.

Readers unfamiliar with the Islamic tradition may not realize the importance of Abraham in that tradition in the context of a polemic with Judaism. As we have seen, the story of Abraham in Genesis already represented him as the common father of both the Jews and the Arabs, the former through his son Isaac by Sarah and the latter through Ishmael by his concubine Hagar. But early Muslims did not accept this story as it is told in the Bible. Various Muslim traditions elaborate on the Genesis story, revising it and "correcting" it in crucial ways. Abraham does not send Hagar and Ishmael away to placate his wife, but follows them into Arabia, where he founds the sanctuary at Mecca. Also, it is not Isaac but Ishmael whom Abraham is called upon to sacrifice. At length he returns to resume his biblical tasks. But the crucial point is made, as Michael Cook puts it: "they endow Arabia and the Arabs with an honoured place in monotheist history, and one genealogically independent of the Jews and Christians."[4]

In other words, through the paternity of Abraham, Islam makes a claim to *displace* Judaism. Medieval Muslim apologists exploited the fact that Abraham (Ibrâhîm in the Arabic) was not a Jew—there were no "Jews" yet—but only a Semitic monotheist in order to make the bold claim that he was, therefore, the first Muslim (!), and furthermore that the son that he was called upon to sacrifice was not Isaac (Ishâq), but Ishmael (Ismâʿîl). All of these facts, they claim, were distorted in a corrupt Torah, which Muhammad was sent to straighten out once and for all. The great sin of the Jews (and the Christians) is their refusal to set aside their corrupt scriptures and accept the final edition of monotheism with the "corrections" that Muhammad delivered.

If we now return to "The First Sheikh" we can see a number of similarities between it and the story of Abraham in Genesis 16–22. The wife, like Sarah, does not give birth to a son, and so the sheikh, like Abraham, takes a mistress who does bear a son for him, like Hagar. The sheikh's son is almost sacrificed on what the text calls *ʿîd Allâh al-akbar*. This we must take to be *al-ʿîd al-kabîr*, the tenth day of the month of *Dhû 'l-ḥijjah*, a feast that marks the end of the pilgrimage season, and that also, more importantly, commemorates the sacrifice of Abraham—the near-sacrifice of his son, that is. These and other links we can describe in terms of the processes of condensation and displacement. As with dream-work, we can say that as the figure of Abraham is condensed in the first sheikh, so too is Ishmael condensed in the son of the concubine. Knowing this much, it is no surprise that the story follows the story line of the medieval Muslim tradition about Abraham: it is the son of the concubine—that is, Hagar's son Ishmael—who is almost sacrificed, while the figure of Isaac is wholly absent.

Yet this is not all, for as we have seen the story's relation to Genesis 16–22 is mediated by the Islamic revision of that story. Hence, insofar as the medieval Muslim version of the story looms as well, the sheikh condenses both biblical Abraham and Muslim Ibrahim. And the same goes for his wife and the biblical and Muslim figures of Sarah, and the concubine and the son and Hagar and Ishmael/Ismaʿil. A glance at one of the most important dreams in *The Interpretation of Dreams*, the dream of "Irma's Injection," shows the same sort of condensations. In the dream figure of Irma, Freud identifies, besides Irma herself, at least four other figures: a child he had examined in a neurological department, a woman acquaintance of Freud (whom he wished to psychoanalyze), one of his daughters, and his wife. As he writes of Irma: "None of these figures whom I lighted upon by following up 'Irma' appeared in the dream in bodily shape. They were concealed behind the dream figure of 'Irma' " (*SE*, 4:293).

The story of the first sheikh also involves a number of displacements that relate to both the biblical and the Islamic tales. The sacrifice is not demanded by God but by the jealous wife—by "Sarah," we might say—while the departure of the mistress's son is not accomplished by the wife but is only weakly motivated by the death of his wife, the herdsman's daughter. Finally, we might note again the fate of Isaac/Ishaq. Biblical Isaac is, from the Muslim standpoint, wittily ejected from the tale, repressed, we might say—his expulsion from the text being a displacement of sorts of the expulsion of Ishmael in the "corrupt" biblical version.

One might think that the first sheikh's story alludes to the story in Genesis only through the medium of the Islamic version, but the conclusion, I think, suggests otherwise. In the version Shahrazad tells, "Sarah" is frustrated in her attempt to get rid of the son of the mistress—though not of the mistress, let us note. Yet the son still wanders off at story's end. Why? As a comic tale, one might expect the story to end with the marriage of the herdsman's daughter to the son and the transformation of the wife into a gazelle. But the story goes on to narrate the death of the daughter-in-law and the subsequent departure of the son who wanders off into a foreign land, India (*bilâd al-Hind*). This serves, as I said, to weakly motivate the sheikh's trip that will bring him to the scene of the merchant and the jinni. But it is hardly necessary for that purpose; he could very well have simply departed on a business trip again, as he did the time his wife bewitched the mistress and the son. However, the story tells us that the sheikh *searches* for his son, and a glance at the biblical story suggests why the story insists upon this point.

When Sarah sees Isaac and Ishmael playing together one day, she says to Abraham, "Cast out this slave woman with her son; for the son of this slave woman shall not be heir with my son Isaac" (Genesis 21:10). Abraham hesitates, but God insists that he get rid of them. He leaves them in the desert, and there they almost die of thirst before an angel of God shows them a well. The last we hear of Ishmael, he wanders off to the wilderness of Paran and takes a wife from the land of Egypt. There he becomes the ancestor of the Arabs. And we hear no more of him until the rise of Islam—the return of the repressed, one might say. Yet, by including this last episode, which at first glance might seem superfluous in the Arabic story, the biblical story is revised—from a Muslim point of view we might even say it is "improved." While in the Hebrew Bible, Abraham reluctantly writes off Ishmael, in the Arabic revised version, we may say that Ibrahim now goes in search of Isma'il. Thus, it seems the story works from both versions—or, to put it another way, the condensations of both biblical Abraham and Islamic Ibrahim into the first sheikh entail a further narrative displacement since those two stories have different and incompatible endings. If this is right, the wandering off of the sheikh's son lingers as a remnant of the biblical story but is also put to work as motivation for the sheikh's trip.

There is, finally, one more detail that shows the presence of Abraham. The detail, however, concerns not the first sheikh but the merchant. The latter obtains his reprieve by insisting that he must return home to pay his debts; and his sense of integrity, bespoken by this, is underscored when he keeps his promise to return and submit to his death. These things impress both the jinni and the sheikhs. Qur'an 53:36 mentions Abraham in this way: "Abraham who upheld his obligations" (*Ibrâhîm alladhî waffâ*). Thus, Abraham is, so to speak, overdetermined here; he looms behind both the first sheikh and the merchant.

In any event, by uncovering this "dream-work" in the form of the biblical and Islamic elements condensed and displaced in the story of "The First Sheikh," we may discern why "The Merchant and the Jinni" is the first story that Shahrazad tells.[5] Since the frame story is derived from Indian and Persian material (as Cosquin showed a century ago), the immediate introduction of a story that is, on one level at least, an Arab-Muslim revision of Hebrew-Jewish material may be a way of asserting the identity of the book. The stories promise to reenact the manner in which Islamic culture borrows from all of these cultures to create a new cultural synthesis.

It should be noted too that these successive displacements of the plot are accompanied by another process, a displacement from scripture to fiction, from sacred writing to secular entertainment. For through its comic transformation of the biblical story, the Arabic story does not thereby seek to replace the former à la Qur'an, but to make something else of it. Indeed, the story works on the Muslim legend of Abraham in the same way, even if it does not revise it as thoroughly as it does the biblical version. On which point, those who know the marginalized place of *The Thousand and One Nights* in both medieval Islam and in the modern Arab world may find an irony in the way that this book, rather like Ishmael in the Bible, has remained an outcast from the literary tradition that gave birth to it.

The Second and Third Sheikhs

When the first sheikh has finished his tale, the second sheikh steps forward and strikes a similar deal with the jinni but with the condition that his story must be more amazing yet. Similar sorts of condensations and displacements involving other texts also figure in the stories of the other two sheikhs, and a brief discussion is in order before returning to the story of the merchant and the jinni.

The second sheikh, a successful merchant, is envied and betrayed by his two older brothers, who are financial failures. When the second sheikh takes a beautiful wife while on a voyage of trade, the two brothers throw him and his wife overboard. The wife turns out, however, to be a jinniyah (a female jinni, that is, and a good Muslim also), and she saves the younger brother and punishes the two older brothers by having them changed into dogs. The story shares the basic plot of a younger sibling who is envied and betrayed by older siblings with a good number of other stories in *The Thousand and One Nights*, notably the stories of "The First Lady" in "The Porter and the Three Ladies of Baghdad," "Abdallah ibn Fadil," "Judar and His Brothers," and "Ahmad and Peri Banou." The Cinderella story of two jealous older sisters and their younger sister is, as Stith Thompson says, "one of the most popular of oral tales, being distributed over nearly the whole world."[6] The story of Joseph and his brothers in the Old Testament, excepting the number of brothers, is of course based on the same plot, and since, as we have seen, that story looms in the frame story, it may also figure as palimpsest here—though except for the brothers' trying to get rid of their sibling while on a trip, no other specific elements seem to be present here.

The third sheikh begins his story by pointing to the mule: "That is my wife," he tells the jinni. In his story, the third sheikh comes home from a business trip and finds his wife in bed with a black slave. She quickly changes her husband into a dog and chases him out of the house. He ends up in a butcher shop, where the butcher's daughter recognizes him for a man and frees him from the spell. Then she gives him a magic potion, which he uses to change his wife into a mule. Again there is the repetition of the man leading the "ensorcelled" person in the form of an animal, and, as in "The First Sheikh," there is the motif of the daughter breaking the spell. But much more importantly, there is the repetition of the central event of the frame story, the discovery of the wife and her lover, the black slave. What is more, it is told to Shahriyar who, we thereby assume, feels the effect also. Comparison of this story with the second sheikh's story suggests that a distinction must be kept in mind. The various repetitions, doublings, and condensations in the *Nights* can function on two planes; sometimes the repetitions and doublings may exist merely for the reader—as the modern reader can see the Cinderella plot in the second sheikh's story—but at other times the repetitions may also be noted by a character within the text. Indeed, comparison of the first episode in "The Merchant and the Jinni" with yet another story in Genesis will show how condensations and displacements can arise for the reader quite apart from any allusive intention on the storyteller's part.

Date Pits

The beginning is one of my favorite episodes in *The Thousand and One Nights*:

> So he sat down beneath a tree and took a piece of bread and a date from his leather sack. He ate the bread and the date, and when he was finished eating the date, he threw the pit away. Then all of a sudden there appeared a towering jinni, brandishing a sword. Advancing toward the merchant, he said, "Stand up so that I can kill you as you have killed my son!" (1:10)

Many of the virtues of narrative style in *The Thousand and One Nights* as a whole are apparent in this brief and startling event. Foremost here is the swift and effortless transition in mood. If a story generally begins with the disruption of the routine by something out of the ordinary, here and throughout the *Nights* the narrator excels at the sudden disruption of the routine with the most startling sorts of events.[7] In the frame story it is from Shahzaman's gloom to the proto-Sadean orgy; here it is from eating a snack to death. But that is not all. The transformation also contrives to join many other disparate elements in it; the mundane (bread crusts, date pits) is linked to the fantastic (a towering jinni), and comedy and terror are brought together, fused in such a way that one cannot really separate them. The words of the jinni create for the reader a sense of wonder (though perhaps not fear) similar to that of the merchant. How on earth, one wonders, did this poor man kill the jinni's son? Which, of course, is just what the merchant asks, and the jinni's reply is superb: "When you ate the date and threw the pit, it entered my son's chest. Just like that! One moment he was walking, and then he died instantly!" The jinni's reply is superb not because it is such a fine answer, for it is only an answer to the merchant's question in the most literal sense; it explains—sort of—how the jinni's son died. It is superb because, precisely insofar as it fails as explanation beyond a very limited, literal reach, it creates yet more questions, or better, it creates an enigma. The jinni's answer brings into relation two events and two realms whose relation to one another is incommensurable. That the jinni in his visible form should be so huge, towering over him as he does, and yet when he was invisible, that he and his son might be so small that, presumably, a date pit should kill one of them as though it were a huge boulder; that one and the same creature is now invisible, now visible, now tiny, now enormous and, of course, now alive, now dead—and, as with life and death, that there should be no intermediate stage; and that all these transformations are caused by nothing more than the casting of a date pit—it is uncanny, and yet strangely pathetic and funny. The comedy results, of course, mainly from the disproportionate relations between cause and effect. This impossible, enigmatic event puzzled more than one scholar. It provoked the nineteenth-century scholar Victor Chauvin to wonder in a perplexed footnote, "*Peut-on tuer avec des noyaux de dattes?*" [8] And D. B. MacDonald tried to explain the episode in terms of Muslim beliefs that jinn were beings made of fire covered with a thin skin, and that a missile such as a date stone, if well aimed—or if it is merely a lucky hit—could pierce a jinni's skin, causing him to flare up and burn to a cinder.[9]

But to answer Chauvin we shall read the episode as a travesty of another story with a different sort of "date" in it. The second story here is another biblical story, but one less well-known than the stories of Abraham and Joseph. The exercise will show even more clearly how a story in the *Nights* can evoke for the reader another story on account of chance similarities, similarities that can be understood in terms of condensation and displacement. In other words, this last example of dream-work is likely my own invention, yet by means of it the story of "The Merchant and the Jinni" will show in relation to the biblical tale some of the same "rebus"-like elements of which Freud speaks in *The Interpretation of Dreams*. At the very least the exercise will show us how a story in the *Nights* may summon stories and plots besides those that its writer consciously used.

The story is that of Judah and his sons, Er, Onan, and Shelah, and the girl named Tamar. A certain similarity of plot structure will be seen if we consider the first ten verses of Genesis 38:

> 1: It happened at that time that Judah went down from his brothers, and turned in to a certain Adullamite, whose name was Hirah. 2: There Judah saw the daughter of a certain Canaanite whose name was Shua; he married her and went into her. 3: And she conceived and bore a son, and he called his name Er. 4: Again she conceived and bore a son, and she called his name Onan. 5: Yet again she bore a son, and she called his name Shelah. She was in Chezib when she bore him. 6: And Judah took a wife for Er his first-born, and her name was Tamar. 7: But Er, Judah's first-born, was wicked in the sight of the Lord and the Lord slew him. 8: Then Judah said to Onan, "Go and perform the duty of the brother-in-law to her, and raise up offspring for your brother." 9: But Onan knew that the offspring would not be his; so when he went in to his brother's wife he spilled the semen on the ground, lest he should give offspring to his brother. 10: And what he did was displeasing in the sight of the Lord, and he slew him also.[10]

These verses are the prologue to the story of Judah and Tamar. As Von Rad writes in his commentary, the verses give "the reader the most necessary facts in a rather dry enumeration and without particular vividness . . . the narrator dispenses with all causes and motivations in this section and limits himself to giving the bare facts."[11] Robert Alter ties this brief story to the recurrent theme in Genesis that the first-born are "losers."[12] The verses do not tell us what Er did, but in the *midrash* we are told that God killed him "because he ploughed on roofs"—that is, he practiced anal intercourse.[13] Onan's sin is explicit, however. He refuses his duty under the institution of levirate marriage wherein the brother-in-law must marry the widow. The purpose, as Von Rad explains, is that "the son begotten by the brother is then considered the son and heir of the deceased man, 'that his name may not be blotted out of Israel' (Deuteronomy 25:6). But the practice has also been explained in the interest of preserving property."[14] As we all know, poor Onan's punishment is twofold. First, he suffers the death penalty, and second—and what is worse, for, after all, he would have died anyway—he suffers the ignominy of his name becoming synonymous with an abominable practice he doesn't even commit.

Tamar, the name of Er's wife, is of course the Hebrew cognate of the Arabic word *tamrah*, and has the same meaning in Hebrew, "date-palm" or simply "date." And let us now say that the merchant, like Onan, has taken the seed out of Tamar and thrown it on the ground, and even as Onan thus "slays Er's son," so too the merchant slays the jinni's son. So, is the Arabic story a conscious revision of the biblical story as "The First Sheikh" is a conscious revision of the Abraham story?

It seems not. For unlike the story of Abraham, which was central in medieval Islamic culture, and which certainly looms behind the story of "The First Sheikh," the story of Judah and his sons and Tamar does not seem to be known in medieval Islam—yet the striking correspondence remains.[15] It has two bases. On the one hand, a fundamental resemblance exists because both episodes are variants of the same plot; both the merchant and Onan "kill" another's son and are sentenced to die for this by a supernatural being. But the chance and uncanny resemblance between the two episodes results from more than simply the shared "plot"; in considerable measure it derives from the role of the cognate *tamrah* in both narratives. It is a kind of "involuntary repetition." It seems mere chance, and yet the fortuitous link established by the word suggests how the story of the merchant could have been written—and can be read—as a comic revision of the Onan-Tamar story, as a *joke*, that is. Hence, the reading here is a creative one, and the reading of the hypothetical joke's structure in terms of condensation and displacement will reveal other thematic links between the two stories. In particular it will show a similarity between Tamar and the date that surpasses the coincidence of the cognate.

While the two episodes share a plot situation, the comic transformation of our hypothesized travesty depends on a piece of wordplay. *Tamrah,* a word that comes to be a feminine name because of its auspicious meaning as a staple fruit in the Near East, would be the linchpin that holds it all together. Its role here matches numerous examples cited by Freud in his chapter on joke techniques under the rubric of words with a "double-meaning." As I have noted before, such transformations are accomplished elsewhere in medieval Arabic stories and give some warrant to our procedure here.[16] Such transformations impart to the stories that rebus-like aspect that Freud describes in dreams and which proceeds from what Lacan calls the "materiality of the signifier."

Once the transformation of Tamar to *tamrah* is accomplished, those of the other biblical figures would be equally clear in our comic version. Even as the date *condenses* Tamar the biblical heroine, the merchant condenses the figure of Onan, while the jinni obviously condenses that of Er and the Lord. However, I would argue that Judah, the father, is also condensed in the jinni. Why? A closer look at the biblical version reveals another similarity between the two tales. As Von Rad notes, it seems clear that after the death of his first-born Er and his second-born Onan, Judah's reluctance to marry his last son Shelah to Tamar results from his suspicion that Tamar bears some sort of curse; for, in a sense, it is as though Tamar has killed his sons. In which case Judah is also akin to the figure of the jinni insofar as the *tamrah* has killed the latter's son. More importantly, the reduction of Tamar to an object, to *tamrah* in the Arabic story, brings out something of fundamental importance in the biblical story. The transformation, based on the similarity of their roles in the plot and on the name they happen to share, does not thereby make an object of Tamar. Tamar is already an object no less than the date is; for they are both objects possessed by men. As Von Rad says, the point of levirate marriage is that "the wife [of the deceased] is also a capital asset. . . ."[17] Or as Lacan puts it: "The fact that the woman is thus bound up in an order of exchange in which she is object is really what accounts for the fundamentally conflictual character, I wouldn't say without remedy, of her position—the symbolic order literally subdues her, transcends her" (*S,* 2:262). Thus, our travesty points to the problematic position of the woman in all these narratives, in the Bible, in *The Thousand and One Nights*—and, indeed, in marriage in general. For the purpose of marriage, the woman is exchanged like an object. But—she is an object who also happens to be a subject, that is, a creature that speaks. And all of Judah's subsequent difficulties follow from the fact that she speaks, that she can invoke the law to Judah, who owes something for her, a son-in-law to Tamar's father. Judah would like to forget the whole thing, but his "date" speaks.Tamar is thus an object of exchange no less than the *tamrah* is one. The transformation simply strips her of her subjectivity. Yet, we should note that although the *tamrah* in the Arabic story does not speak, it still has its effect. The symbolic effect of Tamar, the claim of the law, becomes in our travesty a real effect, the crushing effect of the date pit—which we may take as a strangely appropriate metaphor for the weight of the law.

The nineteenth-century Orientalist Edward Lane tried to find the merchant culpable on this account, an opinion Lane based on the custom of nineteenth-century Egyptian peasants, saying "*Dastûr!*" before they tossed date pits away—*dastur,* in familiar Egyptian usage, meaning "permission."[18] Hence, the merchant's omission of this word makes him guilty in Lane's view. Of course, the story is probably half a millennium older, and although traditions tell us of Muhammad throwing date pits, they make no mention of him uttering the word *dastur* or any other precautionary formula.[19] I think it is more profitable to reflect on the merchant's plight from a different angle, that aspect of the law emphasized in the last chapter, law as unappeasable superego, Žižek's "law qua 'irrational' pressure, the force of culpabilitization totally incommensurable with our actual responsibility . . ."[20]

These similarities concern only the episode of Onan and Tamar, of course, and are not meant to efface the differences between "The Merchant and the Jinni" and the larger story of Judah and Tamar in Genesis 38. In the biblical story of Tamar, competing claims under the law are weighed and Judah is found to have sinned more; in "The Merchant and the Jinni," the emphasis falls on setting aside the claims of the law, at least *lex talionis*. And here a final repetition must be emphasized. Even as Shahrazad shows her willingness to submit to death by marrying King Shahriyar (and so rejects the role of slave), so too the merchant has shown his willingness to submit to death. And even as the jinni shows himself willing to set aside revenge and accept the ransom of narration, so, in the case of one bent on a revenge that exceeds the law, a fortiori.

The dreamlike effect of the various sorts of repetitions and recurrences is strengthened by at least one other characteristic of the *Nights*: the anachronisms that abound in the book from the very first story. The kings Shahriyar and Shahzaman are said to be Sasanian monarchs, but the Sasanian dynasty was pre-Islamic, brought down in the Islamic conquests. Yet Shahrazad later in the tale says that she must save the daughters of the Muslims. And soon enough she is telling Shahriyar stories about Harun al-Rashid and Ja'far the Barmecid, Harun being the fifth of the Abbasid caliphs, the second great Islamic dynasty. And some of the latest additions to the book will introduce tobacco and gunpowder. The numerous anachronisms remind us of the way our dreams falsify time to bring forth another sort of truth: that of the unconscious, where, as Freud insists, there is no time.

The repetitions and anachronisms together give a unique sort of unity to the book, binding together thematically the otherwise disparate narratives that Shahrazad recounts. The uniqueness can be seen by comparing *The Thousand and One Nights* with other collections of stories from Europe and the medieval Arab Islamic world. Most such collections avoid the impression of total randomness by sorting the stories according to various thematic and exemplary rubrics. *The Decameron* offers a notable example in European literature, and a collection like *Happiness after Hardship* by Tanukhi offers a similar method of coping with disparate narratives in medieval Arabic literature. Yet *The Thousand and One Nights* succeeds in holding together its disparate tales without any such device. Perhaps the most important means of doing so is through the repetitions that proliferate in the text in a dreamlike way. A more overtly didactic mode of organization is avoided, yet unity is not thereby sacrificed. The unity of *The Thousand and One Nights* is like the fragile unity of a dream whose various threads, with all their condensed and displaced meanings, threaten to unravel in a thousand and one different directions.

9

The Destroyer of Delights

> "Heav'n but the Vision of fulfill'd Desire,
> And Hell the Shadow of a Soul on Fire,
>   Cast on the Darkness into which Ourselves
> So late emerg'd, shall so soon expire."
> —Edward Fitzgerald, *The Rubaiyat of Omar Khayyam*

SHAHRAZAD CONCLUDES HER LAST STORY, "MAʿRÛF THE COBBLER," with a sentence the reader has already encountered:

> "And they lived the most comfortable of lives; times were serene and joys were sweet until there came to them the destroyer of delights and the separator of societies, the wrecker of homes and dwellings, the maker of orphans. Glory be to the living one who never dies, whose hands hold the reins of power of kingship and dominion."
>
> (*wa-aqâmû muddah fî arghad ʿaysh wa ṣafat lahum al-awqât wa ṭâbat lahum al-masarrât ilâ an atâhum hâdim al-ladhdhât wa mufarriq al-jamâʿât wa mukharrib al-diyâr al-ʿâmirât wa muyattim al-banîn wa ʾl-banât fa-subḥâna ʾl-ḥayy alladhî lâ yamût wa bi-yadihi maqâlîd al-mulk wa ʾl-malakût*)

This version, with its mention of orphans and of kingship and dominion, seems tailored to the epilogue, for these things would seem to be key issues in understanding Shahriyar's transformation there after one thousand and one nights of narrative as it stands in the Second Calcutta text. Shahriyar is, after all, a king, one who marries a woman every night and kills her in the morning so as to be certain that no one else enjoys her sexual favors. A king in Arabic is a *malik,* a word that derives from the root *m-l-k,* whose fundamental meaning is "to possess." The verbal noun *mulk* mentioned in the coda sentence means "dominion, control," and Shahriyar's story is very much a story about the control of one's good. For him the experience of this *detour,* what his brother shows and tells him, is that the object of desire betrays one in the most painful and humiliating way. Shahriyar's solution has been to eliminate the detour—and hence the narrative—and to proceed immediately from the "they lived happily" in the coda sentence to death. In this, Shahriyar's crisis exemplifies Lacan's reading of Freud, that subject and object come into being through a conflict. For which reason, the object is from the very beginning not a simple "good" but a traumatic "thing" associated with the subject's constitutive alienation, and, hence, the true test of possession is the ability to deny others the enjoyment of the object.

How does the epilogue resolve these matters? In mundane terms, the solution is marriage. But Shahriyar has been married before—quite a few times, as a matter of fact—so how does this marriage differ? For one thousand and one nights Shahrazad, through narration, suspends Shahriyar's practice of marriage and murder. Then, on the one thousand and first night, when she finishes the story of "Maʿruf the Cobbler," we learn that she has given birth to three sons. This is a bit of a surprise. Her pregnancies and births have not interrupted her storytelling, and if Shahriyar noticed, the narrator has neglected to mention it until this moment. It might be argued this revelation could be taken as yet another dreamlike element, akin to those sudden transformations in dreams whereby one place suddenly becomes another, or one person suddenly metamorphoses into another—though some of my readers, at this point, may think it is an all-purpose justification for all manner of non sequiturs. Nevertheless, such transformations, as we know, do not unduly disturb the dreamer. It is only the waking subject who muses on the remarkable turn of events.

In any case, with this Shahrazad has their three children brought forth, and then she asks Shahriyar for a favor on their behalf. She asks him to lift the sentence of death from her as a favor to his own children. "For," as she says, "if you kill me, they shall be motherless, and they will find no other woman to raise them well." And now we can see how the version of the coda sentence at the end of "Maʿruf" with its mention of orphans seems designed to prepare the way for this scene. And Shahriyar agrees to this, although he says a curious thing: "By God, Shahrazad, I had already pardoned you [*qad ʿafawtuʿanki*] before these children arrived, because I found you chaste and pure, noble and pious. God bless you and your father and mother and your whole family, root and branch. I swear before God that I free you from anything that might harm you." But what sin has Shahrazad committed? Nothing—though if this occurs to anyone present, he keeps quiet, presumably on the grounds that "all's well that ends well."

But what does Shahriyar's pardon mean at this point in the proceedings for us? I would say it means that he accepts her as ultimately "beyond" his *mulk*, insofar as the object of desire remains other, and thus defies his sovereignty and possession. And this is why this version of the coda sentence mentions *mulk* and *malakut*, so as to point towards the epilogue's resolution. For Shahriyar in all his previous "marriages" has refused to accept any limit to his desire—which means they were not truly marriages. When Shahriyar "forgives" Shahrazad it means he accepts her lock, stock, and barrel, and submits his desire to the Law—and it is only then that he is truly married. He accepts that even his *mulk* is not truly "his," but exists *outside* him, beyond him, as the coda sentence says, beyond life and pleasure—in death. In other words, Shahrazad has made Shahriyar see the value of the detour—confirmed by the presence before him of his three sons—without denying its risks and its limits.

Nevertheless this conclusion does disappoint certain readers. Grotzfeld speaks of the conclusions of the ZER manuscripts—all similar to that of the Second Calcutta—as "artless, simple or poor."[1] And, indeed, in other manuscripts he found other conclusions, of which at least one version is intriguing enough to merit our attention here. In this version, the last story Shahrazad tells is a slightly disguised form of Shahriyar's own story.[2] Burton translates it in his *Supplemental Nights* and the key passage is of interest here:

> On the fifth night she told him anecdotes of Kings and Wazirs and Notables. Brief, she ceased not to entertain him many days and nights, while the king still said to himself, "Whenas I shall have heard the end of the tale, I will do her die," and the people redoubled their marvel and admiration. Also the folk of the circuits and cities heard of this thing, to wit, that the king had turned from his custom [of slaying his wives] and from that which he had imposed upon himself and had renounced his heresy, wherefor they rejoiced and the lieges returned to the capital and took up their abode therein, after they had departed thence; and they were in constant prayer to Allah Almighty that He would stablish the king in his present stead. "And this," said Shahrazad, "is the end of that which my friend related to me." Quoth Shahriyar, "O Shahrazad, finish for us the tale thy friend told thee, inasmuch as it resembleth the story of a King whom I knew; but fain would I hear that which betided the people of this city and what they said of the affair of the king, so that I may return from the case wherein I was." Shahrazad replied, "With love and gladness!" Know, O auspicious king and lord of

> right rede and praiseworthy meed and prowess of deed, that, when the folk heard how the king had put away from him his malpractice and returned from his unrighteous wont, they rejoiced in this with joy exceeding and offered up prayers for him. Then they talked one with other of the cause of the slaughter of the maidens [and they told this story and it became obvious for them, that only women had caused all that] and the wise said, "Women are not all alike, nor are the fingers of the hand alike."[3]

The effect, as Grotzfeld says, is that "the king comes to himself and awakens . . ."[4] And one must admit there is a certain logic to this conclusion, at least with respect to what Freud had to say about repetition and remembering. Shahriyar's repetitious killing ends when Shahrazad's story makes him conscious of himself—when he "remembers," as it were. Yet note the child is missing from this solution. I should be more hesitant to dismiss the role of the child. Consider that the first story Shahrazad tells begins with the death of the son of a powerful being, the jinni. It seems reasonable to assume that Shahriyar's "malpractice" of killing his wives after deflowering them has similarly "killed" his own sons (since he continued this for three years, it seems quite possible that some of the wives might have conceived sons). Hence, when Shahrazad introduces their children, nothing could make the benefit of quitting this practice clearer for Shahriyar.

We have come full circle. For I began by speaking of the elusiveness of this work, and if nothing else, consideration of the relative merits of the two endings helps one to understand why the translators have found it so difficult to resist tinkering with the stories—a fact often bemoaned by scholars. For reading this other version, one begins to daydream, "Now what if Shahrazad told that story *and* then also had her children brought to the king—or perhaps she should summon the children first, and then . . ." More than any other book I have read, the *Nights,* with its tantalizing "beyond" of variants, of "supplemental nights," of analogues, of "frauds" tempts the reader to imagine a new "definitive version that would once and for all . . ." But this is a hopeless and impossible dream.

The sort of desire for some ultimate fiction that is aroused in the reader by such stories is itself the subject of the prologue to "Sayf al-Mulûk" (3:589–663). When Muhammad ibn Sabâ'ik, the king of Khurasan, is scolded by his vizier for the sums of money he spends obtaining stories, he shows his vizier that he is still boss by commissioning Hasan the Merchant to seek out the most amazing story ever. Hasan, in turn, sends Mamluk slaves off to the ends of the earth, but only one succeeds. In Damascus he acquires the story of Sayf al-Muluk. But those who are tempted to "complete" the *Nights* are far more likely to meet the failure of the first four Mamluks. And this may be for the best after all—for Burton reports the popular belief that whoever reads the entire book will die.

The title itself, *The Thousand and One Nights*—the Arabic literally translates "A Thousand Nights and a Night"—seems to allude to this elusive promise of the book. Borges compared the title to the English phrase "forever and a day," and to the line Heine wrote to a woman, "I will love you eternally and even after."[5] The title seems to allude in the same way to a paradoxical "beyond": "and a Night"—the "night" is paradoxical precisely because it seems superfluous after "a thousand nights." It is like Žižek's "last grain of sand" that constitutes the "heap": "We can never be sure which grain of sand is the last one [that makes it a heap]; the only possible definition of the heap is that *even if we take away one grain, it will still be a heap*. So this "last grain of sand" is by definition superfluous, but none the less necessary—it constitutes a 'heap' by its very superfluity."[6]

The sentence that concludes "Ma'ruf the Cobbler"—and, indeed, many other stories—as a sort of coda also speaks of a "beyond" in relation to narrative. The most elaborate version of the sentence I have found comes at the end of "Sindbad." Because of the rhymed prose or *saj'* involved, I will give the Arabic as the rhymes cannot be reproduced in the English:

> "And they lived in companionship and affection with waxing pleasure, happiness and ease until there came to them the destroyer of delights, the separator of societies, the wrecker of mansions and the populator of tombs, he who is the cup of death."
>
> (*wa lam yazâlû fî 'ashîrah wa muwaddah ma'a basṭ zâ'id wa faraḥ wa inshirâḥ ilâ an atâhum hâdim al-ladhdhât wa mufarriq al-jamâ'ât wa mukharrib al-quṣûr wa mu'ammir al-qubûr wa huwa ka's al-mamât*) (3:82–83)

The version that concludes the book adds: "Glory be to the one whom the cycles of Time do not destroy, who knows no change or variation." While the coda sentence's mention of God and its emphasis on his omnipotence and his changelessness are typically Islamic, the image of death as the destroyer of pleasures is not particularly Islamic. On the contrary, the emphasis in many medieval Islamic works is on the delights of Paradise that await the believer after death. In a book where one often senses various cultural strata in a single story, here too one senses a stratum beneath the Islamic one, perhaps a palimpsest of pre-Islamic Arabic poetry with its pagan view of life wherein the pleasures of life are snatched away by the *manâyâ*, the furies.

With its contrast of pleasure and death, the sentence might have furnished an epigraph for *Beyond the Pleasure Principle*, wherein Freud introduces a death drive in response to the problem of certain sorts of traumatic repetition that seemed to defy the sovereignty of the pleasure principle:

> The attributes of life were at some time evoked in inanimate matter by the action of a force of whose nature we can form no conception. It may perhaps have been a process similar in type to that which later caused the development of consciousness in a particular stratum of living matter. The tension which then arose in what had hitherto been an inanimate substance endeavored to cancel itself out . . . For a long time, perhaps, living substance was thus being constantly created afresh and easily dying, till decisive external influences altered in such a way as to oblige the still surviving substance to diverge ever more widely from its original course of life and to make ever more complicated *détours* before reaching its aim of death. (*SE,* 18:49)

At the very basis of Freud's conception of the mind and the drives is the definition of pleasure or *Lust* as the removal of a tension felt as displeasure—as *Unlust*, that is. In *Beyond the Pleasure Principle*, Freud goes so far as to hypothesize life itself as the tension that seeks to annul itself. Life as a fateful detour forced upon the organism. In framing his hypothesis in this way, Freud at the same time makes life and narrative almost "consubstantial." For in such a theory, every narrative departs from and returns to the monotony of routine events in precisely the same way that Freud envisioned life as a deviation from non-being.[7] And even as none of us dies "in general," but each dies his own particular sort of death, so too in narrative, the beginning in its *singularity* is exactly what must be addressed by the narrative's conclusion. Or, to say it in Hegel-ese, narrative is yet another form of negation—it transforms what is given and cancels it, but in such a way that the given, the beginning, is still present in the end. Hence, all of the transformations of which a theorist like Todorov speaks can be reduced to the formula $A \rightarrow -A$, insofar as every narrative is a *negation* of an initial state.

Likewise, the coda sentence situates narrative in relation to a "beyond"—every time we hear this refrain at a story's end we may recall that from the very outset of the book the relation between Shahrazad and Shahriyar is structured as a wager whose stakes are life and death. As Todorov noted, in *The Thousand and One Nights* "narrative equals life."[8] In the coda sentence, time, change, and pleasure are placed on the side of narrative; on the other side of death are God and immutability. Indeed, the peculiar narrative structure of *The Thousand and One Nights* exemplifies the point that for narrative the "death drive" is not a metaphor—it is *the* metaphor. Because human consciousness of death is a sine qua non for narrative; Shahrazad tells her stories just because she is conscious of her own death. Death "gives birth" to narrative—until, in the final sentence of *The Thousand and One Nights*, "*ilâ an atâhum hâdim al-ladhdhât*," the tension between *Erzählzeit* and *erzählte Zeit* collapses, and narration and life end.

Of all the points made in the foregoing analyses, this one seems central: the stories repeatedly define desire in relation to death. This suggests how we might amend Lacan's remark that Freud "questioned life as to its meaning . . . not to say that it has none . . . but to say that it has only one meaning" so as to apply it to the *Nights*. *The Thousand and One Nights* has many meanings, but central among them is that in which "desire is borne by death." As the somber coda of "*ilâ an atâhum hâdim al-ladhdhât wa mufarriq al-jamâʿât*" tells us.

Notes

1. *Alf Laylah wa Laylah*

1. Jorge Luis Borges, *Seven Nights*, trans. Eliot Weinberger (New York: New Directions, 1980), p. 54.

2. First described by Nabia Abbott in her article "A Ninth-Century Fragment of the Thousand Nights: New Light on the Early History of the Arabian Nights," *Journal of Near Eastern Studies* 8 (1949), pp. 129–64.

3. Al-Mas'ûdî, *Murûj al-dhahab*, ed. and trans. C. Barbier de Meynard and Pavet de Courteille, as *Les prairies d'or* (Paris: Imprimerie imperiale, 1861–1877), vol. 4, pp. 89–90.

4. Ibn al-Nadîm, *The Fihrist of Ibn al-Nadim*, trans. Bayard Dodge (New York: Columbia University Press, 1970), vol. 2, p. 714.

5. Samuel Goitein, "The Oldest Documentary Evidence for the title *Alf layla wa layla*," *Journal of the American Oriental Society* 78 (1958), p. 301.

6. Al-Maqrîzî, *Al-Khiṭaṭ* (Cairo: Bulaq, 1854), vol. 1, p. 484.

7. D. B. Macdonald, "The Earlier History of the Arabian Nights," *Journal of the Royal Asiatic Society* (July 1924), pt. 3, pp. 353 ff.

8. The similarities were first noted and discussed by H. F. Amedroz in his article "A Tale of the Arabian Nights Told as History in the 'Muntazam' of Ibn al-Jawzî," in *Journal of the Royal Asiatic Society* (1904), pp. 273–93. Muhsin Mahdi has recently discussed them in his book *The Thousand and One Nights* (Leiden: E.J. Brill, 1995), in appendix 3, "From History to Fiction," pp. 164–80.

9. This and other transformations of the *madirah* plot tell us something of the plasticity of the material in the hands of the medieval storyteller, matters I discuss in an article called "A Mighty and Never Ending Affair," *Journal of Arabic Literature* 24, pt. 2 (July 1993), pp. 139–59. One finds other echoes in the *Maqamat* of al-Hamadhani: in "The Hunchback" the barber brings the apparently dead hunchback back to life, and in al-Hamadhani's "The *Maqamah* of Mosul," the trickster Abu 'l-Fatḥ comes upon a corpse and also tells an astonished crowd, "This man is not dead!" He promises to raise him within two days, but he fails—the man is dead after all.

10. Al-Khatîb al-Baghdâdî, *Al-Bukhalâ'* (Baghdad: Al-Majma' al-'Ilmî al-'Iraqî, 1964), p. 148.

11. The *Maqâmât* are written in a style of rhymed prose peculiar to Arabic known as *saj'*, and are rich in word play and rhetorical tricks. Al-Hamadhani's eleventh century work *Al-Maqâmât* (Beirut: Dâr al-Mashriq, 1986) is the first example.

12. The story in al-Isḥâqî's *Accounts of . . . Egypt* (*Akhbâr al-uwal fî man taṣarrafa fî Miṣra min arbâb al-duwal*) (Cairo: Al-Maṭba'ât al-Fakhrah, 1859) begins on p. 129. The anecdote in al-Iṣfahânî's *Al-Aghânî* (Cairo: Bulaq, 1868–69) is in vol. 9, p. 131.

13. Al-Isḥâqî, *Akhbâr al-uwal fî man tasarrafa fî Misra min arbâb al-duwal*, p. 91.

14. *Book of the Thousand and One Nights Commonly Known as "The Arabian Nights Entertainments" Now for the First Time Published Complete in the Original Arabic,* ed. W. H. Macnaghten (Calcutta: Thacker, 1839–1842), vol. 4, p. 730. Unless otherwise noted, all references to an Arabic text will be to this edition, the so-called Second Calcutta, giving volume and page numbers in the text.

15. In *Al-Faraj ba'd al-shiddah* (Cairo: Khanji, 1956), pp. 23–24. I discuss this and other examples in "In the Second Degree: Fictional Technique in Tanukhi's *Al-Faraj ba'd ash-shiddah," Journal of Arabic and Middle Eastern Literatures* 1, no. 2 (July 1998), pp. 125–39.

16. Georges May, *Les Mille et une nuits d'Antoine Galland* (Paris: Presses universitaire de France, 1986), pp. 8–23.

17. *Kitâb alf layla wa layla*, ed. Muhsin Mahdi (Leiden: E.J. Brill, 1984), and *The Thousand and One Nights*, (Leiden: Brill 1995).

18. The Mamluk dynasty ruled Egypt from 1258 to 1517.

19. Robert Irwin, *The Arabian Nights: A Companion* (New York: Penguin, 1995), pp. 55–56.

20. Ibid., pp. 57–62.

21. Eva Sallis, *Sheherazade through the Looking Glass* (London: Curzon, 1999), p. 34. Sallis even speculates that by the close of the twelfth century that work "incorporated most probably literally one thousand and one nights . . . and around two hundred tales" (p. 27). It is certainly possible, but then again—who knows?

22. Hussain Haddawy, *The Arabian Nights* (New York: Norton, 1990), p. xii.

23. Hussain Haddawy, *The Arabian Nights II* (New York: Norton, 1995).

24. They are called "popular" *sirah*s to distinguish them generically from works like the first biography of Muhammad, also a called a *sirah*. They are long fictions of chivalry, relating the adventures of a hero/knight; *'Antar* and *Sultan Baybars* are notable examples of which at least parts are now available in English and French. In my view, these works do not have the formal brilliance of *The Thousand and One Nights*, and while individual episodes may be entertaining enough, in the aggregate, they take on a monotonous character.

25. Even measured against other works of a hitherto denigrated "popular literature," *The Thousand and One Nights* is a rather singular work. More typical representatives of that literature are the "popular *sîrahs*" mentioned above.

26. S. A. Bonebakker considers the problematic status of fiction in his essay "*Nihil obstat* in Storytelling?" found in the recent volume *The Thousand and One Nights in Arabic Literature and Society*, ed. Richard C. Hovannisian and Georges Sabagh (New York and Cambridge: Cambridge University Press, 1997), pp. 56–77. But he seems to think the question is an open one. I think I have shown that something does tend to obstruct it in my articles on parody and lying, on Tanukhi, and on early Muslim historical traditions. I am more or less going over the same ground here.

27. This, despite the fact that the greater portion of "legal" traditions or *ḥadîth*s and much of the "historical" ones are now known to be "fictions."

28. Abdelfattah Kilito, *L'oeil et l'aiguille* (Paris: Éditons la Découverte, 1992), p. 14.

29. The same can be said of attempts to distinguish between different forms of the fantastic that would act as criteria. It is not a question of forms of the fantastic per se, but of forms that would be unmistakable indices of fictionality. Joseph Sadan's review, in *Journal of Arabic Literature* 25 (March 1994), pp. 81–83, of a book by Wiebke Walther discusses some of these questions.

30. Cited by Mohammed Arkoun in *L'Islam, morale et politique* (Paris: Desclée de Brouwer, 1986), p. 12.

31. Ibn Isḥâq, *Sîrat an-nabî*, trans. Alfred Guillaume, *The Life of Muhammad* (London: Oxford University Press, 1955), pp. 135–36, p. 308.
32. Eva Sallis, *Sheherazade through the Looking Glass*, p. 40.
33. Irwin, *The Arabian Nights: A Companion*, p. 169.

2. The Imaginary, the Symbolic, and the Real

1. Slavoj Žižek, *The Sublime Object of Ideology* (London and New York: Verso, 1989), p. 50.
2. In a paper he gave at the fourteenth International Psychoanalytical Congress in Marienbad. A later version of this paper can be found in the *Écrits*, trans. Alan Sheridan (New York: W.W. Norton, 1977) pp. 1–7. Henceforth references to the *Écrits* will be given in the text in the form (*E*, page number).
3. *The Seminar of Jacques Lacan: Book II, The Ego in Freud's Theory and in the Technique of Psychoanalysis*, ed. Jacques-Alain Miller, trans. Sylvana Tomaselli, annotated by John Forrester (New York: W.W. Norton, 1991), p. 49. Henceforth references to Lacan's seminars will be given with the abbreviation *S* followed by a roman numeral, which designates the seminar. Less frequent references to French editions will be given in notes.
4. Alexandre Kojève, *Introduction to the Reading of Hegel*, ed. Allan Bloom, trans. James H. Nichols, Jr. (Ithaca: Cornell University Press, 1980), p. 40.
5. Richard Boothby, *Death and Desire* (Baltimore: Johns Hopkins University Press, 1991), pp. 145–55.
6. Boothby, *Death and Desire*, p. 149.
7. Jacques Lacan, *Seminar on "The Purloined Letter,"* trans. Jeffrey Mehlman in *French Freud: Structural Studies in Psychoanalysis: Yale French Studies* (New Haven: Yale University Press, 1972), p. 40.
8. Žižek, *Sublime Object of Ideology*, pp. 4–5.
9. Sigmund Freud, *The Interpretation of Dreams*, in *The Standard Edition of the Complete Psychological Works*, translated under the general editorship of James Strachey (London: Hogarth Institute, 1953–1974), vol. 12, p. 71. Henceforth, references to Freud will be to this English edition using the abbreviation *SE* followed by volume and page number in parentheses.
10. *Verwurfung* is usually translated as "rejection"; the French word Lacan uses is precisely *foreclusion*.
11. Lacan, *The Four Fundamental Concepts of Psycho-Analysis*, trans. Alan Sheridan (New York: W.W. Norton, 1981), p. 55. The book is in fact Lacan's eleventh seminar. Henceforth citations to this work will be given in the text with the abbreviation *FFC*.
12. Malcolm Bowie, *Lacan* (Cambridge: Harvard University Press, 1991), p. 102.
13. Slavoj Žižek, *Tarrying with the Negative* (Durham, NC: Duke University Press, 1993), p. 280, n. 1.

3. King, Queen, Master, Slave

1. Discussions by Jerome Clinton, F. Farag, and Bruno Bettleheim are examples of the former, while those of F. Malti-Douglas and F. Mernissi are representa-

tive of the latter. I will deal with Clinton, Farag, and Malti-Douglas by and by. Bettleheim's analysis is in *The Uses of Enchantment: The Meaning and Importance of Fairy Tales* (New York: Knopf, 1976), pp. 86–90. The first feminist reading (mentioned by Irwin) is M. Lahy-Hollebecque's *Le Feminisme de Scheherezade* (Paris: Radot, 1927). Judith Grossman's article "Infidelity and Fiction: The Discovery of Women's Subjectivity in the Arabian Nights," *Georgia Review* 34, no. 1 (Spring 1980), pp. 113–26 can also be mentioned. In the work of the Moroccan feminist Fatima Mernissi, Shahrazad crops up repeatedly.

2. Fedwa Malti-Douglas, *Woman's Body, Woman's Word* (Princeton: Princeton University Press, 1991), p. 13.

3. Irwin, *The Arabian Nights: A Companion*, p. 191.

4. Two facts linked by Jacqueline Guy-Heinemann and Abdellah Bounfour in "La Fracture de l'un-pere: essai sur l'origine de la fratrie dans *Les Mille et une nuits*," *Journal of Arabic Literature* 24, pt. 2 (July 1993), pp. 160–72.

5. Boothby, *Death and Desire*, p. 26.

6. In the Second Calcutta text no tree is mentioned, but this seems an oversight. The tree is found in other versions, and without the additional slave the arithmetic of the orgy is affected, there would be twenty-one females and twenty males—though we may presume it would never be the queen who was reduced to mere spectator.

7. The gaze is a commonplace of feminist criticism, which emphasizes how the one who sees occupies a position of power which transforms the person who is seen into an object. But, as Slavoj Žižek notes, this emphasis misses the dialectic of the gaze whereby the one who sees may be transformed into a helpless object. See *Metastases of Enjoyment* (London, New York: Verso, 1994), pp. 73–74. Bentham's scheme for a "Panopticon" has become the *locus classicus* for it.

8. Peter Brooks, *Reading for the Plot* (Cambridge: Harvard University Press, 1984) p. 99.

9. Abdelfattah Kilito makes a very apposite comparison with an anthropologist's discussion of the reactions of a Crow and a Hopi to their wives' infidelities. The Hopi calls on God to cause all rain to cease and destroy the human race, whereas the Crow simply cuts off the nose of his wife. *L'oeil et l'aiguille* (Paris: Éditions la Découverte, 1992), pp. 11–12.

10. It is here, I should say, that F. Farag goes astray in his article "*Al-Taḥlîl al-nafsî wa Alf layla wa layla*" ("Psychoanalysis and *The Thousand and One Nights*"), *Fusûl* (Winter 1994), p. 118, where he says, "Thus, the man is the master and the woman is the slave" (*fa'r-rajulu huwa al-sayyidu wa 'l-mar'atu hiya al-'abdu*). Although it's true that Lacan sometimes considers the relation of husband and wife in relation to Hegel's master-slave dialectic, he does not *reduce* the first relation to the second. Even within the scope of a medieval Arabic story—where, if one were inclined, one might argue that in some areas of Islamic law, the conjugal relation may approach that as a kind of limit. It is perhaps due to this reduction that, soon enough, Farag's analysis finds nothing else to do but simply tag the various characters in the way of much psychoanalytic criticism: Shahriyar is a paranoid, the kidnapped girl a nymphomaniac, and so on.

11. *'abd aswad* = "black slave"; best known in the Kharijite formula for who qualifies to be Caliph, but found elsewhere in Muslim traditions also. It is used by a follower of the Prophet to signify the most humble sort of person imaginable: *Ṣaḥîḥ*, Muslim, ed. 'Abd al-Bâqî (Cairo: Dâr al-*Ḥadîth*, n.d.), vol. 4, *Kitâb a-faḍâ'il*, *ḥadîth* no. 136, pp. 1832–33.

12. The quote from Mas'udi's *Akhbâr al-zamân* (Beirut: Dâr al-andalus, 1966)

p. 88, is taken from Al-Munsif bin Hasan's work, *Al-ʿAbîd wa'l-jawârî fî ḥikâyât Alf laylah wa laylah* [Slaves in *The Thousand and One Nights*] (Tunis: Céres Editions, 1994) p. 62. For those who read Arabic, this work is a thorough treatment of slavery in the *Nights*.

13. Kojève, *Introduction to the Reading of Hegel,* p. 40.

14. Ibid., p. 41.

15. Ibid., p. 42.

16. As Fedwa Malti-Douglas does, in *Woman's Body, Woman's Word*, p. 18.

17. See Patricia Crone's *Slaves on Horses* (Cambridge: Cambridge University Press, 1980) for the historical development of the Mamluk system of government.

18. Walter Andrews, *Poetry's Voice, Society's Song* (Seattle: University of Washington Press, 1985), p. 90.

19. Ibid., p. 202 n.

20. Malti-Douglas, *Woman's Body, Woman's Word*, "On one level, their role has been assimilated to that of the slave," p. 18.

21. Ibid., p. 18.

22. The word "wife" (*zawjah*) is used in the Mahdi text (p. 64), but is not found in Second Calcutta or Bulaq; given my point of view, I would say the ZER storyteller is *afras*, more insightful, than the Syrian storyteller.

23. Rather as Tamar demands Judah's signet ring after they have had sex in Genesis 38:18, a story we will discuss in a later chapter in relation to "The Merchant and the Jinni."

24. Several of the points in this paragraph were suggested to me by Walter Andrews in a letter.

25. *Kitâb Alf Layla wa Layla*, ed. Muhsin Mahdi, p 64.

26. For example, Jerome Clinton, "Madness and Cure in *The Thousand and One Nights,*" in *Studia Islamica* 61 (1985), pp. 107–25.

27. Farag says he suffers from paranoia. Schreber was a judge and a paranoid schizophrenic with the classic symptom of auditory hallucinations, "voices." He wrote a book about his illness *Denkwurdikeiten eines Nervenkranken* subsequently translated into English as *Memoirs of My Nervous Illness* by I. Macalpine and R. A. Hunter (London: William Dawson, 1955). Freud discussed Schreber's book (*SE,* 12:3–82), and Lacan devoted his third seminar to psychosis with the Schreber book as its centerpiece. The seminar has been translated, and a condensed version can also be found in the translation of the *Écrits,* "On a question preliminary to any possible treatment of psychosis," pp. 179–225.

28. Again, the phrase was suggested by Walter Andrews in a letter.

29. As Abdelkebir Khatibi argues in *La blessure du nom propre* (Paris: Denoël, 1986), pp. 168–69.

30. Gérard Genette in *Narrative Discourse* (Ithaca: Cornell University Press, 1980) also distinguishes three main types of relations between what he terms diegetic and metadiegetic levels, pp. 232–34.

4. The Mirror of Love

1. One might contend that the pious tales found in the *Nights* are similarly proximate, but these short anecdotal tales make up a very small portion of the material in the book whereas love stories form one of the largest genres.

2. Andras Hamori, *On the Art of Medieval Arabic Literature* (Princeton: Princeton University Press 1974), p. 38.

3. Vadet's work is *L'Esprit courtois en Orient dans les cinq premiers siècles de l'Hégire* (Paris: G.P. Maisonneuve et Larose, 1968). Giffen's work is *Theory of Profane Love among the Arabs: the Development of the Genre* (New York: New York University Press, 1971).

4. "Ptolemaic" rather than "Neo-Platonic" because the issue is whether the psychology manifest in these tales is to be discarded on scientific grounds.

5. For example, a common poetic cliché is that women's eyes "shoot arrows" whose aim is unerring. The issue of the veil—still with us—also suggests that the effect on the "seer" is inescapable, as does also the lesser-known issue of "averting the eyes" (*ghaḍḍ al-naẓar*). Against those who upheld the permissibility of '"just looking," Ibn al-Qayyim argued that while an "inadvertent look" (*naẓar al-faj'ah*) was not sinful, to look again after that was akin to drinking liquor. The effect was sure-fire, so to speak. Discussion of these and related issues can be found in Giffen's *Theory of Profane Love among the Arabs*, the issue of "averting the eyes" is found in pt. 3, chapter 2.

6. André Miquel, *Sept contes des Mille et une nuits ou Il n'y a pas de contes innocents; suivi d'entretiens autour de Jamaleddine Bencheikh et Claude Brémond* (Paris: Sindbad, 1981), p. 222.

7. Many other means that could serve the same purpose can be found in the work *The Ring of the Dove* by Ibn Ḥazm (994–1064), trans. Arthur Arberry (London: Luzac, 1953).

8. Aristophanes' myth of love in *The Symposium*, for example; Bencheikh discusses the physical similarity of the lovers against that myth in his book, *Les mille et une nuits ou la parole prisonnière* (Paris: Éditions Gallimard, 1988), pp. 106–7.

9. Burton's translation, slightly amended, found in *A Plain and Literal Translation of . . . the Book of the Thousand Nights and a Night* (London: Shammar Edition, The Burton Club, 1900), vol. 3, p. 236.

10. Though we only learn this later, when Maymunah claims victory: " 'My beloved is better than yours, but I forgive you!' Then she wrote for him a document that she freed him" (1:837–38).

11. He is said to be one of the Banu Sasan, descendants of the last Persian dynasty, the Sasanid. They are the stuff of legend and anecdote in medieval Arabic literature under the name of the *Banî Sâsân*. Oddly enough, in time, the latter name becomes associated with a group of lowlifes, vagabonds, con men, and such. But ʿAli ibn Bakkar obviously is far removed from those.

12. In *The Thousand and One Nights in Arabic Literature and Society* (Cambridge and New York: Cambridge University Press, 1997), p. 26, n. 9.

13. Burton's translation again, *A Plain and Literal Translation* . . , vol. 3, p. 165.

14. This and the rest of the translations of verse are my own. Necessarily the poetry is sacrificed for the meaning.

15. Needless to say, those holding this view claim the same a fortiori with respect to marriage.

16. *Diwân Jamîl Buthaynah*, ed. Mahdi Muhammad Nasir al-Din (Beirut: Dar al-kutub al-ʿarabiyah, 1987), p. 19.

17. Giffen, *Theory of Profane Love among the Arabs*, pp. 119–20.

18. A real poet of the ninth century.

19. Giffen, *Theory of Profane Love among the Arabs*, p. 120, n. 7.

20. Gerhardt says that the enigmatic jewel provides "a hint of the marvelous" so as to motivate Qamar al-Zaman's unflagging search for it (*The Art of Storytelling*, p. 293). Hamori says the jewel might be "an image of anxiety about sexual possession" or "an encoding of fears about inadequacy" In "The Magian and the Whore," in *Essays on the 1001 Nights* (Cambridge: Dar Mahjar, 1985), p. 34.

21. Žižek, *Metastases of Enjoyment*, p. 33.

22. Jacques Lacan, *La relation d'objet* (Paris: Éditions de Seuil, 1994), p. 170. In this instance, my translation.

23. Gerhardt, *The Art of Storytelling*, p. 294.

24. Al-Sarrâj, *Maṣâri' al-'ushshâq*, ed. A. Najati and A. Mashali (Cairo: Maktabah al-Anglo al-Miṣriyah, 1956), p. 5.

5. Double Trouble

1. The double is the subject of Otto Rank's *The Double: A Psychoanalytical Study* (London: Karnac, 1989). Rank stresses the narcissism involved in the theme and the ambivalent feelings of love and hate which the double embodies. Literary expressions may emphasize one or the other. Rank's ideas are more or less givens here; the following discussion attempts to go further by means of Lacanian concepts.

2. Chauvin, *Bibliographie des ouvrages arabes* (Liège: H. Vaillart-Carmanne, 1902), vol. 5, p. 100.

3. Søren Kierkegaard, *Either/Or, vol. 1* (New York: Doubleday, 1959), p. 30.

4. *Al-Mufaḍḍalîyât*, ed. A. Shâkir (Cairo: Dâr al-Ma'ârif, 1942), p. 149.

5. I discuss the story in the article "In the Second Degree: Fictional Technique in Tanukhi's *Al-Faraj ba'd ash-shidda*," in *Journal of Arabic and Middle Eastern Literatures*.

6. Al-Jâḥiẓ, *Rasâ'il*, ed. 'Abdu 'l-Amîr Mahannâ (Beirut: Dâr al-Ḥadâthah, 1988), vol. 2, pp. 96–97.

7. "The Sleeper Awakened" is not found in either Second Calcutta or Bulaq; I have used the Breslau edition edited by Habicht, *Tausend und Eine Nacht* (Breslau: Hirt, 1825–38), vol. 4, pp. 134–89. References in the text will be given with the abbreviation *B* followed by the page number.

8. J. G. Hava, *Al-Farâ'id Arabic-English Dictionary* (Beirut: Dar al-Mashreq, 1986), p. 181.

9. Burton's translation, *The Supplemental Nights*, vol. 1, p. 35.

10. A resemblance observed by Ferial Ghazoul in *Nocturnal Poetics* (Cairo: American University in Cairo Press, 1996), p. 112. I might add that this is the sort of evidence that Mahdi's thesis overlooks; even a story such as this, found in no extent Arabic manuscript of the *Nights* shows signs of adaptation to the frame story and signs of a coherence beyond the narrow limits Mahdi would set to the collection.

11. Although Gerhardt finds "The Sleeper Awakened" "as different as possible" from "Khalifah."

12. Ghazoul explores the relation between this story and the opening scene of *The Taming of the Shrew*, which makes use of the same plot.

13. René Descartes, *Meditations on First Philosophy*, trans. Elizabeth S. Haldane and G. R. T. Ross (London: Routledge, 1993), p. 45.

14. I assume Descartes was influenced by Spanish literature, specifically Calderón and Cervantes. While the madman who imagines himself a king is a stock character, it is also a fact that Calderón's play was published in 1635/6 and was translated into Dutch and Italian the same year, 1636, five years before Descartes published the *Meditations*. In the case of Descartes's mention of persons "made of glass" it seems to me even more certain that he is referring here to "Master Glass," the Cervantes story of the scholar who thinks he is made of glass. His *Exemplary*

Novels containing that story was published in 1613. Moreover, Don Quixote himself speaks of "evil enchanters" in the famous episode of the windmills.

15. Descartes, *Meditations,* pp. 46, 47.

16. Amélie Oksenberg Rorty, "The Structure of Descartes' *Meditations,*" in *Essays on Descartes' Meditations*, ed. Amélie Oksenberg Rorty (Berkeley and Los Angeles: University of California Press, 1986), p. 14.

17. Descartes, *Meditations,* pp. 46, 47.

18. Ibid., p. 47.

19. Ibid., pp. 49–50.

20. It seems useful to speak of "narrative" in both cases. The *Meditations* are, after all, meditations—not a straightforward treatise. Two essays, "The Structure of Descartes' *Meditations*" by Amélie Oksenberg Rorty and "The Naive Narrator" by L. Aryeh Kosman in the collection mentioned above, *Essays on Descartes' Meditations,* have been very useful for me on this and other literary aspects of Descartes's work.

21. Michael Williams, "Descartes and the Metaphysics of Doubt," in *Essays on Descartes' Meditations*, p. 126.

22. Rather as King Shahriman imprisons his son Qamar al-Zaman in a tower. This presumably is one of the "Oriental elements" that Gerhardt mentions in connection with Calderón's play.

23. The drug is the same also; Calderón mentions a drug cocktail containing henbane.

24. Žižek, *Tarrying with the Negative,* p. 160.

25. Ibid.

6. The Circuit of Desire

1. Georges Bataille, *Erotism*, trans. Mary Dalwood (San Francisco: City Lights Books, 1991), p. 47.

2. Žižek, *Sublime Object of Ideology,* p. 180.

3. Readers familiar with Tzvetan Todorov's famous essay "Narrative-Men" will note that his account of this chain of narrators differs since he used Khawam's translation:

Scheherazade tells that
Jaafer tells that
the tailor tells that
the barber tells
that his brother tells that . . .

The Poetics of Prose, trans. Richard Howard (Ithaca: Cornell University Press, 1977), p. 71.

4. Bataille, *Erotism*, p. 57.

5. In *The Purloined Poe*, ed. John P. Muller and William J. Richardson (Baltimore: Johns Hopkins University Press, 1988), trans. Jeffrey Mehlman, p. 51.

6. As I mentioned in the first chapter, a version of "The Steward's Story" is also found in the work of Tanukhi, where it is given as fact.

7. A head count saves his neck; an anecdote telling the same story is found in another work by al-Tanukhi, *Nishwâr al-muḥâḍarah* [*The delight of conversation*] (Beirut: Dâr Ṣâdir, 1971).

8. Andrews, *Poetry's Voice, Society's Song*, p. 93.
9. Todorov, *Poetics of Prose*, p. 74.
10. See Boothby's discussion in *Death and Desire*, p. 136.
11. Friedrich Nietzsche, *Philosophical Writings*, ed. Reinhold Grimm and Caroline Molina y Vedia, trans. Maximillian Mugge (New York: Continuum, 1995), p. 91.

7. The Sublime Wound

1. Žižek, *Sublime Object of Ideology*, p. 169.
2. A sentence that Ferial Ghazoul discusses at length in *Nocturnal Poetics*, pp. 30–31.
3. Of course, that story is more or less the same as the latter part of the story of "The Third Qalandar."
4. The writer says it is the right eye—a "Homeric nod" after telling us that the qalandars have lost their left eyes.
5. Žižek, *Sublime Object of Ideology*, p. 58.
6. Babylonian astronomers discovered that the Pleiades disappeared for a forty-day period. It rained on Noah for forty days, and the children of Israel wandered in the desert for forty years. Of the doomed boy's period of fifty days, I know of nothing in Near Eastern traditions except that fifty in Leviticus is associated with the jubilee year in which strife was to disappear. Of the jinn's period of appearance and disappearance, nine days + one = ten, I have only the obvious suggestion that ten is another number strongly associated with perfection in all traditions of numerology, Islamic as well. Hence, the qalandar's inability to be satisfied with nine may suggest a doomed desire for inhuman perfection. Annemarie Schimmel's *The Mystery of Numbers* (New York: Oxford University Press, 1993) is my source for some of the more arcane associations here.
7. Hence, the camel's rather self-satisfied "smile."
8. *Letters from the Earth*, ed. Bernard DeVoto (New York: Harper & Row, 1962), p. 16.
9. C. Brémond has done a comparative study of the three stories, "*En deçà et au delà d'un conte: le devenir des thèmes,*" published in the collection previously mentioned, *Mille et un contes de la nuit*, which contains two other long essays by J. Bencheikh and A. Miquel.
10. El-Said Al-Badawi and Martin Hinds, *Dictionary of Egyptian Arabic* (Beirut: Librarie du Liban, 1986), p. 315.
11. *Oxford English Dictionary*, 2nd ed. (New York: Oxford University Press, 1989), vol. 20, p. 469.
12. Hamori, *On the Art of Medieval Arabic Literature*, p. 179.
13. Gerhardt, *The Art of Storytelling*, pp. 133–37, and Bencheikh, *Mille et un contes de la nuit*, pp. 289–310.
14. Bencheikh, *Mille et un contes*, p. 294.
15. Bencheikh, *Mille et un contes*, p. 304.
16. Ibid., p. 305.
17. Ibid., p. 301.
18. Ibid., p. 289
19. Burton, A Plain and Literal Translation, vol. 9, p. 37, n. 2.
20. The third sheikh in "The Merchant and the Jinni" is an example; in Mahdi's Syrian manuscript he lacks a story, but the Egyptian manuscripts give him one.

21. Immanuel Kant, *Philosophical Writings*, ed. Ernest Behler, trans. J. C. Meredith (New York: Continuum, 1986), p. 214.
22. Žižek, *Tarrying with the Negative*, p. 46.
23. Žižek, *Tarrying with the Negative*, p. 46–47.
24. Žižek, *Sublime Object of Ideology*, p. 43.

8. *Peut-on tuer avec des noyaux de dattes?*

1. Sandra Naddaf, *Arabesque: Narrative Structure and the Aesthetics of Repetition in 1001 Nights* (Evanston, Ill.: Northwestern University Press, 1991).
2. I should note that some readers slight this story. D. B. Macdonald, in "The Earlier History of the Arabian Nights," wrote: "It has often been remarked that Shahrazad certainly did not put her best foot foremost in her storytelling. . ." *Journal of the Royal Asiatic Society* (1924), p. 376. And Mia Gerhardt says, "Shahrazâd is given a surprisingly insignificant piece for a beginning." *The Art of Story-Telling*, pp. 402–3.
3. Edward Lane, *Arabic-English Lexicon* (Cambridge: Islamic Texts Society, 1984), vol. 1, p. 131. Emil Homerin pointed this similarity out to me.
4. Michael Cook, *Muhammad* (New York: Oxford University Press, 1990), p. 38.
5. And this may answer the objections of Macdonald and Gerhardt to the "pride of place" given "The Merchant and the Jinni."
6. Stith Thompson, *The Folktale* (New York: Dryden Press, 1946), p. 126.
7. Or, as Genette would say, with a shift from the "iterative" to the "singulative"; *Narrative Discourse: An Essay in Method* (Ithaca: Cornell University Press, 1980), pp. 113 ff. The narrative transition from the mundane to the amazing leans on an entire genre of medieval Arabic literature. See Roy Mottahedeh's " *'Ajâ'ib* in The Thousand and One Nights," in *The Thousand and One Nights in Arabic Literature and Society*, pp. 29–39.
8. Victor Chauvin, *Bibliographie des ouvrages arabes* (Liége: H. Vaillant-Carmanne, 1902), vol. 7, p 23, n.1.
9. D. B. MacDonald, "From the Arabian Nights to Spirit," *Moslem World* 9 (1919), p. 341. Philip Kennedy was kind to point this article out to me.
10. *The Oxford Annotated Bible* (New York: Oxford University Press, 1962), p. 48.
11. Gerhard Von Rad, *Genesis: A Commentary*, trans. John H. Marks (Philadelphia: Westminster Press, 1972), p. 357.
12. Robert Alter, *The Art of Biblical Narrative* (New York: Basic Books, 1981), p. 6.
13. *Midrash Rabbah*, ed. H. Freedman and M. Simon (London: Soncino Press, 1951), vol. 2, p. 792.
14. Von Rad, *Genesis: A Commentary*, p. 358.
15. On the other hand, a professor of Judaica at the University of Toronto informed me that the story of Onan and Er and Tamar was a prominent one in medieval Jewish exegesis and lore—which would increase the possibility of its transmission into Muslim culture.
16. I might mention also the review titled "Midrash Mishmash" by Frank Kermode of a recent book, *The Bible As It Was* by James Kugel. Kugel and Kermode speak of the humor involved in some of the *midrash* and how a certain rabbinic reading of a verse from Amos produces "a joke-like structure"; *New York Review of Books*, April 23, 1998, p. 45.

17. Von Rad, *Genesis: A Commentary*, p. 358.

18. I was recently informed that they still say this.

19. For example, see the *Musnad* of Ibn Ḥanbal, (Cairo: Bulaq, 1893), vol. 4, p. 189. Those unacquainted with Islamic law might be surprised that the throwing of a date pit, trivial as it seems, should be a matter of law, but every action of Muhammad is potentially a matter of law and a model for all Muslims to imitate. In any case, against Lane, I would argue that it is permitted to throw date pits without uttering *dastur*, noting that tradition does not record any preemptive utterance by Muhammad in connection with this act. However, the case of throwing a real stone that causes a woman to miscarry is dealt with in traditions: al-Bukhârî, *Ṣaḥîḥ*, ed. Dr. M. M. Khan (Medina: n.d.), vol. 9, *diyât* 25, p. 32.

20. Žižek, *Tarrying with the Negative*, pp. 46–47.

9. The Destroyer of Delights

1. H. Grotzfeld, "Neglected Conclusions of the *Arabian Nights*," in *Journal of Arabic Literature* 16 (1985), p. 77.

2. Which recalls Borges's statement that on the 602nd night Shahrazad tells her own story, a statement that has sent readers such as Kilito and myself on a frustrating search for this story (in Second Calcutta she tells one that has some similarities to it).

3. Burton, *The Supplemental Nights*, vol. 12, pp. 268–69.

4. Grotzfeld, *"Neglected Conclusions,"* p. 80.

5. Borges, *Seven Nights*, p. 46.

6. Žižek, *Sublime Object of Ideology,* p. 221.

7. The narrative detour is usually signaled by the shift from an iterative tense that condenses repeated events ("For a long time I used to go to bed early") to a perfect tense that singles out the event that ruptured the routine ("one day when he had come to see us after dinner in Paris . . ."); see Gerard Genette's discussion in *Narrative Discourse: An Essay in Method*, pp. 113–27. The "perfect" here would be what Genette calls the "singulative."

8. Todorov, *Poetics of Prose*, p. 74.

Bibliography

The Thousand and One Nights

Arabic Editions

Alf laylah wa laylah. Edited by W. Macnaghten. 4 vols. Calcutta: Thacker, 1839–42.

Alf laylah wa laylah. Edited by Shaykh Muḥammad Qiṭṭah al-ʿAdawî. Cairo: Bûlaq, 1835.

Kitâb Alf laylah wa laylah. Edited by Muhsin Mahdi. Leiden: E. J. Brill, 1984.

Tausend und Eine Nacht. Edited by M. Habicht. Breslau: Hirt, 1825–38.

English Editions

Burton, Richard. *A Plain and Literal Translation of the Arabian Nights' Entertainments now entitled The Book of the Thousand Nights and a Night*. London: Shammar Edition, the Burton Club, 1900 (including *The Supplemental Nights*).

Dawood, N. J. *The Thousand and One Nights*. New York: Penguin, 1973.

Haddawy, Hussain. *The Arabian Nights*. New York: W.W. Norton, 1990.

Lane, Edward W. *The Arabian Nights' Entertainments*. London: 1859. Reprinted, New York: Bigelow, Brown, 1914.

Mathers, Powys. *The Thousand Nights and One Night*. New York: Routledge, 1989.

Arabic Literature, Islamic Culture

Abbott, Nabia. "A Ninth-Century Fragment of the Thousand Nights: New Light on the Early History of the Arabian Nights." *Journal of Near Eastern Studies* 8 (1949), pp. 129–64.

Amedroz, H. F. "A Tale of the Arabian Nights Told as History in the '*Muntazam*' of Ibn al-Jawzî." *Journal of the Royal Asiatic Society* (1904), pp. 273–93.

Andrews, Walter. *Poetry's Voice, Society's Song*. Seattle: University of Washington Press, 1985.

Arkoun, M. *L'Islam, morale et politique*. Paris: Desclée de Brouwer, 1986.

Al-ʿAttar. *The Conference of the Birds*. Translated by Afkham Darbandi and Dick Davis. New York: Penguin, 1984.

Al-Badawi, El-Said, and Martin Hinds. *Dictionary of Egyptian Arabic*. Beirut: Librarie du Liban, 1986.

Al-Baghdâdî, al-Khaṭîb. *Al-Bukhalâ*ʾ [The Misers]. Baghdad: Al-Majmaʿ al-ʿIlmî al-ʿIrâqî, 1964.

Bâqî, Muḥammad. *Al-Muʿjam al-Mufahras*. Cairo: Dâr al-Ḥadîth, 1988.

Beaumont, Daniel. "In the Second Degree: Fictional Technique In Tanukhi's *Al-Faraj baʿd ash-shidda*." *Journal of Arabic and Middle Eastern Literatures* 1, no. 2 (1998), pp. 125–39.

———. "Hard-Boiled: Narrative Discourse in Early Muslim Traditions." *Studia Islamica* 83 (February 1996), pp. 5–31.

———. "Parody and Lying in Medieval Islam: Jahiz's Book of Misers." *Studia Islamica* 74 (1994), pp. 27–49.

———. "The Return of the Repressed: The Trickster in the Maqamat." *Edebiyat* (Spring 1994), pp. 1–14.

———. "A Mighty and Never Ending Affair: Comic Anecdote and Story in Medieval Arabic Literature." *Journal of Arabic Literature* 24, (July 1993), pt.2, pp. 139–59.

Bencheikh, Jamal Eddine. *"Les mille et une nuits" ou la parole prisonnière*. Paris: Gallimard, 1988.

———. Claude Brémond, and André Miquel. *Mille et un contes de la nuit*. Paris: Gallimard, 1991.

Ibn Buṭlân. *Daʿwat al-aṭibbâʾ*. Edited by Felix Kleine-Franke. Wiesbaden: Harrasowitz, 1985.

Chauvin, Victor. *Bibliographie des ouvrages arabes*. Liége: H. Vaillant-Carmanne, 1902.

Clinton, Jerome. "Madness and Cure in *The Thousand and One Nights*." *Studia Islamica* 61 (1985) pp. 107–25.

Cook, Michael. *Muhammad*. New York: Oxford University Press, 1990.

Cosquin, Emmanuel. "Le Prologue-cadre des mille et une nuits." *Études folkloriques*. Paris, 1922.

Crone, Patricia. *Slaves on Horses*. Cambridge: Cambridge University Press, 1980.

Elisséeff, Nikita. *Thémes et motifs des "Mille et une nuits": Essai de classification*. Beirut: Institut Français de Damas, 1949.

Encyclopedia of Islam, New Edition. Leiden: E.J. Brill.

Farag, Aḥmad, "Al-Taḥlîl al-nafsî wa *Alf laylah wa laylah*." *Al-Fuṣûl* (Winter 1994) pp. 114–29.

Gerhardt, Mia. *The Art of Storytelling*. Leiden: E.J. Brill, 1963.

Ghazoul, Ferial. *Nocturnal Poetics*. Cairo: American University in Cairo Press, 1996.

Giffen, Lois. *Theory of Profane Love among the Arabs*. New York: New York University Press, 1971.

Goitein, Samuel. "The Oldest Documentary Evidence for the title *Alf layla wa layla*." *Journal of the American Oriental Society* 78 (1958), pp. 301–2.

Grossman, Judith. "Infidelity and Fiction: The Discovery of Women's Subjectivity in the *Arabian Nights*." *Georgia Review* 34, no. 1 (Spring 1980), pp. 113–26.

Grotzfeld, Heinz, "Neglected Conclusions of the *Arabian Nights*." *Journal of Arabic Literature* 16 (1985), pp. 73–87.

Guy-Heineman, Jacqueline, and Abdellah Bounfour. "La Fracture de l' un-pere: Essai sur l'origine de la fratrie dans *Les Mille et une nuits*." *Journal of Arabic Literature* 24 (July 1993), pt. 2, pp. 160–72.

Al-Hamadhânî. *Al-Maqâmât* (The Seances). Beirut: Dâr al-Mashriq, 1986.

Hamori, Andras. *On the Art of Medieval Arabic Literature*. Princeton: Princeton University Press, 1974.

———. "Notes on Two Love Stories from the *1001 Nights*." *Studia Islamica* 43 (1976), pp. 65–80.

———. "A Comic Romance from the *1001 Nights*." *Arabica* 30 (1983), pp. 38–56.

———. "The Magian and the Whore: Readings of *Qamar al-Zaman*." In *Essays on the 1001 Nights: Critical Essays and Annotated Bibliography*. Cambridge, Mass.: Dar Mahjar, 1985.

Ibn Ḥanbal, Aḥmad. *Musnad*. Cairo: Bulaq, 1893–1894.

Al-Ḥarîrî. *Al-Maqâmât*. Photocopied edition of DeSacy's edition with Zamakhsharî's commentary. N.p., n.d.

Bin Hasan, Al-Munsif. *Al-ʿAbîd wa'l-jawârî fî ḥikâyât Alf laylah wa laylah* [Slaves in the stories of *The Thousand and One Nights*]. Tunis: Céres Editions, 1994.

Ibn Hazm. *The Ring of the Dove*. Translated by A. J. Arberry. London: Luzac, 1953.

Hovannisian, Richard C., and Georges Sabagh. *"The Thousand and One Nights" in Arabic Literature and Society*. Cambridge: Cambridge University Press, 1997.

Irwin, Robert. *The Arabian Nights: A Companion*. New York: Penguin, 1994.

Al-Iṣfahânî, Abû 'l-Faraj. *Al-Aghânî* [The songs]. Cairo: Bûlâq, 1868–1869.

Ibn Isḥâq. *The Life of the Prophet*. Translated by Alfred Guillaume. London: Oxford University Press, 1955.

Al-Isḥâqî. *Akhbâr al-uwal fî man taṣarrafa fî Miṣra min arbâb al-duwal*. Cairo: Al-Maṭbaʿât al-Fakhrah, 1859.

Al-Jâḥiẓ. *Rasâ'il*. Edited by Abd al-Amîr Mahannâ. Beirut: Dâr al-Ḥadâthah, 1988.

Kilito, Abdelfattah. *L'oeil et l'aiguille*. Paris: Éditions la Découverte, 1992.

Lane, Edward. *Arabic-English Lexicon*. Cambridge: Islamic Texts Society, 1984.

Macdonald, D. B. "The Earlier History of the *Arabian Nights*." *Journal of the Royal Asiatic Society* (July 1924), pt. 3, pp. 353–97.

Mahdi, Muhsin. *The Thousand and One Nights*. Leiden: E. J. Brill, 1995.

Malti-Douglas, Fedwa. *Woman's Body, Woman's Word*. Princeton: Princeton University Press, 1991.

Ibn Manẓûr. *Lisân al-ʿarab*. Beirut: Dâr Ṣâḍir, n.d.

Al-Maqrîzî. *Al-Khiṭaṭ*. Cairo: Bulaq, 1854.

Al-Masʿûdî. *Murûj al-dhahab*. Edited and translated by C. Barbier de Meynard and Pavet de Courteille (as *Les prairies d'or*). Paris: Imprimerie Imperiale, 1861–1877.

May, Georges. *Les mille et une nuits d'Antoine Galland, ou, Le chef-d'oeuvre*. Paris: Presses universitaire de France, 1986.

Al-Mufaḍḍalîyât. Edited by A. Shâkir. Cairo: Dâr al-Maʿârif, 1942.

Ibn al-Muqaffaʿ. *Kalîlah wa Dimnah*. Beirut: Dâr al-Masîrah, 1987.

Muslim. *Ṣaḥîḥ*. Edited by Muhammad Fu'ad ʿAbd al-Bâqî. Cairo: Dâr al-Ḥadîth, 1955–1956.

Naddaf, Sandra. *Arabesque: Narrative Structure and the Aesthetics of Repetition in "1001 Nights*." Evanston, Ill.: Northwestern University Press, 1991.

Ibn al-Nadîm. *The Fihrist of Ibn al-Nadim*. Translated by Bayard Dodge. New York: Columbia University Press, 1970.

Sallis, Eva. *Sheherazade through the Looking Glass*. London: Curzon, 1999.

Schimmel, Annemarie. *The Mystery of Numbers*. New York: Oxford University Press 1993.

Sharḥ Dîwân Jamîl Buthaynah. Edited and annotated by Mahdî M. Nâsir al-Dîn. Beirut: Dâr al-Kutub al-ʿIlmiyah, 1987.

Al-Tanûkhî. *Al-Faraj baʿd al-shiddah* [Happiness after hardship]. Cairo: Al Khangi, 1956.

———. *Nishwâr al-muḥâḍarah* [Delight of conversation]. Edited by M. Shaljî. Beirut: Dâr Ṣâḍir, 1971.

Vadet, J. C. *L'Esprit courtois en Orient dans les cinq premiers siècles de l'Hégire*. Paris: G.P. Maisonneuve et Larose, 1968.

Wensinck, *Concordance et indices de la traditions musulmane*. 2nd ed. Leiden: E.J. Brill, 1992.

General Works

Alter, Robert. *The Art of Biblical Narrative*. New York: HarperCollins, 1981.

Bataille, Georges. *Erotism*. Translated by Mary Dalwood. San Francisco: City Lights Books, 1991.

Bettleheim, Bruno. *The Uses of Enchantment: The Meaning and Importance of Fairy Tales*. New York: Knopf, 1976.

Boothby, Richard. *Death and Desire*. Baltimore: Johns Hopkins University Press, 1991.

Borges, Jorge Luis. *Seven Nights*. Translated by Eliot Weinberger. New York: New Directions, 1984.

Bowie, Malcolm. *Lacan*. Cambridge: Harvard University Press, 1991.

Brooks, Peter. *Reading for the Plot*. Cambridge: Harvard University Press, 1984.

Calderón de la Barca. "Life Is a Dream." Translated by Edwin Honig. New York: Hill & Wang, 1970.

Cervantes, Miguel. *Exemplary Stories*. Translated by C. A. Jones. New York: Penguin, 1972.

Descartes, René. *Meditations on First Philosophy*. Edited by Stanley Tweyman. Translated by Elizabeth S. Haldane and G. R. T. Ross. London: Routledge, 1993.

Freud, Sigmund. *The Standard Edition of the Complete Psychological Works of Sigmund Freud*. Edited by James Strachey. London: Hogarth Institute, 1955.

Genette, Gérard. *Narrative Discourse*. Translated by Jane Lewin. Ithaca: Cornell University Press, 1980.

Hegel, G. W. F. *The Phenomenology of the Mind*. Translated by J. B. Baillie. New York: Harper & Row, 1967.

Kant, Immanuel. *Philosophical Writings*. Edited by Ernest Behler. Translated by J. C. Meredith. New York: Continuum, 1986.

Kierkegaard, Søren. *Either/Or*. Vol. I. Translated by David F. Swenson and Lilian Marvin Swenson. New York: Doubleday, 1959.

Kojève, Alexandre. *Introduction to the Reading of Hegel*. Edited by Allan Bloom. Translated by James H. Nichols, Jr. Ithaca: Cornell University Press, 1969.

Lacan, Jacques. *Écrits*. Translated by Alan Sheridan. New York: W.W. Norton, 1977.

———. *The Seminar of Jacques Lacan, Book I: Freud's Papers on Technique 1953–1954*. Edited by Jacques-Alain Miller. Translated by John Forrester. New York: W.W. Norton, 1988.

———. *The Seminar of Jacques Lacan, Book II: The Ego in Freud's Theory and in the Technique of Psychoanalysis 1954–1955*. Edited by Jacques-Alain Miller. Translated by Sylvia Tomaselli. New York: W.W. Norton, 1991.

———. *The Seminar of Jacques Lacan, Book III: The Psychoses*. Edited by Jacques-Alain Miller. Translated by Russell Grigg. New York: W.W. Norton, 1997.

———. *The Seminar of Jacques Lacan, Book VII: The Ethics of Psychoanalysis*. Edited by Jacques-Alain Miller. Translated by Dennis Porter. New York: W.W. Norton, 1997.

———. *The Four Fundamental Concepts of Psycho-Analysis*. Translated by Alan Sheridan. New York: W.W. Norton, 1981.

———. *La Relation de l'objet*. Edited by Jacques-Alain Miller. Paris: Éditions du Seuil, 1994.

Midrash Rabbah. Edited by H. Freeman and M. Simon. London: Soncino Press, 1951.

Muller, John P., and William J. Richardson. *The Purloined Poe*. Baltimore: Johns Hopkins University Press, 1988.

Nietzsche, Friedrich. "On Truth and Falsity in the Extramoral Sense." In *Philosophical Writings*, edited by Reinhold Grimm and Caroline Molina y Vedia. New York: Continuum, 1995.

Oxford Annotated Bible. New York: Oxford University Press, 1962.

Oxford English Dictionary. 2nd ed. Prepared by J. A. Simpson and E. S. C. Warner. New York: Oxford University Press, 1989.

Plautus. *Amphityron*. Translated by Paul Nixon. Cambridge: Harvard University Press, 1966.

Rank, Otto. *The Double: A Psychoanalytical Study*. London: Karnac, 1989.

Rorty, Amélie Oksenberg. "The Structure of Descartes' *Meditations*." In *Essays on Descartes' Meditations*, edited by Amélie Oksenberg Rorty. Berkeley and Los Angeles: University of California Press, 1986.

Thompson, Stith. *The Folktale*. New York: Dryden Press, 1946.

———, ed. *Motif-Index of Folk-Literature*. Bloomington: Indiana University Press, 1955.

Todorov, Tzvetan. *The Poetics of Prose*. Translated by Richard Howard. Ithaca: Cornell University Press, 1977.

Twain, Mark. *Letters from the Earth*. Edited by Bernard De Voto. New York: Harper & Row, 1962.

Žižek, Slavoj. *The Sublime Object of Ideology*. New York: Verso, 1989.

———. *Tarrying with the Negative*. Durham, N.C.: Duke University Press, 1993.

———. *The Metastases of Enjoyment*. New York: Verso, 1994.

———. *The Plague of Fantasies*. New York: Verso, 1997.

Index

(Note: for purposes of alphabetization, the article "al-," "Abu" ("father"), and "Ibn" ("son") are ignored for Arabic names; thus, "Ibn al-Qayyim" will be found under "q")